PATRICK   DESMOND,
H I G H   M E A D,
HILLFIELD DRIVE,
LEDBURY,   HR8 1AG
Tel: LEDBURY 2988

Desmond MacCarthy

Desmond MacCarthy

DESMOND MacCARTHY

THE MAN AND HIS WRITINGS

Introduced by
DAVID CECIL

CONSTABLE
LONDON

First published in Great Britain 1984
by Constable and Company Limited
10 Orange Street London WC2H 7EG
Copyright © 1984 by David Cecil
Dermod MacCarthy, Chloe MacCarthy
Introduction copyright © by David Cecil
ISBN 0 09 465610 X
Set in Linotron Baskerville 11 pt
by Rowland Phototypesetting Ltd
Bury St Edmunds, Suffolk
Printed in Great Britain
by St Edmundsbury Press
Bury St Edmunds, Suffolk

To Dermod MacCarthy

CONTENTS

ILLUSTRATIONS

EDITOR'S NOTE

The contents of this volume first appeared in volume form in the following collected editions:

From *Portraits*, published by Putnam in 1931
    Dedication: To Desmond MacCarthy, Henry James, Conrad, George Meredith, Asquith, Disraeli, Goethe, Herbert Spencer, Strindberg

From *Criticism*, published by Putnam in 1932
    Samuel Butler, Boswell, Unity of effect, Gertrude Stein, The artistic temperament, Literary Snobs, Literary Booms, From a critic's daybook

From *Memories*, published by MacGibbon & Kee in 1953
    Hardy, Max Beerbohm, Kipling, Shooting with Wilfrid Blunt

From *Humanities*, published by MacGibbon & Kee in 1953
    Swinburne, Ibsen, Chekhov, James Joyce's *Exiles*, Reviewers and Professors

From *Experience*, published by Putnam in 1935
    Eton, Two trials, The crowds at Burlington House, Ugliness

Most of the second part of the Introduction has already been published in my preface to the selection from Desmond MacCarthy's writings entitled *Humanities*.

INTRODUCTION

For two reasons Desmond MacCarthy deserves the attention of posterity. He was one of the most distinguished men of his time in two ways: as a writer and as a man, a personality. Yet none of his writings are still in print, nor has anyone left an adequate record of the impression he made as a man. The purpose of this volume is to make a start at filling these gaps. It is therefore divided into two parts, one containing a selection from his writings and the other giving a sketch – it is no more – of the man and his life.

I

Let me begin with the man. Desmond MacCarthy was the only child of Charles MacCarthy, a man of Irish extraction and a Sub-Agent of the Bank of England, and of his wife Isa de La Chevalerie, half French and half German. Thus on two sides Desmond was by blood more foreign than English. Born in 1877, he was educated at Eton and Trinity College, Cambridge; at both he was happy, popular and showed signs of exceptional charm and intelligence. Cambridge was to prove the more important in his life, for it was there that his personality first fully flowered. He became a member of the famous and exclusive intellectual society called the Apostles, made some remarkable friends including Bertrand Russell, Roger Fry, and, most important, the philosopher G. E. Moore who was to be the strongest and most permanent influence in forming his moral and intellectual beliefs. After leaving Cambridge with only an aegrotat degree – he had fallen ill during his final examinations – he settled down to follow for the rest of his life the career of a literary journalist. At first this was in a leisurely, easy-going fashion with plenty of time left over to cultivate his tastes, make friends, and satisfy his curiosity about the world around him. But in time he was to learn that literary journalism is a precarious and worrying profession; all the more so, as his father had died in 1893 leaving his son very little money to live on if he was out of work. In consequence he was liable to get into financial difficulties. This became a growing trouble after 1906 when he married Mary, more generally known as Molly, Warre Cornish, daughter of the Vice-Provost of Eton, so that he soon had a wife and three children – Michael, Rachel and Dermod – to support and educate by his earnings. In spite of these difficulties, Desmond gradually made a name for himself as a literary and a dramatic critic, notably of the Vedrenne-Barker productions at the Court Theatre, where there first appeared plays by some of the most interesting dramatists of the period: Shaw, Galsworthy, and Barker himself. As time passed, Desmond also became known as a successful contributor to various periodicals: the *New Quarterly*, the *Eye Witness*, and in 1913, the *New Statesman*. In 1911 he also got into the news for the help he gave to Roger Fry in producing the sensational first exhibition of Post-Impressionist paintings.

His career was interrupted by the outbreak of the 1914 war, during which he worked first in France with the Red Cross and later at the Admiralty. Afterwards he returned to literary journalism, and with growing success. In 1920 he became literary editor of the *New Statesman*, and in 1928 he brought out and edited *Life and Letters*, a new literary journal which managed, as few such publications do, to be at the same time intellectually impressive and agreeable reading. Finally in 1929, on the death of Edmund Gosse, Desmond was made literary critic of the *Sunday Times*, and remained for the rest of his life the acknowledged leading literary journalist of England. Meanwhile, and indeed ever since he left Cambridge, his other and personal claim to fame had gradually made itself known. Born by nature sociable and gregarious, he combined an instinctive liking for his fellow men and women and an enjoyment of their company with a natural ability to make them take pleasure in his. All sorts of company too: because at Cambridge he had made some lifelong friends who were later to found the nucleus of the so-called Bloomsbury Circle. Desmond is sometimes spoken of as belonging to it. This was not so. As he himself said, 'Bloomsbury has never been a spiritual home to me.' Its characteristic attitude to the world was alien to him; its exclusiveness, its intellectual pride, the inability of its members to feel at ease with anyone but each other. Further, after Cambridge days he was soon moving in other circles and making new friends as close as those of the past. Some of these were writers: Hilaire Belloc, Logan Pearsall Smith, Max Beerbohm, and Maurice Baring, to name only a few. Soon he began to acquire a wide reputation as an unusually agreeable man, and this in turn opened for him the doors of the great world of politics and fashion. He found himself making new close friends there; with members of the Asquith family, in particular Violet (afterwards Lady Violet Bonham-Carter), Asquith's daughter, and also with his daughter-in-law Cynthia, with Duff and Diana Cooper and, though less intimately, with Winston Churchill. However Desmond was always wonderfully indifferent to worldly reputation, whether intellectual, political, or social, and throughout his life he also managed to keep up with a number of old friends that few people but himself had ever heard of. The fact that he belonged to no particular group meant that his intimates were drawn from diverse categories – famous and obscure, male and female, old and young. For as he himself grew older he liked making friends with young persons – Raymond Mortimer and Cyril Connolly are examples – to whom he would give advice; considered sympathetic, unpatronizing advice, about their work and their lives.

It was as such a young person that I myself first made his acquaintance. We met in various houses; in the late 'twenties acquaintance warmed into friendship. It began one evening at a big house party given by Lady Desborough, a celebrated hostess of the period. Though I had not yet published a book, I had already started on a biography of William Cowper. Desmond asked me about this and our conversation became so absorbing that later, when it was time to go upstairs to bed, we went on with it in his bedroom till 2 o'clock in the morning. It led to his inviting me, in the following week, to lunch with him in London at a little restaurant in Soho. The lunch went on till well after 4 o'clock that afternoon, and in consequence I was soon showing him the first chapter of my book. I was impressed and gratified by the way he gave his whole mind to it, together with precise and valuable advice about almost every paragraph. This was the start of a friendship which was to be enriched and strengthened when, two or three years later, I married his daughter Rachel.

It would be conceited and misleading to suggest that even during our first meetings we talked only, or mainly, about myself and my writings. On the contrary our conversation ranged over many topics. The impression he made on me by his personality was captivating and stimulating to the highest degree. It was also a complex impression. At this time Desmond was writing a weekly *causerie* for the *New Statesman* signed 'Affable Hawk'. This was not a bad name for him. There was something hawk-like in his keen, dark-eyed, aquiline head

surmounting an active and stockyish figure. But this hawk was
'affable'; there was nothing of the bird of prey about it; its
expression was friendly and benignant. A similar combination
characterized his views. His judgements were acute, concerned
only to discover the truth even if this was painful or disillusioning. Yet they never seemed unduly harsh and were never
scornful. Moreover the tone in which he offered them was
genial and sympathetic, quick to understand other people's
points of view and, if he could, to enter into them. 'I am
exceedingly fond of controversy,' he says somewhere, 'not as a
participant but as a spectator.' He could have extended this
statement to apply to his general reactions to the world he saw
around him. He enjoyed this very much – a power of enjoyment
was one of his outstanding qualities – but as a spectator rather
than as a participant.

This outlook, this personality, expressed itself unforgettably
in his talk. He was a supremely good talker, one of the few
supremely good talkers I have ever met, and equal to the best of
them. In a charming, expressive voice, male and unmannered
but beautifully modulated to convey his ever-changing shades
of thought and feeling, his discourse flowed forth, relaxed,
leisurely, enthralling. He never let the conversation drop, but it
never turned into a monologue either. Desmond was too interested in the person he was talking to to let this happen,
wanted too much to know what he or she had to say. His own
tone varied in mood, now light, now serious, now thoughtful,
now fanciful, now melancholy, now playful. He was humorous
rather than witty, with a delicate, observant humour that
shimmered over any description he might give of a place, a
person, or an experience. The distinctive individual characteristic of his conversation was that it combined substance with
style. It was very substantial; nature and Cambridge training
had taught him to dislike superficial inconsequent talk that, for
fear of becoming boring, jumped from one topic to another
without giving adequate attention to any. He once wrote, 'I like

the company of people who go hacking on at the same subject, even if that is only how to get a lawn in good order. If they go on long enough the subject is usually illuminated, but I notice that most people begin to get bored just when I am becoming interested. I suspect I was born a bore myself; I prefer so distinctly the persistent to the hop-skip talker.' Desmond had no need to fear he had been born a bore. The movement of his mind was too lively for that.

His talk was made even more agreeable by its style, the language in which he embodied it. He delighted in words, and had an extraordinary eye for the right word and a special pleasure in finding it. The search was, more often than not, marked by a typical gesture. Pausing in the midst of a sentence, he would put out his hand with thumb and forefinger joined as if he was trying to pluck the wanted word out of the air. When he succeeded in finding it, he withdrew his hand with a little half-laugh of satisfaction. I remember questioning him about his first visit to an author he admired but whom he heard was formidable. 'How did it go?' I asked. 'Well,' Desmond replied, and paused to stretch out his thumb and forefinger; then as he withdrew them, 'I was ushered into a very *inauspicious* front hall,' he said. Again, I recall him pausing to define the quality that made a friend of his especially sympathetic. 'He is not exactly intellectual,' said Desmond, 'but', after a pause, 'he has a *clever heart.*' It was in his sense of words that the artist in Desmond MacCarthy manifested itself most clearly and vividly; and more easily in his talk than in his writing. This was true of its matter as well as its manner. The creative impulse in him fulfilled itself less readily in writing, which he found painfully uphill work, than when, sparked off in the give-and-take of conversation, it took fire in the unpremeditated, improvised mode of spontaneous speech.

One more distinguishing quality of his talk must be mentioned; its sincerity. Desmond combined an innate desire to please with an equally innate inability to give an opinion or judgement that was not what he thought to be true. Cyril Connolly has spoken of Desmond's 'strangely bleak and forbidding' expression when he was reading something he thought 'bosh'. If someone he was talking to said something he thought bosh, Desmond did not reply bleakly; he would have disliked hurting the speaker's feelings too much for that. So when possible he kept silent. But if asked directly for his opinion, he gave it courteously but truthfully. This sincerity it was that made his conversation morally impressive as well as interesting and entertaining.

To the end of his life Desmond's career continued to prosper. In middle age he made a brilliant name for himself in the new role of broadcaster; he was knighted in 1951, and in 1952 – what must have especially gratified him – his own university of Cambridge gave him an Honorary Doctorate. A few days after this he died suddenly; a lucky end for what must have seemed to the world a successful life. Yet, for him, its second half was less sunlit than its first. His old friends noticed that, though his company remained delightful, it had lost the high spirits that had marked it in youth. Often there seemed to hang over him a slight shadow of sadness. The reason was that, whatever others might think of him, in his own eyes he was a failure, both as man and as author. He had not fulfilled the hopes and dreams that he had cherished when young. Though he had planned and even begun several full-length works – more than one novel, as well as studies of Byron and Tolstoy – he had never completed any of them. Looking back on his personal life too, he found much to regret in it. All too often his friends had reproached him for being unreliable and forgetful; his marriage, too, had passed through some troubled phases. Desmond was too modest and too honest not to recognize where he thought he had been to blame and to feel guilty about it.

He was wont to accuse himself of being lazy and feckless. Here he was mistaken. These weaknesses suggest he was irresponsible; in fact he had an acute sense of responsibility, which was why he felt guilty. But he did suffer from one besetting weakness: an unusual capacity to respond intensely and immediately to experience went along with an almost uncontrollable inability to restrain his responses enough to keep him steadily on any course of action he had planned to follow. 'I have gulped down experience like a thirsty man,' he says somewhere; and, he implied, all too recklessly. In consequence his was a disorganized life. He had little sense of priorities, he muddled engagements, missed appointments, left work unfinished to the last hurried moment. If he became interested in a conversation, he forgot any previous commitment for the same time. I suspect that he was able to spend the whole afternoon with me, after our first enthralling lunch together, because he had forgotten he had an article to finish by that evening, or a contributor waiting to interview him at the *New Statesman* office.

It was partly because his life was so unplanned that he never seemed to find time to settle down and finish a book. His curiosity about other things was too easily stirred: life called to him as often as art did, and more compellingly. Desmond had the artist's talent; he had not the artist's vocation. He once said that he envied Max Beerbohm because his achievement, though on a small scale, was perfect, and this was because he could dismiss all other considerations in order to concentrate on perfecting it in a way that he, Desmond, could never manage to do. Desmond lacked the final powerful incentive that inspires the truly dedicated writer.

He was in special need of incentive too. As much as any personal weakness, the circumstances of his life were against him as an author – financial circumstances for one thing. He was no more orderly about his money affairs than about anything else: till he was middle-aged he was continually hard-up, a freelance journalist living precariously on a few hundreds a year, on which he had to keep a family in a period where there was no welfare state to pay for health and education. He was too affectionate and conscientious not to take these obligations seriously. The same conscientiousness encouraged him to put the blame less on circumstances than on his own weakness. Indeed, he lacked the basic belief in himself that might have strengthened him to overcome these weaknesses. Successive letters to his wife written over the years marked signs of a growing discouragement. As early as 1907 he was writing, 'I wish I had less to hope for and more to be certain of.' The passage of time was to diminish his hopes and increase his fears. Here he is in 1912 lamenting, 'How could I have wasted so few years of life? How could I be capable of letting myself be blown like a dead leaf into a sheltered corner, and hope to achieve anything?' But he adds, 'Still I am young enough for such regrets to be shot through with the glow of resolution and belief in the future.' Some words written five years later show these hopes, for the moment at any rate, totally extinguished. 'I was born to be a good writer,' he cries, 'and a rare friend. Idleness and fecklessness have spoilt me for myself and others.' A last quotation, though written in 1935 in the full flood of his apparent worldly success, finds him resigned to accept himself as a failure: 'I want to understand life a little before I leave it. I no longer expect to contribute something of this understanding to the world.'

These melancholy remarks must be included in a portrait of Desmond, for they are so characteristic. In themselves, however, they are mostly unjustified. Nor did they represent his prevailing state of mind. Apart from anything else, Desmond did not care all that much about personal success – he was too unegotistic, too lacking both in vanity and ambition – and his judgement was too objective to let him think that his own success was a matter of extreme importance. Moreover, his moods of extreme depression never lasted long. He was never for long wholly unable to enjoy himself and help other people to enjoy themselves too. But, over and above all this, when surveyed through the impartial eyes of posterity, Desmond's view of his achievement is revealed as a mistaken one. Whether considered as a man or as an author he was not a failure but a success.

The nature of his success as an author will be discussed in a later section of this introduction. For the rest, so far as his friendships were concerned, he was wrong to think poorly of himself. His friends might reproach him but their affection for him never cooled, for they never accused him of any serious shortcomings. He might muddle engagements and fail to answer letters, but he could be trusted to be unfailingly sympathetic and understanding; and faithful. Though he was always making new friends he never dropped old ones. On the contrary, he took pains to keep up with them even if he found them difficult or demanding. Altogether, and in every important respect, the story of Desmond's friendships is a happy story.

The story of his marriage cannot be so easily summed up. It was an unusual marriage, primarily because both partners in it were unusual people. Molly, in her own more retired way, was as remarkable and attractive a personality as Desmond; original, gifted, and possessed of a charm that mingled, with delicious unexpectedness, imaginative sensibility and quick perceptive Jane Austen-ish humour. Though too shy to be sociable in the way Desmond was, she had her own smaller group of friends – most of them very interesting people – who played a big part in her life and who enjoyed her company as much as they enjoyed Desmond's. Her writings – for she, too, was a writer – though fewer and slighter than his, had qualities his had not. Nothing he wrote is a complete and finished work of art, as is *A 19th-Century Childhood*, her book of youthful reminiscences. Altogether husband and wife were worthy of each other, and exceptional.

Alas, this very exceptionalness brought with it difficulties. Molly's character was distinguished by admirable qualities: she was unusually loving, just, generous, and truthful. But she was also unusually nervous, highly-strung, prone to fits of melancholy, and, when under strain, to violent outbursts of feeling which she found hard to control; and all the harder because she was a delicate woman who easily felt strains. Moreover, from very early in their marriage she was afflicted by a growing deafness which cut her off from others in a way peculiarly trying to someone as sensitive and quickly responsive as she was. Unluckily Desmond's weaknesses were of a kind that all too readily provoked nervous outbursts: his inability to impose order on his life led him too often to confuse his engagements, miss trains, suddenly change his plans. Added to this there was, deep down in his nature, a streak of detachment which made him unable wholly to identify his life with that of his wife and family as is the way in a perfectly harmonious marriage.

Circumstances intensified these inherent causes of trouble, financial circumstances in particular. Neither Desmond nor Molly was by nature or education good at managing money. The result, especially during their early years together, was that financial crises, mild and less mild, succeeded each other, and during these each partner was liable, with some justice, to suspect the other of managing badly. Sometimes it led each to say so. Desmond's work, too, was of a kind to come between them. Sometimes Molly's health disposed her to live in the country, so that he was often away. This gave him even more opportunity to muddle his plans and disappoint her by failing to come home at the time he had promised. Meanwhile absence led him, almost involuntarily, to develop a social life independent of hers, in the company of his men friends or inveigled to their houses by fashionable hostesses on the look-out for agreeable single men. Even when they were both in London, he went on living an active social life which meant an independent one. Molly did not feel it right to try and deprive him of this, but was too deaf and too delicate to want to take part in it herself; so they still tended to spend too much time apart, and she continued often to miss him.

At one period during the middle years of their marriage her feeling of loneliness was intensified by a new factor. The physical relationship between the two, had never seemed of supreme importance to either; and after a time, apparently by mutual consent, it came to an end. Afterwards both became involved in brief, transitory love affairs. With Molly this happened only once or twice, and without her getting any satisfaction from them; with Desmond it happened more often, and with greater pleasure. Later in middle age he found himself entangled with a demanding, insensitive woman. Molly, suffering at this time from the strain of her change of life, became jealous as never before, and passionately urged Desmond to break off the affair at once. It was broken off, but not at once; meanwhile he explained to Molly that it had never meant enough to him in any way to affect their relationship with each other. Molly's jealousy was understandable in the circumstances, but in fact Desmond spoke the truth; for, as anyone noticed who saw them together over any length of time, the MacCarthy marriage was a true marriage in a way that many less disturbed marriages are not. It was a union founded on a profound affinity of spirit which neither partner shared with anyone else. Even at their most strained moments there was never any question of either drifting apart from the other, let alone of the marriage breaking up: it was too indissolubly close. After a more than unusually stormy incident, Desmond could still write to her, 'Never have you ever said or done anything which has not something about it that, as soon as the pain struck was over, did not make me love and respect you more.' And again, 'Our marriage was based on a perfectly spontaneous delight in each others' natures and minds; and that this has proved lasting, though it has often been buried under pain and dispute, shows that the marriage of true minds is also a lasting marriage.'

These words were written during an unhappy phase. The happy phases were more significant. They grew to be pretty well continuous during Desmond's last years; for then age and weakening health led him to spend most of his time tranquilly at home. 'Dear Moll,' he writes a few years before his death, 'remember as we go downhill together, that in spite of nerves, in spite of scatterbrain moments that we both suffer from, we are closer to each other than to anyone else – we cannot help being more important to each other than to anyone else – we cannot help being all important to each other.' He could have added that, as much as in the past, they could still delight each other. This was one of the things that other people noticed when in their company. With delight went understanding. Even when Molly seemed at her most critical of him, Desmond could sympathetically enter into her thoughts and feelings. So also did she understand him. She shows this in her fictional portrait of him under the name of Fitzgerald in her novel *A Pier and a Band*, where she herself also figures as the heroine, Perdita. Perdita, she says, at first criticized Fitzgerald for not making more of himself. 'He seemed', she says, 'to take no pains whatsoever to keep himself up to the mark, and there was something at once tantalizing and ingratiating in this indifference. He might have been impressive if he had shown the slightest desire to be so; but he never did – a trait which suggested a disconcerting absence of ambition or resolve to use his talents to the greatest advantage . . . Perdita sometimes felt as if he were a full jug without a handle – full of precious liquid, but with no means of pouring it out. But, as she got to know him better, she discovered something strongly supporting in his character. She had never met anyone in whom so much detachment was combined with such readiness to value and enjoy human beings. In his company she found she could face the most disillusioning facts about the world and human nature, and yet feel, if anything, rather more affectionate and hopeful than usual. When with him, she seemed to get all the satisfaction and none of the pain of being perfectly truthful. There did not seem to be a single thing he believed because he ought to believe it. His critical faculty was of the order which usually produces cold indifference or savage impatience, but these characteristics were markedly absent in him.'

These words, published after eleven years of marriage, reveal how much she had come to depend on Desmond for her happiness. She was to go on depending on him always; so much so that in their last peaceful years together she seems at times almost to have forgotten that any trouble had ever overcast their relationship. After his death she told Rachel that, though the last years of her marriage had been the best, she did look back on the whole of it as forty-five years of happiness. Since she was an uncompromisingly honest character, this suggests that her memories of past happiness had grown so radiant as to obliterate all darker recollections. Certainly, after he died, her life seemed to her to have lost value and purpose. Perhaps because of this, her hold on living, never strong, grew weaker. Within two years she too was dead. An old friend of Desmond's in a letter of condolence quoted aptly a couplet by Sir Henry Wotton:

He first deceased; she for a little tried
To live without him, liked it not and died.

Their marriage had been strengthened and cemented by their relationships to their children. Both were very fond of them, very interested in them, and in general agreed with each other in their view of them. They were good parents. Desmond, indeed, was the best father I have ever known; the one who most consistently and affectionately illuminated and enriched his children's lives. When they were little, he enjoyed playing with them and had a turn for entertaining nonsense which made him do this very well. As they grew older, his relationship with them developed. In some ways this was on old-fashioned lines: he liked to instruct and guide them both intellectually and morally, and did not hesitate to do so. His letters to his eldest son, Michael, just in his teens, are almost like those of an eighteenth-century father in the way he points out the advantages of education, urges him to work hard, and warns him against any weaknesses he has noticed in him, especially if his experience has taught him to regret similar faults in his own past. On the other hand he was a 'modern' parent in that, when they were barely grown up, he began to treat his children as equals and to talk to them freely and intimately. When his seventeen-year-old daughter Rachel had left school and was living at home, he and she were often out on their own in the evening, though in different places and at different parties. If he came in later than her, Desmond liked to sit on her bed and the two would compare notes about their experiences that evening, describe and discuss the different characters each had met and the different circles in which each had moved. These conversations, and others, with so subtle and practised an observer of the human scene as Desmond, helped Rachel to acquire a knowledge and perceptive understanding of her fellow creatures granted to very few girls of her age.

She used to confide in him if she had become friendly with a young man and especially if she found herself attracted by him. Attentively Desmond listened and advised; the 'detached' streak in him – a disadvantage sometimes in his relations with Molly – was here nothing but an advantage. It made Rachel feel that his advice was objective, that he was not trying to use his position as her parent to influence her. For this very reason, it did influence her. She used to say that it would have been very difficult for her to marry someone against her father's considered advice; not because she feared his disapproval, but because she trusted his judgement. Once she brought home a young man who was interested in her, to be told by Desmond afterwards that he would be against him as a possible son-in-law, and given his reasons. Her first impulse was to disagree; but the next time she talked to the young man, reluctantly she became aware that Desmond's criticisms were justified.

Equally, he took an interest in his sons' lives and gave advice about them; advice which experience taught them was likely to be valuable. Over and above all this, his three children found his conversation as entertaining and enthralling and informative as his friends did. On his side, Desmond enjoyed the company of his children as much as he enjoyed the company of his friends. His relationship with them for once did nothing to stir up his all-too-active sense of guilt. As a father, even Desmond MacCarthy never found a reason to think himself a failure.

II

Though Desmond MacCarthy never completed any of his predicted full-length books, he did in 1931 reluctantly allow his friend Logan Pearsall Smith to make a selection from his occasional writings, and agreed to their publication. For this he himself wrote a preface which is the first item in the present selection. I have included it because it contributes so vividly to my portrait of him, recalls so exactly the smiling, rueful, unself-pitying sadness with which he spoke of what he regarded as his failure to realize the literary dreams of his youth. But the contents of that first collected volume, together with several more that followed, were proof that this sense of failure was unjustified. They compose an achievement to be proud of.

They suggest for one thing that, though he himself may not have realized it, the form his achievement took was in fact the form most suitable to Desmond's talent. The full-length single book was not the right unit for this to display itself, any more than it had been for Hazlitt or Saint-Beuve. Perhaps he had not the faculty needed for design on a big scale; certainly it would not have given him the chance to exhibit the variety of his interests and sympathies. This variety was extraordinary. Desmond MacCarthy is generally described as a critic, literary and dramatic; and indeed he was an extremely distinguished one. But the term does not properly describe him, for it implies a man primarily interested in the art of literature and drama, whereas Desmond MacCarthy, like Dr Johnson, was first of all a student of human nature. Because he loved and appreciated good writing, he particularly enjoyed studying men as they revealed themselves in books and plays. But he was just as ready to observe them directly, in actual persons and events, and just as well equipped to record his observations in the form of a report or a reminiscence. His account of London at the outbreak of war in 1914 is as good and as representative of his talent as any of his specifically literary studies. Moreover his most characteristic writings cannot be placed neatly into different literary categories. His pieces on authors whom he has known personally, such as Henry James and George Meredith, are pen-portraits of men as well as critical studies of their works; his review of Percy Lubbock's *Shades of Eton* combines an estimate of the book with memories of his own Eton days; is the piece entitled 'The crowds at Burlington House' best described as the account of an experience, or as a reflection on an aspect of human nature? Thus the following collection is no heterogeneous hotch-potch of reviews and reminiscences, but a unity; for, in all but a very few items its author employs different forms to achieve the same end, which was to express his own profound, acute, individual vision of human nature.

It was individual because it was the product of a very individual blend of elements: detachment and sympathy, moral sense and a sense of pleasure. The detachment showed itself in his realism. Partly, it may be, because of his foreign blood, he showed none of what, during his youth at any rate, was the typical Englishman's flinching from painful fact. No doubt much in life was ugly and baffling and disillusioning, but that only made it more interesting to Desmond, only intensified his curiosity to explore it further. To shroud the disagreeable in deceptive and idealizing dreams was feeble and futile. For him, a grain of fact, however harsh, was worth a ton of day-dreams, however beguiling.

This sense of the value of fact had been increased by the mental atmosphere in which he grew to maturity. His years at Cambridge had affected him deeply, and Cambridge in the early part of this century was the home of a liberal rationalism which made it a man's first obligation to search for truth by the light of reason, however chilly might be the conclusions to which this led him. Integrity, rationality, truthfulness – these were the watchwords of the circles in which Desmond Mac-Carthy moved at the university. They are rather depressing watchwords, and on many of his companions they had a depressing effect, imbuing them with a conscientious, joyless, pedantic agnosticism, more respect-worthy than inspiring. Not so Desmond MacCarthy! He accepted the Cambridge principles of thought; intellectually and morally he remained all his life a liberal. But temperamentally he was very unlike the typical English liberal. Here again, his foreign blood may have affected him. Not only was he inexhaustibly inquisitive about life in its every manifestation, but he delighted in it. Seldom can so unworldly a man have taken so much pleasure in the world. Let it be as irresponsible and flamboyant as it pleased; he only responded to it the more. Liberals, for the most part, are more tolerant politically than personally: they believe that every man should be permitted to do as he pleases, but they seldom take pleasure in watching him do it. Desmond MacCarthy did. He enjoyed his fellows all the more because they were diverse.

Further, he liked them. He was not at all put off by the spectacle of human imperfection. The worried, undignified animal called man, bustling about with his unwieldy bundle of inconsistent hopes and fears, virtues and weaknesses, stirred in him the amused, sympathetic affection of one who feels himself akin to him and, therefore, has no reason to look on him with dislike or contempt. Or even with disrespect: there was nothing of the sentimental cynic about Desmond MacCarthy. His firm grip on fact made him recognize the existence of human virtue, and he had a sharp eye to discern it. Instinctively he was always seeking to do so. Life interested him because it exhibited human character, and for him the centre of every character was its moral centre. After he has noted keenly and with enjoyment a man's idiosyncrasies of aspect or temperament, Desmond Mac-Carthy always goes on deeper to discover the moral nature behind them. Then, justly but relentlessly, he makes his judgement. The canons he judged by were appropriate to his own mixed nature. On the one hand he believed in honesty, good sense, and the courage to face facts; on the other in a readiness to respond to life and to feel deeply and delicately. No amount of brilliance could reconcile him to silliness or false sentiment or hard-heartedness. Least of all to hard-heartedness: for all that he appreciated Proust's genius, he could not bring himself to like him, for he perceived in him a fundamental coldness. He found Carlyle more lovable because he discerned, glimmering through all the acrid clouds of bigotry and bias which billowed smokily forth from his personality, the fitful flame of a passionate heart.

It is necessary to stress this moral strain in Desmond Mac-Carthy because it was this which turned his intelligence into wisdom, which gave depth and significance to his charming, humorous, acute observation of men and things. Consider his final comment after watching the crowd at a Burlington House exhibition of paintings. 'People seldom lie more flatly than when they utter with exasperating modesty the familiar formula, "I know nothing about art, but I know what I like." If they spoke the truth they would say, "I have some idea what others think I *ought* to like, but I have not the smallest notion what I do." The safest approach to the art of painting is not through the gate of aspiration or self improvement, but through the humble door of pleasure, and the first step to culture is to learn to *enjoy*, not to know what is best. It is not true that we needs must love the highest when we see it, only vanity ever convinced anyone that it was. Those who do not deceive themselves need no enlightenment on that point.' A similar wisdom reveals itself in the reflections on the evening of the outbreak of the 1914 war, or after attending the trial of Sir Roger Casement.

But inevitably, because he was by profession a critic, it is in his criticism that he is able to display his view of men and things most often and most fully. Though he could write shrewdly and sensitively on any play or book, he liked some sorts better than others: and it is about those he liked that his criticism is most memorable. His preferences were typical. He says somewhere that literature can be divided into the kind that adds the force of reality to imagination, and that which lends the charm of imagination to reality, and that the second is the kind he himself enjoys most. This is true. The books he valued most were those that extended and illuminated his knowledge of human beings. He preferred realism to fantasy; he was more concerned with a writer's matter than his manner, though anything he said about his manner was always acute. For this reason he is more characteristically successful on prose than on poetry. His mode of criticism exhibits first his imaginative sympathy and then his power of judgement. He starts by 'placing' his author, defining his point of view and the range of his talent. He then goes on to examine how far the picture of life revealed in his work squares with the facts of experience as he has himself observed them. Finally, he makes a judgement on the quality of the author's moral reaction to life as shown in his picture of it. Tested by such a process, some authors pass; others, though gifted, fail. D'Annunzio, for instance, fails. The spell he casts by his mastery of language and imaginative exuberance are, in Desmond MacCarthy's eyes, insufficient compensations for a basic intellectual silliness. Swinburne, on the other hand, though apparently a spell-binder of a simi- lar kind, comes off better: 'If one has kept one's intelligence alert in spite of the over-powering swing of his verse, one

As a schoolboy

As a Cambridge undergraduate

is often surprised at the subtlety and coherence of the poet's thought.'

Desmond MacCarthy is most at home, however, with the writers who do not go in for spell-binding; with Tolstoy and Trollope, Ibsen and Chekhov. This last particularly; for, when Desmond MacCarthy wrote about him he was still relatively uncharted ground for the critic to work on, and Desmond therefore had a chance to display his greatest critical gift which was the capacity to understand and expound a new, fresh vision of reality. Desmond MacCarthy has sometimes been counted as a 'conservative' critic, and it is true that he was repelled by the deliberate obscurity and oddness of some contemporary authors. He thought it cut literature off from the central stream of life. But to the end of his days he welcomed any author who ventured out to explore new territories of human experience; and he had an extraordinary power of discovering what they were after. Read the passage in his review of *The Cherry Orchard* in which he examines in detail a piece of dialogue between Madame Ranevsky and the student Trofimov; see how delicately he interprets each casual, fleeting phrase of their conversation, thus teaching us to discern the modulation of mood which directs it. He explains to us Chekhov's mode of expression, and makes us see how it is the perfect vehicle to convey his unique vision of human life. Chekhov was the ideal author for Desmond MacCarthy to criticize, for, like his critic, Chekhov combined an unillusioned realism with an unfailing affectionate amusement at the spectacle of the human comedy. No one could better appreciate Chekhov's ruthless charity than Desmond MacCarthy.

Moreover, he approached him from a point of view acquired by a lifelong acquaintance with the great literature of the past; and was thus able to relate him to it. Because he knows his classics, he can judge in what sense Chekhov is a writer of classic quality. He himself was a 'classical' type of critic; that is to say, he examined literature always in relation to important and permanent aspects of man's experience, and estimated it by rational and timeless standards deeply grounded in the European tradition of culture and not biased by the prejudice of any school or period. Cocteau is not too modern for him or Ruskin too old-fashioned: nonsense is equally deplorable whether he observes it in an Elizabethan playwright or in Gertrude Stein. If would-be critics today want to acquire a classical point of view, they should study the writings of Desmond MacCarthy.

They will learn how to express it too. His writing is a model of what critical prose should be, for he was without the conceit that inspires some critics to expect to find readers when they have taken no trouble to make their books readable. As might be expected from so famous a talker, Desmond MacCarthy's prose style is a conversational style; easy, casual, parenthetical, its unit the sentence rather than the paragraph. Like his talk too, his prose is marked by a subtle feeling for words; at every turn this gleams out in some vivid, felicitous phrase or epithet – 'Swinburne's strong, monotonous melodies', 'Hawthorne's pensive, delicate, collected prose', 'the passion which smoulders in the dark impersonal eyes of Rembrandt's Jewish portraits'. How delightful, too, it is when the steady, substantial good sense of his discourse is lit up by the flicker of his playfulness! 'I myself enjoy Swinburne's prose very much, but this is so exceptional a taste that I have been tempted to insert an Agony Column advertisement, "Lonely literary man of moderate means wishes to meet friend; must appreciate Swinburne's prose."'

To end here is to end my sketch portrait of Desmond on a humorous note. But this is not inappropriate. His humour was an essential element in his outlook; and, since he was right in thinking Swinburne's prose works unjustly neglected, the passage quoted is an example of how he sometimes chose a humorous tone in which to utter his thoughtful, truthful, opinions on books, and plays, and life.

TO
DESMOND MacCARTHY
Aet. 22*

I dedicate this book to you, young man, and you will not be pleased. You will suspect me of laughing at you: I admit to a certain malice. It was you who prevented me from collecting my contributions to the press during the past thirty years, with the result that when I finally made up my mind to do so, I found I had written more than I could read. If Logan Pearsall Smith, whose friendship, in the beginning, I owe to you, had not undertaken to choose for me, this volume and those which are to follow, would never have been got together. When I tried to do the work myself you were at my elbow, blighting that mild degree of self-complacency which is necessary to an author preparing a book for publication. I was afraid of you, for I knew I had nothing to print which would gratify your enormous self-esteem. Why, I ask, did everything I wrote seem to you, not necessarily worthless, but quite unworthy of you? I respect your high standards, but you have behaved to me like an over-anxious mother who prevents her daughter from making the

---

* Dedication, to a collection of his essays and reviews, written at the age of fifty-four to himself as a young man.

most of herself at a party because she is not indisputably a queen among the rest.

How angry you were in 1900 when I hinted that you would be doing splendidly if you ever wrote nearly as well, say, as Andrew Lang? Your dismay convinced me that you would, in that case, never have touched a pen – and yet you were not conceited. You were only hopeful.

Now, I am not writing this letter for your eyes alone, but for young men of your age who long to write books and have to live by literary journalism. That was our case. It is an agreeable profession – provided you get enough work, or your circumstances do not require you to undertake more than you can do; but it had dangers for such as you: the journalist must ever be cutting his thoughts in the green and serving them up unripe, while his work as a critic teaches him to translate at once every feeling into intellectual discourse. But artists know what a meddlesome servant the Intellect can be, and in the Kingdom of Criticism the Intellect learns to make itself Mayor of the Palace. Moreover, to frequent newspaper offices, to live always close to the deafening cataract of books is chilling to literary endeavour. So many good books, let alone the others, are seen to be unnecessary.

Of course you are disappointed with what I have done, though I admit that of each essay as it was written you were by no means an austere judge. Still, I always felt that your praise was conditional upon there being something much better to come – and I have disappointed you. Why? Partly, I maintain, because your hopes (I do you the justice of not calling them expectations) were excessively high. Parents would not be surprised at the difficulty of dissuading their children from the life of letters, if they remembered that there is hardly a masterpiece which a would-be author of your age would not blush to have written. He admires parts of the masterpiece – qualities in it – adoringly, but he hopes that he will be able to make its merits his own and avoid all its defects. Impossible! as critics know.

By the by you never intended me to become a critic, did you? I slipped into it. The readiest way of living by my pen was to comment upon books and plays. At first the remuneration was never more than thirty shillings a week; but the work was easy to me, for I found, whenever I interrogated you (though you continued to insist that there was within you something which ached to find expression), your head was humming with the valuable ideas of others. They were more audible than your own; they were useful to me. Some day, when you came upon a hushed space in life, away from journalism, away from the hubbub of personal emotions, I know you fully intended to listen to yourself; and discovering what you thought about the world to project it into a work of art – a play, a novel, a biography. But confess, you were too careless to prepare that preliminary silence, and too indolent to concentrate. Meanwhile how delightful you found it to imbibe literature at your leisure! And so you read and read. I must say I was grateful to you afterwards, for as a critic I should have run dry long ago if you had not been so lazy.

HENRY JAMES

In Henry James's later letters his voice is audible; nor is this surprising, for his letters were often dictated, and his conversation, in its search for the right word, its amplifications, hesitations and interpolated afterthoughts, resembled dictation. This sounds portentous, not to say boring; indeed, it was at times embarrassing. But – and this made all the difference – he was fascinating. The spell he exercised by his style was exercised in his conversation. Phrases of abstruse exaggerated drollery or of the last intellectual elegance flowered in it profusely. At first you might feel rather conscience-stricken for having set in motion, perhaps by a casual question, such tremendous mental machinery. It seemed really too bad to have put him to such trouble, made him work and weigh his words like that; and if, through the detestable habit of talking about anything rather than be silent, you had started a topic in which you were not interested, you might be well punished. There was something at once so painstaking, serious and majestical in the procedure of his mind that you shrank from diverting it, and thus the whole of your little precious time with him might be wasted. This often happened in my case during our fifteen years' acquaintance, and I still regret those bungled opportunities.

In conversation he could not help giving his best, the stereotyped and perfunctory being abhorrent to him. Each talk was thus a fresh adventure, an opportunity of discovering for himself what he thought about books and human beings. His respect for his subject was only equalled, one noticed, by his respect for that delicate instrument for recording and comparing impressions, his own mind. He absolutely refused to hustle it, and his conversational manner was largely composed of reassuring and soothing gestures intended to allay, or anticipate, signs of impatience. The sensation of his hand on my shoulder in our pausing rambles together was, I felt, precisely an exhortation to patience. 'Wait,' that reassuring pressure seemed to be humorously saying, 'wait. I know, my dear fellow, you are getting fidgety; but wait – and we shall enjoy together the wild pleasure of discovering what "Henry James" thinks of this matter. For my part, I dare not hurry him!' His possession of this kind of double consciousness was one of the first characteristics one noticed; and sure enough we would often seem both to be waiting, palpitating with the same curiosity, for an ultimate verdict. At such moments the working of his mind fascinated me, as though I were watching through a window some hydraulic engine, its great smooth wheel and shining piston moving with ponderous ease through a vitreous dusk. The confounding thing was that the great machine could be set in motion by a penny in the slot!

I remember the first time I met him (the occasion was an evening party) I asked him if he thought London 'beautiful' – an idiotic question; worse than that, a question to which I did not really want an answer, though there were hundreds of others (some no doubt also idiotic) which I was longing to ask. But it worked. To my dismay it worked only too well. 'London? Beautiful?' he began, with that considering slant of his massive head I was to come to know so well, his lips a little ironically compressed, as though he wished to keep from smiling too obviously. 'No: hardly beautiful. It is too chaotic, too –' then followed a discourse upon London and the kind of appeal it made to the historic sense, even when it starved the aesthetic, which I failed to follow; so dismayed was I at having, by my idiot's question, set his mind working at such a pitch of concentration on a topic indifferent to me. I was distracted, too, by anxiety to prove myself on the spot intelligent; and the opportunity of interjecting a comment which might conceivably attain that object seemed to grow fainter and fainter while he hummed and havered and rolled along. How should I feel afterwards if I let slip this chance, perhaps the last, of expressing my admiration and my gratitude! At the end of a sentence, the drift of which had escaped me, but which closed, I think, with the words 'finds oneself craving for a whiff of London's carboniferous damp,' I did however interrupt him. Enthusiasm and questions (the latter regarding *The Awkward Age*, just out) poured from my lips. A look of bewilderment, almost of shock, floated for a moment over his fine, large, watchful, shaven face, on which the lines were so lightly etched. For a second he opened his rather prominent hazel eyes a shade wider, an expansion of the eyelids that to my imagination seemed like the adjustment at me of the lens of a microscope; then the great engine was slowly reversed, and, a trifle grimly, yet ever so kindly, and with many reassuring pats upon the arm, he said: 'I understand, my dear boy, what you mean – and I thank you.' (Ouf! What a relief!)

He went on to speak of *The Awkward Age*. 'Flat' was, it appeared, too mild an expression to describe its reception. 'My books make no more sound or ripple now than if I dropped them one after the other into mud.' And he had, I learnt to my astonishment, in writing that searching diagnosis of sophisticated relations, conceived himself to be following in the footsteps, 'Of course, with a difference,' of the sprightly Gyp! Hastily and emphatically I assured him that where I came

[40]

from, at Cambridge, his books were very far from making no ripple in people's minds. At this he showed some pleasure; but I noticed then, as often afterwards, that he was on his guard against being gratified by appreciation from any quarter. He liked it – everybody does, but he was exceedingly sceptical about its value. I doubt if he believed that anybody thoroughly understood what, as an artist, he was after, or how skilfully he had manipulated his themes; and speaking with some confidence for the majority of his enthusiastic readers at that time, I may say he was right.

He was fully aware of his idiosyncrasy in magnifying the minute. I remember a conversation in a four-wheeler ('the philosopher's preference,' he called it) about the married life of the Carlyles. He had been rereading Froude's *Life of Carlyle*, and after remarking that he thought Carlyle perhaps the best of English letter-writers, he went on to commiserate Mrs Carlyle on her dull, drudging life. I protested against 'dull,' and suggested she had at least acquired from her husband one source of permanent consolation and entertainment, namely the art of mountaining mole-hills. A look of droll sagacity came over his face, and turning sideways to fix me better and to make sure I grasped the implication, he said: 'Ah! but for that, where would *any of us* be?'

Once or twice I went a round of calls with him. I remember being struck on these occasion by how much woman there seemed to be in him; at least it was thus I explained the concentration of his sympathy upon social worries (the wrong people meeting each other, etc., etc.), or small misfortunes such as missing a train, and also the length of time he was able to expatiate upon them with interest. It struck me that women ran on in talk with him with a more unguarded volubility than they do with most men, as though they were sure of his complete understanding. I was amazed, too, by his standard of decent comfort; and his remark on our leaving what appeared to me a thoroughly well-appointed, prosperous house, 'Poor S., poor S.

– the stamp of unmistakable poverty upon everything!' has remained in my memory. I never ventured to ask him to my own house; not because I was ashamed of it, but because I did not wish to excite quite unnecessary commiseration. He would have imputed himself; there were so many little things in life he minded intensely which I did not mind at all. I do not think he could have sat without pain in a chair, the stuffing of which was visible in places. His dislike of squalor was so great that surroundings to be tolerable to him had positively to proclaim its utter impossibility. 'I can stand,' he once said to me, while we were waiting for our hostess in an exceptionally gilt and splendid drawing-room, 'a great deal of gold.' The effects of wealth upon character and behaviour attracted him as a novelist, but no array of terms can do justice to his lack of interest in the making of money. He was at home in describing elderly Americans who had acquired it by means of some invisible flair, and on whom its acquisition had left no mark beyond perhaps a light refined fatigue (his interest in wealth was therefore the reverse of Balzacian); or in portraying people who had inherited it. Evidence of ancient riches gave him far more pleasure than lavishness, and there we sympathized; but above all the signs of tradition and of loving discrimination exercised over many years in conditions of security soothed and delighted him. 'Lamb House', his home at Rye, was a perfect shell for his sensibility. He was in the habit of speaking of its 'inconspicuous little charm', but its charm could hardly escape anyone; so quiet, dignified and *gemütlich* it was, within, without.

But an incident comes back to me which struck me as revealing something much deeper in him than this character-istic. It occurred after a luncheon party of which he had been, as they say, 'the life'. We happened to be drinking our coffee together while the rest of the party had moved on to the verandah. 'What a charming picture they make,' he said, with his great head aslant, 'the women there with their embroidery, the . . .' There was nothing in his words, anybody might have spoken them; but in his attitude, in his voice, in his whole being at that moment, I divined such complete detachment, that I was startled into speaking out of myself: 'I can't bear to look at life like that,' I blurted out, 'I want to be in everything. Perhaps that is why I cannot *write*, it makes me feel absolutely alone. . . .' The effect of this confession upon him was instantaneous and surprising. He leant forward and grasped my arm excitedly: 'Yes, it is solitude. If it runs after you and catches you, well and good. But for heaven's sake don't run after *it*. It is absolute solitude.' And he got up hurriedly and joined the others. On the walk home it occurred to me that I had for a moment caught a glimpse of his intensely private life, and, rightly or wrongly, I thought that this glimpse explained much: his apprehensively tender clutch upon others, his immense preoccupation with the surface of things and his exclusive devotion to his art. His confidence in himself in relation to that art, I thought I discerned one brilliant summer night, as we were sauntering along a dusty road which crosses the Romney marshes. He had been describing to me the spiral of depression which a recent nervous illness had compelled him step after step, night after night, day after day, to descend. He would, he thought, never have found his way up again, had it not been for a life-line thrown to him by his brother William; perhaps the only man in whom he admired equally both heart and intellect. What stages of arid rejection of life and meaningless yet frantic agitation he had been compelled to traverse! 'But,' and he suddenly stood still, 'but it has been good' – and here he took off his hat, baring his great head in the moonlight – 'for my genius.' Then, putting on his hat again, he added, 'Never cease to watch whatever happens to you.'

Such was Henry James the man. For Henry James the writer I shall attempt to find a formula.

He was a conscious artist, who knew more clearly than most English novelists what he wished to do and how he must set about it. That fiction need not be formless, and that a novelist's mastery is shown in unfolding a situation to which every incident contributes, was the lesson that his books could teach a generation, persuaded to the contrary by dazzling achievements in an opposite manner. To Henry James the novel was not a hold-all into which any valuable observations and reflections could be stuffed; nor was it merely peptonized experience. He was an artist and a creator. Of course the world he created bore a vital relation to experience, as all fiction must if it is to bewitch and move us; but the characters in that world, in whose fate and emotions he interested us, existed in a medium which was not the atmosphere we ordinarily breathe. That medium was his own mind. Just as there is a world called 'Dickens', another called 'Balzac', so there is a world called 'Henry James'. When we speak of the 'reality' of such worlds, we only mean that we have been successfully beguiled. We are really paying homage to the shaping imagination of a creator. How independent of the actual world are characters in fiction, and how dependent for their vitality upon the world in which they are set, becomes clear the moment we imagine a character moved from one imaginary world into another. If Pecksniff were transplanted into *The Golden Bowl*, he would become extinct; and how incredible would 'the Dove' be in the pages of *Martin Chuzzlewit*! The same holds good of characters constructed piecemeal from observation, when introduced into a world created by an overflow of imagination. They become solecisms, either they kill the book or the book kills them. The unforgivable artistic fault in a novelist is failure to maintain consistency of tone. In this respect Henry James never failed. His characters always belonged to his own world, and his world was always congruous with his characters. What sort of a world was it? And what were its relations to our common experience which made it interesting? There is no need to separate the answers to these two questions, which the work of every creative artist prompts. The answer to the one will suggest the answer to the other.

It is important to emphasize at once Henry James's power of creating his own world because, in every novelist who possesses that power, it is the most important faculty. Yet in his case it has often been overlooked. Critics have found in his work so much else to interest them: his style, his methods, his subtlety. From their comments it might be supposed that his main distinction lay in being a psychologist, or an observer, or an inventor of a fascinating, but – so some thought – an indefensible style. Yet to regard him primarily as an observer or psychologist or as a maker of phrases, is not only to belittle him, but to make the mistake we made when first Ibsen came into our ken. It seems hardly credible that we should have taken Ibsen for a realist, but we did. Despite his rat-wife, wild-duck, his towers and ice-churches; despite the strange intensity of his characters, which alone might have put us on the right track; despite the deep-sea pressure of the element in which they had their being; despite the perverse commonness of the objects which surrounded them – as of things perceived in some uncomfortable dream – it was under the banner of realism that Ibsen's battle was fought for him. Because his characters threw such a vivid light on human nature and our predicaments, we mistook them for photographs. And yet what we meant by 'an Ibsen character' was as clear to us as what 'a Dickens character' meant. The fact that we understand each other, when we speak of a 'Henry-James character', is the proof that his imagination, too, was essentially creative.

Most great novelists have given to their creations an excess of some faculty predominant in themselves. Thus Meredith's characters are filled to an unnatural degree with the beauty and courage of life, while Balzac gives to his a treble dose of will and appetite. The men and women in Henry James's novels, the stupid as well as the intelligent, show far subtler powers of perception than such men and women actually have. It was only by exaggerating, consciously or unconsciously, that quality in them, that he could create a world that satisfied his imagination. With this exception his work is full of delicately observed actualities. His men and women are neither more heroic, nor single-hearted, nor more base than real people; and, if allowance be made for their superior thought-reading faculties and the concentration of their curiosity upon each other, events follow one another in his stories as they would in real life. The reader may sometimes find himself saying: 'Would anyone, without corroborative evidence act on such a far-fetched guess as that?' But he will never find himself saying (granted of course the super-subtlety of these people), 'That is not the way things happen.' Whether his characters are children of leisure and pleasure, jaded journalists, apathetic or wily disreputables, hard-working or dilatory artists, they are all incorrigibly preoccupied with human nature; with watching their own emotions, and the complex shifting relations and intimate dramas around them. There is a kind of collected self-consciousness and clairvoyance about them all. They watch, they feel, they compare notes. There is hardly a minor character in his later books, not a butler or a telegraph clerk, who, if he opens his lips twice, does not promptly show the makings of a gossip of genius. There are other equally important generalizations to be made about the people of Henry James's world, but this is the most comprehensive. For the critic this peculiarity has a claim to priority, not on aesthetic grounds, but because it leads to the centre of his subject: what was the determining impulse which made Henry James create the particular world he did?

In that astonishing record of imaginative adventure, *The American Scene*, he continually refers to himself as the 'restless analyst', speaking of himself as a man 'hag-ridden by the twin demons of observation and imagination'. The master faculty of Henry James was this power of analysing his impressions, of going into them not only far but, as they say in Norse fairy-tales, 'far and farther than far'. Indeed, there are only three other novelists whom a passion for finality in research and statement has so beset, for whom the sole condition of a Sabbath's rest was the assurance that everything that there was to be said had been at any rate attempted: – Proust, Balzac (with whom the later Henry James had more sympathy than with any other fellow-craftsman) and Dostoevsky. The last two were very different men from himself, labouring in other continents. Dostoevsky's subject is always the soul of man, and ultimately its relation to God; his deepest study is man as he is when he is alone with his soul. In Henry James, on the contrary, the same passion of research is directed to the social side of man's nature, his relations to his fellow-men. The universe and religion are as completely excluded from his books as if he had been an eighteenth-century writer. The sky above his people, the earth beneath them, contains no mysteries for them. He is careful never to permit them to interrogate these. Mr Chesterton has called Henry James a mystic; the truth is that he is perhaps the least mystical of all writers who have ever concerned themselves with the inner life. Mysticism would have shattered his world; it is not the mystical which attracts him, but a very different thing, the mysterious, that is to say, whatever in life fascinates by being hidden, ambiguous, illusive and hard to understand. And this brings us again straight up to the question of his directing impulse as an artist.

It was to conceive the world in a light which (a religious interpretation of man's nature being excluded) would give most play to his master faculties of investigation. It was an impulse, or rather a necessity, to see people in such a way as made them, their emotions and their relations to each other, inexhaustible subjects for the exploring mind. A single formula for a writer is justly suspect; but entertain this one for a moment on approval. It may prove to be 'the pattern in the carpet'.

In the first place, it explains his choice of themes. His long career was a continual search for more and more recondite and delicate ones. He begins with cases of conscience, and in these already the shades seemed fine to his contemporaries, and the verdicts to depend upon evidence not always visible to 'twelve good men and true'. Then the formula explains his early fondness – long before he had found a method of constructing a world of recondite possibilities – for ending with that substitute for mystery, the note of interrogation. It explains also his excitement in discovering Europe, especially those secluded corners of European society where dark deposits of experience might be postulated without extravagance. (In *his* America everything was depressingly obvious.) It explains his passionate interest in the naïve consciousness of his Americans when confronted with Europeans who possessed more complex standards and traditions. Did they or did they not understand? It explains his later interest in children, in whom it is so puzzling to fix the moment of dawning comprehension. It explains his marked preference for faithful failure as a subject over the soon exhausted interest of success. It explains in a measure his comparative lack of interest in the life of the senses (there is no mystery in the senses compared with the mind); also his efforts to keep in the background, so that they might gather an impenetrable portentousness, crude facts, such as professional careers, adulteries, swindles and even murders, which nevertheless, for the sake of the story, had sometimes to go through the empty form of occurring in his books. It explains the attraction a magnificently privileged class had for his art, his 'Olympians', whose surroundings allowed latitude to the supposition of a wonderfully richer consciousness. It explains the almost total exclusion from his world of specimens of labouring humanity, to whom no such complexity can be with any plausibility attributed – a dustman in the world of Henry James is an inconceivable monster. It accounts, too, for the blemishes in his books; for his refusal to admit that such a thing as a molehill *can* exist for a man with eyes in his head, and (how it seems to fit!) for his reluctance, even when occasion demanded it, to call a spade anything so dull and unqualified as a spade. It explains the fascination of his style, which conveyed amazingly the excitement of a quest, the thrill of approaching some final precision of statement. And above all, it explains why he came to endow his men and women with more and more of his own penetration, tenderness and scrupulousness, till at last he created a world worthy of his own master faculty, in which human beings, when confronted, saw mysteries in one another's gestures, and profundities in their words, and took joy in each other's insight, like brave antagonists in each other's strength; a world in which they could exclaim about one another that they were 'wonderful' and 'beautiful', where they belonged to, or fought with each other, on levels of intimacy which had never been described before.

The words, which he found to describe the characters in this world that he loved, are unrivalled for revealing delicacy. His method is to present them to us through some other character dowered with his own power of appreciation. Mrs Stringham in *The Wings of the Dove* is, for instance, the medium through which we first catch a glimpse of Milly. She is first conscious of the immense rich extravagant background of New York from which Milly springs, and of which 'the rare creature was the final flowering'; next of 'a high, dim, charming ambiguous oddity which was even better' in Milly herself, who seemed, on top of all that, to enjoy boundless freedom, the freedom of the wind in the desert. 'It was unspeakably touching to be so equipped and yet to have been reduced by fortune to little humble-minded mistakes. . . . She had arts and idiosyncrasies of which no great account could have been given, but which were a daily grace if you lived with them; such as the art of being almost tragically impatient and yet making it light as air; of being inexplicably sad and yet making it clear as noon; of being unmistakably gay and yet making it as soft as dusk.'

Although this world is peopled with subtler men and women than that of any other novelist, the crown does not go to the clever. It is tempting to describe him as an inveterate moralist, who, finding ordinary scales too clumsy to weigh finer human qualities, employs instead aesthetic weights and measures. The consequent reversal of the verdict was one of his favourite themes. 'There are no short cuts', he seemed to say, 'to being beautiful; to be beautiful you must be really good.' He made us understand better the meaning of intimacy and the beauty of goodness.

If one were to attempt to suggest the morality or philosophy behind his books in a sentence, 'There are no short cuts to a good end' would serve the purpose. What are Maggie Verver and 'Milly' but beautiful examples of 'the long road', or Kate Croy and Charlotte Stant but instances of the disastrous 'short cut'? Where does the failure and vulgarity of the set in *The Awkward Age*, Mrs Brookenham and her friends, lie? Surely, in their attempt to take by storm the charms of refinement and the refinements of intimacy. In many short stories, recent and early, we find the same drama; the contrast between the charms and superiorities (even the physical beauties) which have been won, paid for, as it were, by suffering, thought and sympathy, and those which have been appropriated by money, sheer brute brain, or self-assertion. Whether the contrast is between houses or manners or faces or minds, the same law is insisted on that *there is no short cut to beauty*. It is curious that just as no other author has noted so subtly the liberating power of wealth, those aspects of it in which it may be even symbolized by 'the wings of a dove', bringing the inaccessible within reach, enabling a noble imagination to gratify itself, lending sometimes to a character, through the consciousness of its possession, an intensified charm, making some virtues just what they ought to be by making them easy; so no other author has insisted more subtly upon the beauty which wealth cannot buy, cannot add to, cannot diminish. How often in his books the failures are the successes, and the man or woman 'who gets there' is, to the artist's eye, the one who fails!

Up to the age of seventeen, like most boys, I read not only without discrimination, but without any clear idea that any-body ever discriminated in such matters. I had only one classification for novels, the 'good' and the 'rotten'. The latter were a very small class; nearly all were 'good'. Dickens was, of course, superbly good; but Wilkie Collins was also good, and so were Miss Corelli, Stanley Weyman, Scott, Miss Braddon, and a host of others whose names are forgotten. *Vanity Fair* was good, but so was *The Deemster* and *She*. It never entered my head that people did not say and do what in books authors made them, or that the writer ever left out anything which would have made the situation or characters more interesting. My attitude (except where Dean Farrar's school stories were concerned) was one of boundless acceptance. It never struck me that the explanation why life, as reflected in novels, was sometimes dull, could be that it was not reflected in them properly. I was very fond, however, of 'good expressions', a phrase which in my private vocabulary covered indifferently any words which pleased me, wherever I found them – in Milton, Dickens, Keats, or Sir William Harcourt's public speeches. I often missed them in books which I otherwise thoroughly enjoyed. One day I had to make a slow long cross-country journey from Eton, and m'tutor lent me two small volumes called *The American*, just the right size for the side pocket. These, I found, were full of 'good expressions'. The book (but not for this reason) had, I see now, a profound effect on me. At the time I thought I had merely enjoyed it very much, but something else had happened – I had discovered the art and the resource of the observer. Henceforward life was to be not merely a matter of doing things and wanting things, or of things happening to oneself; there was another resource of inexhaustible interest always to hand – one could stand still and take things in.

Nevertheless my own generation, when we discovered Henry James, read him on the whole for his substance, for precisely that side of his work which appears now to be wearing thin. Our generation, at least that part of it with which I was best acquainted and most at home, was interested in those parts of experience which could be regarded as ends in themselves. Morality was either a means to attaining these goods of the soul, or it was nothing – just as the railway system existed to bring people together and to feed them, or the social order that as many 'ends' as possible should be achieved. These ends naturally fined themselves down to personal relations, aesthetic emotions and the pursuit of truth. We were perpetually in search of distinctions; our most ardent discussions were attempts to fix some sort of a scale of values for experience. The tendency was for the stress to fall on feeling rightly rather than upon action. It would be an exaggeration to say we cared not a sprat either for causes or for our own careers (appetite in both directions comes with eating, and we had barely begun to nibble); but those interests were subordinate. Henry James was above all a novelist of distinctions; he was, indeed, the master in fiction of the art of distinguishing. His philosophy amounted to this: to appreciate exquisitely was to live intensely. We suspected, I remember, that he over-valued subtlety as an ingredient in character, and was perhaps too 'social' in his standards, employing, for instance, 'charm' too often as the last test of character. But whether or not we always agreed with his estimate of values, he was pre-eminently interested in what interested us; that is to say, in disentangling emotions, in describing their appropriate objects and in showing in what subtle ways friendships might be exquisite, base, exciting, dull or droll. That his characters were detached from the big common struggling world, that its vague murmur floated in so faintly through their windows, that they moved and had their being in an environment entirely composed of personal relations, aesthetic emotions, and historic associations, seemed to us unimportant limitations to his art. Nor were we particularly interested in the instincts or the will compared with the play of the intelligence. What was the will but a means, a servant? Or what were the instincts but the raw stuff out of which the imagination moulded a life worth contemplating?

It still seems to me, on the whole, a sound philosophy; only the fiction which reflects these things to exclusion of all else now appears to me to shut out much which is both more absorbing and more important than I once supposed – even also to falsify the flavour of those very experiences on which it exclusively dwells.

I have described Henry James's youthful audience during those years when his books in his later manner were appearing, because such a description indicates the angle from which his work must always appear important. He cared immensely for spiritual decency; nothing in life beguiled him into putting anything before that. He had a tender heart, an even more compassionate imagination, but a merciless eye.

I knew him for over fifteen years, but I only saw him at long intervals. In spite of admiration and curiosity, I left our meetings entirely to chance, for I soon discovered two daunting facts about him. Firstly, that he was easily bored (not merely in an ordinary but in an excruciating sense of the word), and secondly, that he minded intensely the dislocations and disappointments which are inevitable in all human relations. They made him groan and writhe and worry. The measure of how much he minded them could be read in the frequency, extravagance and emphasis of his signals that all was really well, across even those small rifts (to him they had the horror of gulfs) which absence and accident open up between people. Many have not understood the elaborate considerateness which is so marked in his correspondence. As I read Henry James, it was his sense both of the gulf between human beings and the difficulty of bridging it which made him abound in such reassurances. Like many remarkable men, while drawn towards others, he was conscious also of his own aloofness. There is a kind of detachment (it is to be felt in the deeply religious, in some artists, in some imaginative men of action), which seems to bring the possessor of it at once nearer to his fellow beings than others get, and at the same time to remove him into a kind of solitude. I think Henry James was aware of that solitude to an extraordinary degree.

His manner of receiving you expressed an anxiety (sometimes comic in desperate thoroughness of intention) to show you that whatever might have happened in the interval, on his side, at least, the splinters had kept new and fine; so that if your half of the tally was in a similar condition, the two would dovetail at touch. I have seen him keep a lady in a paralysed condition for five minutes while he slowly recalled everything about her. And if your talk with him had been something of a failure, his farewell expressed that what you had wanted, yet failed to get, he had also wanted, and that nothing must blind you to his recognition of any affection or admiration you might be so generous as to feel for 'your old Henry James'.

I imagine being interrupted here by a pointed question, 'But did not this agitated anxiety to signal, defeat its own end and make complications?' It often did so, just as some of his letters, long as they are, were sometimes almost entirely composed of signals and gestures. But to many sensitive natures who find the world only too full of callous, off-hand people, this exquisite and agitated recognition of their own identity and of their relation to himself was a delightful refreshment. To say that he was a magnet to muffs would be a grievous injustice to his friends, but certainly those who were most easily attracted to him were the sort who are excoriated by the rough contacts of life. He himself was clearly one of the most sensitive of men. The importance to him of urbanity, money, privacy, lay in the fact that they were salves. His art was a refuge to him as well as the purpose of his life. He was horrified by the brutality and rushing confusion of the world, where the dead are forgotten, old ties cynically snapped, old associations disregarded, where one generation tramples down the other, where the passions are blind, and men and women are satisfied with loves and friendships which are short, common and empty. I picture him as flying with frightened eyes and stopped ears from that City of Destruction, till the terrified bang of his sanctuary door leaves him palpitating but safe; free to create a world which he could people with beings who had leisure and the finest faculties for comprehending and appreciating each other, where the reward of goodness was the recognition of its beauty, and where the past was not forgotten. His sense of the past – of the social world's, of his own – which he recorded with a subtlety and piety never excelled in autobiography, was almost the deepest sense in him. Such reverence for human emotions is usually associated with the religious sense; yet that, as I have said, is singularly absent from his work. While we read his books, only the great dome of civilization is above our heads – never the sky; and under our feet is its parti-coloured mosaic – never the earth. All that those two words 'sky' and 'earth' stand for in metaphor is absent.

One word on the style and method of Henry James's stories. He is the most metaphorical of writers and 'metaphysical' in the sense in which that term was applied to Cowley and Donne. He abounds in 'conceits', that is to say, he often follows a metaphor or verbal association to its furthest ramifications, and ingeniously forces them to help him carry on his thought, which in this way takes many turns and twists in approaching a particular point. The characteristic of his later style is a spontaneous complexity. The sentences are often cumbrous and difficult, struggling through a press of hints and ideas which gather round every word and are carried on to help elucidating the situation; this end, however, they only achieve for those who take the trouble to see their bearing; and this requires close attention. But apart from the frequency of happy and beautiful phrases, both his style and his method of telling a story have often a charm usually associated with a very different kind of imaginative work. The charm of all writing which has the quality of improvisation is that, in such writing, the reader catches the author's own excitement in the development of his idea, shares his delight in dallying with it, in turning it round and round, or if it is a simple story, he feels it growing at the same time as he enjoys the tale. It is a quality which cannot be illustrated by extracts; but that much of Henry James's writing has this charm and merit, which usually accompanies simplicity of thought, is clear to anyone who analyses the pleasure he gets from reading him. He does not clip his ideas or cut his coat according to his cloth, but he weaves it as he goes along. As he follows this idea wherever it leads him, his readers are sometimes landed in strange places, and those who are capable of a psychological glow, experience again something like the thrill with which they used in their childhood to read such phrases as 'as soon as his eyes grew accustomed to the darkness . . .' what on earth is he going to see next!

When I look up and see the long line of his books, the thought that it will grow no longer is not so distressing (he has expressed himself) as the thought that so many rare things in the world must now go without an appreciator, so many fine vibrations of life lose themselves in vacancy.

CONRAD

I

I only saw Conrad once. I lunched and spent the afternoon with him one spring day two years before his death. The orchards of Kent were in blossom, the poles of its hop-fields bare when the train took me down to Canterbury. It was a drive of some miles from there to his new home, a large, airy, Georgian rectory, a few strides from its church – one of those short, heavy-towered little country churches which lie like great grey dogs about the fields and among the trees of England. His face was already familiar to me, though he was among the least photographed, least paragraphed of celebrities – for, once seen, his photograph was not easy to forget. The length of his head from chin to crown struck me, and this was accentuated by a pointed greyish beard, which a backward carriage of his head on high shoulders projected forwards. Black eyebrows, hooked nose, hunched shoulders gave him a more hawk-like look than even his photograph had suggested. His eyes were very bright and dark when he opened them wide, but unless lit and expanded by enthusiasm or indignation, they remained half-hidden, and as though filmed in a kind of abstruse slumberous meditation. Very quiet in voice and gesture, somewhat elaborate in courtesies, his manner was easy without being reassuring. He had the kind of manners which improve those of a visitor beyond recognition. He was very much the *foreign* gentleman. He evidently expected others not only to respect his dignity (that went without saying) but their own. I surmised that, like his own people, the Poles, and like the Irish, he might be lavish in compliment, but that anyone would be a fool who did not divine that his delicious generosity of praise might hide reserves of caustic severity. Following the sea had not left a trace of bluffness in his manner. His talk was that of a man who cares for what is delicate, extreme, and honourable in human nature – and for the art of prose. Intellectually, he seemed something of a Quietist; he did not enjoy provoking discussion. He praised, I remember, Henry James, and admiration in that direction might have been anticipated. For though the worlds of the two novelists were so different, their literary methods were not unlike, and again and again 'the point of honour' provided both with subjects. Moreover they had the same kind of devotion to their calling. His scorn, which in his seafaring days would have withered a slack-twisted officer whose heart was not in his ship, was ready now to strike the counterpart of such a character in the world of letters. Clearly in life and literature *noblesse oblige* was Conrad's motto, and I doubt if he would have been able to decide which of the two, life or literature, subjected men to the more stringent tests. It was evidently a necessary passport to his literary esteem to be able to write a fine sentence.

II

Though it would be absurd on the strength of an hour or two of desultory conversation, part of which was in French (a French lady was present), to pronounce upon Conrad's literary preferences; still I did get an impression that originality of mind in an author counted for little with him, if unaccompanied by an aesthetic sense. Perhaps, however, this is really a deduction (and a fairly safe one) from his own writing, which shows so strong a love of the sentence engraved as on a cameo. He would have understood Henry James's pathetic cry, 'I have sweated blood to give an amusing surface to my style!' I surmise Conrad 'sweated blood' too in the same endeavour, so laudable, yet so often a waste of pains. And on the top of that he felt himself impelled to attempt an intenser vividness in description. Try, just try, so to describe something that the inattentive reader must see it, and the attentive one can never forget that he has seen it. You will find it an exhausting task; especially if you are also determined your sentences shall run sonorously and gracefully. The easiest half of Conrad's life was that he spent at sea, hard though that had often been.

I remember thinking it characteristic that he should have expressed disgust at an eminent author, remarkable for gay candour, because on his first visit he had described how his father had taken to drink. This appeared to have shocked Conrad both as a sign of insensibility in his visitor, and as a breach of good manners, their relations not warranting such confidences. More obviously characteristic was his remark when, after lunch, he hobbled with me up a paddock avenue of elms. The spring wind was fluttering the daffodils at their roots and blustering in their budding tops; he stopped, lifted his face, and said: 'I walk here for the sake of that sound; it reminds me of the sea.' This peaceful nook in Kent did not seem his natural home; nor in the neat, white, quiet rooms did I perceive the impress of his peculiar personality – a sailor's tidiness, cleanliness, perhaps, nothing more. Of course, in the case of men who live in the imagination, it is silly to look for something characteristic in their surroundings; still, when I read his account of his leaving that home, on the eve of the war, for a long-delayed journey to Poland, I recognized there something that had dimly struck me about the setting in which I had seen him. 'All unconscious of going towards the very scenes of war, I carried off in my eye this tiny fragment of Great Britain; a few fields, a wooded rise, a clump of trees or two, with a short stretch of road, and here and there a gleam of red wall and tiled roof above the darkening hedges wrapped up in soft mist and peace. And I felt that all this had a very strong hold on me as the embodiment of a beneficent and gentle spirit; that it was dear to me not as an inheritance, but as an acquisition, as a conquest in the sense in which a woman is conquered – by love, which is a sort of surrender.' The last words remind me that his profound appreciation of English character was also 'a sort of surrender'. He sprang himself of a race which is effusive, touchy, superlative, electric; in early life he had come into close fellowship with English seamen, who, by nature and tradition, are undramatic in speech and gesture, gentle and steady, among whom the highest commendation possible is the signal, 'well done'.

The contrast between what their matter-of-fact persistence and corporate loyalty could endure, and the little fuss they made over it, inspired in him an admiration all the deeper since, however completely he had identified himself with their traditions, he remained in temperament a fierce, independent, sensitive, magniloquent Pole, with a far-ranging speculative imagination. He loved them so well, partly because he was so different himself. He saw their ordinary characteristics as strange attributes. He drew them, praised them, better than Kipling, because he was more disinterested and unlike Kipling, free from self-conscious national pride. His imaginative outlook was not limited by patriotism; England and that tradition were dear to him 'not as an inheritance, but as an acquisition'.

If you read *A Personal Record* and *Notes on Life and Letters*, you will come nearer to understanding Conrad and the relation in which his way of thinking stood to his work, than by reading his critics. Indeed, most of the penetrating things that have been written about his work you will find in those two books – and the authority is better.

It is superficial to class him, in the ordinary sense, among the writers of adventure stories, for though his stories are adventurous, the point of the adventure is ever the same: the spirit of loyalty in men, struggling, sometimes victoriously, sometimes vainly, either against the forces of nature, or the power of mean persons. In all his stories the 'immortal ruler' dispenses 'honour and shame'; 'shame' it may be to the stronger, 'honour' perhaps to the frustrated. Conrad is a profoundly ethical writer, though in the written word he always sought, arduously, for the beautiful. But this truth about him has been somewhat obscured by the fact that, unlike most writers whose inspiration is passionately moral, he does not postulate that the universe is on the side of good. On the contrary, his universe is utterly indifferent.

Many passages express directly what his stories exhibit imaginatively: a judgement which is passionately ethical and a conception of nature as indifferent to human values. In a universe, beautiful in an inscrutable way, but without justice and honour, it is man's glory to have put justice and honour. 'That is our concern.' There is no occasion for despair, for in defeat man also is great, and the spectacle of the struggle is sublime to the contemplating mind. Conrad then has no 'message'. He has, as these passages show, a philosophy of life, but it is not the kind which drives a man to win converts. He was also singularly free from worldly ambition, and he certainly did not write to amuse an idle hour. We must look, therefore, elsewhere for the impulse which made him a writer. He was born with a love of words, but there was, I think, in his case yet another. The Sibyl's writing is on leaves which the wind scatters, but memory flies after them and catches and collects them. I think it was because he had seen so many things in human nature and the world that he did not wish to be forgotten or to forget, that Conrad, to our great gain, became a writer.

III

Conrad's relation towards the public was more dignified than that of most of the eminent novelists. He did not volunteer opinions on subjects on which his view was of no value; he was also scrupulous in speaking only about those sides of art which he understood, showing thus a respect for art itself which appears to be rare. Possibly his early training in the merchant service taught him the difference in value between, say, the mate's views on navigation and those of the intelligent passenger. He seldom parted with his signature in any cause, and he respected his own craft so sincerely that he did not think it necessary for his manhood publicly to express strong views on the problems of London traffic, diet, or foreign exchanges. He modestly supposed that there were others who, compared with him, might be as well up in these matters as he knew himself to be in regard to story-telling and prose; and he seems to have held that an artist's work is so important that it ought to absorb him. In allowing this conviction to influence his conduct, he missed many opportunities of obtaining cheap advertisement and produced some very remarkable books. He lived for his work; and since hard work of any kind keeps alive in us a sympathetic consciousness of our common destiny, he never became dehumanized. I dwell on the point because his concentration was of rare intensity, and such devoted artists are scarce in England. Though he died at an age far from ripe as modern longevity goes, he had created his world and completed his personal contribution to literature. It is unlikely that his talent would have developed in any new direction; but men of letters have lost by his death that heartening thing – a living example.

IV

This achievement, the creation of his own world, places Conrad at once among important imaginative writers. The implications of that useful critical phrase are that the writer's imagination has left so vivid an impress on all he describes, that his reader finds it easy to adopt temporarily the same way of feeling and judging, and is aware of an inner emotional consistency, not necessarily logical, in the author's whole response to experience. It may be a bubble world, but it holds together. There is an indefinable congruity between the author's moral values, his sense of beauty, his sense of humour. The reader feels that it is inevitable that the man who sees human nature in that particular way should also see nature and inanimate objects as he does, should grieve or rage over a particular event, or sing a *Nunc dimittis* on such and such occasions. This is the difference between a creatively imaginative work and work which is the product of intelligence. Intelligence is a modest selective faculty; it borrows and envies 'this man's skill and that man's scope'; it can achieve wonders, but it cannot do one thing – it cannot create that unity of apprehension which is the life-breath of a work of art.

It was not the exploitation of tropic forests or tropic seas which made Conrad a remarkable novelist, but this power of thus creating a world dyed through and through with his own imagination; his Soho was as much part of this world as the Amazon. Of his contemporaries only Meredith, Henry James, and Hardy have done the same; they, too, have blown great comprehensive, iridescent bubbles, in which the human beings they describe, though they have of course a recognizable resemblance to real people, only attain in that world their full reality.

These several worlds may have different values for us; the relation of each to what interests us most in life may be more significant in one case than another; but the point is that such authors have at least qualified for greatness. Afterwards let us by all means measure, if we can, or compare the diameters of their minds; but unless we recognize that such imaginative writers are in a class by themselves we shall get the scale of criticism all wrong, and exalt most absurdly in comparison work which appeals to us because it happens to suit the intellectual or aesthetic fashion of the moment, or discourses upon matters much talked about. The same is of course true of history and biography. I am by no means sure that the mind of Gibbon was remarkably wide; but his history is self-subsisting, a marvel of intellectual and moral coherence. The work of Mr Lytton Strachey is another case in point. Its lasting merit does not lie in its being an expression of that wave of anti-hero-worship irony which is running across minds now rapidly qualifying as 'the elder generation', but in the imaginative coherence of the picture he gives of the past; its saturation throughout with the same quality of feeling, so that historic figures, however different in themselves, are presented as inhabitants of the same world. Such work may vary in repute (the appearance of another, and of course different, Carlyle might quickly put the nose of Mr Strachey out of joint); but it remains as a challenge, an interpretation, to which men may return suspiciously or enthusiastically – that does not matter – and which has henceforth to be reckoned with. I have stressed this point in connection with Conrad, because there is always a trough after a crest in the fame of imposing writers, and in a short time extravagantly denigrating things may be said of him, if it is not remembered that he has taken his place as a writer who has after all recorded an imaginative interpretation of life.

V

The last novel published in Conrad's lifetime, *The Rover*, was greatly enjoyed and not a little carped at – respectfully of course. I have no doubt that, had *The Rover* appeared not very long ago, reviewers and readers would have been so occupied with its fine imaginative qualities, that they would have hardly stopped to pick holes. Yet holes can in fairness be picked. I

In his late twenties

Mary MacCarthy
shortly after her marriage

In later life

enjoyed it immensely myself; yet when a friend said to me casually, 'I have just finished listening to a performance on the Conrad,' I saw what he meant, and recognized the justice of the criticism. Artistically, it resembles more a voluntary on a powerful organ to show its compass than a musician's constructed masterpiece. All the famous Conrad stops are pulled out one after another. We are given the familiar scene of passion, almost mystically imaginative and supersensual, tinctured perhaps with melodrama but never with a drop of sentiment, in which Conrad's lovers seem to fall together through the crust of ordinary experience into a shadowy grander world, where men and women grow to the stature of gods. We are given the scene of tempted and exalted honour. We are given the familiar contrast between the curt, mild-spoken English sailor and the turbulent, darker, more imaginative highly-strung man. We meet the enigmatic woman. Above all, we are given those descriptions of scene and place which create in us such a strange expectancy; the clean, large, empty room, or the sun-scorched yard of a lonely farm-house, which seem to wait like a stage for something to happen there; and horizons – changing, beckoning, beautiful horizons. This is his master faculty as an imaginative writer; this power of evoking a scene, a gesture, or the confrontation of two people, so that the moment seems charged with all the significance of what is to come, just as scenes vividly recalled by memory are apt to seem to us laden with what was to happen. When we remember how, long ago, someone looked up or turned away, or only, it may be, a hat and pair of gloves on the table, suddenly it may seem to us, that, even then, we must have already understood although we did not know it. Our own memories now and then create these magic moments for ourselves; Conrad could create them for others. It seems to me incomparably his rarest gift. I value such moments in his stories far more than his tremendous set pieces of storms and long breathless tropic nights. I become confused while reading *Typhoon* and the hurricane in *The Nigger of the*

Narcissus; too much, much too much happens. I forget how badly the ship has been already smashed; I forget how overwhelming the last wave but one was compared with the one I see coming. The little cup of my imagination was full long ago, but the waterfall goes on pounding down into it.

Conrad's subject was not adventure as his readers first supposed. It was the idea of loyalty. He said himself, 'There is nothing more futile under the sun than adventure. . . . Adventure by itself is but a phantom, a dubious shape without a heart.'

GEORGE MEREDITH

I

Turning over the Meredith letters, and reading here and there in them, brings back in pictures a December afternoon, still vivid to me across a considerable gap of years. I had long been promised a visit to the man whom of all living English writers I then revered the most, and at last the day had come.

Hero-worship some say is the duffer's virtue, though by no means all heroes are of that opinion. Is not Victor Hugo reported to have said of some young poet, 'He will never write well; he did not turn pale on meeting me.' Certainly the heroes would resent the imputation that the ardour of their worshippers had its root in incompetence. No: the saying evidently originates from those formidable people of whom the first thing to be said, and often the last, is that they are not duffers. But if they are right, it certainly needed someone with a touch of the duffer about him to share my excitement on seeing the smoke from the roof of Flint Cottage, that late December afternoon, as my friend and I ran up the rise of ground which brings the small

[67]

five-windowed house in view. Well worth envying that moment
was.

One who is young and a hero-worshipper approaches the
home of a writer who has fired his imagination with feelings
very like a lover's. Trees look as though they were expecting
him, and to pull the bell is a momentous action. On the
doorstep the lover's incredulity comes over him. Can the person
he will see the next minute really be inside? Savages have a
word we might adopt for this significance which clings about
certain places; they say that a place or person has *mana*. For me
the high box hedges, the damp gravel drive, the quiet house
with its black speckless windows, all had *mana*. The next
moment we were in a narrow passage-hall, hanging up our caps
and coats, and through a thin door on the right I heard the
resonant rumble of a voice. The great man was talking to his
dog.

He was sitting to one side of the fire, dressed in a soft, quilted
jacket, with a rug upon his knees. On a little rickety table by his
side stood two candles and one of those old-fashioned eye-
screens which flirt out green wings at a touch; a pile of
lemon-coloured volumes lay beside it. His face beneath a
tousled thatch of grey hair, soft as the finest wood-ash, and
combed down into a fringe upon a high round forehead, had a
noble, ravaged handsomeness. The vanity and delicacy, as of a
too aesthetic *petit maître*, which marks Watts's portrait of him
was not discernible; rather a noteworthy boldness. I guessed
him to be one of those men who seem bigger seated than when
on their legs. At this time he could not rise from his chair. That
keen look in profile, as of an upward-pointing arrow, had gone.
Old age had blurred his eyelids, and his eyes, once blue, were
faded and full of 'the empty untragic sadness of old age'; but
that vitality which had inspired many a packed page still
vibrated in his powerful voice, and told in the impetuosity of his
greeting. His talk was full of flourishes and his enunciation
grandiose, as though he loved the sound of his own words. This

characteristic at first, I remember, somewhat disconcerted me. It struck me that he talked with a kind of swagger, and I was not prepared for that. Copy-book biographies always insist upon modesty as a sign of true greatness. I had certainly found out that humility was not the invariable accompaniment of power and insight, but I still clung to the idea that great men were always as biographers say, 'simple'. Now 'simple' Meredith was not, nor was he 'natural', 'unaffected'; in fact none of the adjectives of obituary respect would apply to him. He was almost stone-deaf, which accounted for the exaggerated loudness of his voice, and the continuity of his discourse, which rolled elaborately along; but the eagerness with which he would now and again curve a hand round his ear and stoop forward to catch an interjection, showed that he was not a born monologist, and that he missed the give and take; though he was, I expect, one likely in any company to follow the sequence of his own thoughts.

My Irish name set him off upon the theme of Celt and Saxon. The English were not in favour with him just then; the Boer War (he detested it) was dragging lamely on, and he belaboured the English with the vigour and bitterness of a disillusioned patriot: few men thought more often of their country, or felt more need of pride in her than Meredith. He accused the English of lack of imagination in statecraft, and abused their manners and their unsociability, their oafish contempt of friendly liveliness and wit, the sluggish casual rudeness that passed among the wealthy for good form; mouthing out sentences he had used, I felt, before, and throwing himself back, before a burst of laughter, with the air of one saying, 'There, what do you think of *that*?' to watch upon our faces the effect of some fantastic, hammered phrase.

Then came the question of refreshments. What would we drink? Tea? Beer? – a list of wines ending with champagne (pronounced in French fashion, with a gusto that brought foam and sparkle before the eyes). I forget the beverage we drank, for, shouting like a boatswain in a gale, I was directing the chasing waters of his discourse to irrigate fresh subjects. I wanted to hear him talk of his famous contemporaries. Had he met Disraeli? No, he wished he had, 'he would have amused me very much'. Then followed an account of the most remarkable Jew he had ever met, a scholar of prodigious erudition and dirtiness, who had begun by tending goats upon the mountains of Romania.

By this time I had come to feel rather the zest behind his elaborate phraseology than its artificiality, and to marvel at and enjoy his determination to strike a spark from every topic, astounding in a paralysed old man, and in one to whom physical decay must have been the most depressing of all humiliations. Scraps of his talk I still remember. Speaking of Gladstone, he said he was 'a man of most marvellous aptitudes but no greatness of mind'; of Swinburne and his emotional mobility, that 'he was a sea blown to a storm by a sigh'; of Dickens's face, when he laughed, that the surprise of it was like the change in a whitebeam 'when a gust of wind shivers it to silver' – this spoken with rapid gesticulation, which suggested the vehemence of his talk in youth.

Indeed, there was still such a fund of invincible vitality in him, that it was incongruous to hear him bemoaning himself as one already dead and better buried: 'Nature cares not a pin for the individual; I am content to be shovelled into the ditch.' I remember how in the midst of such discourse, solemn as the wind in the pines, with a humorous growl in it, for an under-note, he looked towards the black uncurtained window, past which a few large snowflakes came wavering down, and that the animation of sudden interest was like a child's. It was a momentary interruption, on he went: yes, the angel Azrael was standing behind him, and he hoped he would touch him on the shoulder. It was, however, a nurse who appeared and stood over him, with a graduated glass containing some dismal fluid in her hand; and we, who had forgotten we had been listening for two hours to an old invalid, took our leave. I looked from the door. He had sunk back in his chair; and with a wave of his hand he sketched an Oriental salaam. Had we tired him unconscionably, we asked ourselves anxiously outside the door? As I was hoisting on my coat, I heard again that resonant rumble. He was talking to his dog.

I saw him several times after that, sometimes alone, sometimes in company with others. I thought I recognized the origin of that loud ostentatious enunciation which had startled me on my first visit; it was an echo, an imitation of the haw-haw drawl of the swell of the 'sixties. His small sitting-room when I first entered it was full of women's photographs; later one photograph reigned alone. He was a born amorist, and his most characteristic utterance that I remember, was *à propos* of the most intimate relation between man and woman; 'It cannot be,' he said, 'too spiritual or too sensual for me.'

II

The middle-aged usually suppose that to be 'young' means to have the same tastes and enthusiasms they had once themselves. This is rash, as anyone may discover by confiding his own youthful admirations to his juniors. To be young in one generation is not the same thing as being young in another. Yet youth has certain tendencies in common, its peculiar predicaments and susceptibilities; and to these the poetry of Meredith must appeal, so long as his ideas have not fallen too far behind the times.

This has already happened, but twenty, twenty-five years ago, Meredith's poems meant much to the young generation; his thought was inspiring The young are preoccupied with two subjects, love and philosophy. It is necessary for them to get some conception of their relation to the universe; also, some idea of what can be made of their own passions. Questioning, no doubt, becomes muted into a more or less passive process of getting used to life, and passions and desires are accommodated or snuffed out; but as long as any condition worthy to be called 'Youth' persists, so long is hope alive, rebellious or wistful, that there are stakes to be played for, and that something admirable, not to say astonishing, can be made out of the mixed stuff each young man feels himself to be. Therefore the didactic poet who can invest his judgements with beauty appeals especially to the young. His interpretations and the values he affixes to emotions, must of course suit the times; but granted they do, by combining thinker and artist in himself, he will kindle the young. (Witness D. H. Lawrence today.) What matter if he is difficult! To get at his meaning they will read and reread poems which to less ardent curiosity are indigestible. They will bring a jemmy and dark-lantern to his obscurest passages; nor will the swiftest allusion seem too elusive to the young reader who has caught the gleam of a revelation on a page. A hint will suffice:

> Show him a mouse's tail, and he will guess,
> With metaphysic swiftness at the mouse.

Meredith found such readers among my generation. And in their ears the assertion that 'he was not of the centre', that reading his poems was as tedious to the mind as oakum-picking to the fingers; that they were composed in shorthand if not cipher, sounded like the mumblings of Struldbruggs, or the peevish petitions of the Mr Woodhouses of literature, for a smoother and warmer gruel.

Meredith's themes were matters most urgent to them: how to make the most of that extraordinary agglomeration of feelings called being in love; how some kind of reconciliation between Nature's beauty and her laws could be reached and maintained; how, penned in by practical circumstances, room could be found for youth's herd of passions, hopes and desires – a problem which soon presses, raising dismay only paralleled, perhaps, by Noah's feelings while he watched the procession of beasts wind slowly towards the limited accommodation of the Ark; and finally how to learn to face the fact that the best things do not last, without losing faith either in them or in life itself.

This theme was one upon which Meredith was never tired of enlarging. He loved his own poem, 'The Day of the Daughter of Hades', because it taught in picture and story that even one day upon earth was good, and the beauty of earth satisfying even to one like Skiagenia herself, who must return to darkness. Death and destruction, the Scriptures say, have heard the sound of wisdom with their ears; it was Meredith's theme that only he who has been close up to them could catch the music of energy and joy that rolls through all creation. He was essentially a religious poet, and a religious poet who appealed especially to those who felt embarrassed when pressed to affirm anything about the nature of the universe or the soul, but remained by instinct loyal to life. 'God is not in his heaven (indeed, that is the last place where a God whom I could worship would be); but all *is* right with the world. . . . No; perhaps not all – but it is right enough.' Some such words would express the creed or no-creed of those to whom Meredith was a satisfying poet. How sustaining he was in great calamities I do not know. I suspect he might fail one then, because it was, above all, the mood of triumph that he was born to express. Only when you had struggled up out of the dark defile would he meet you again; then, there is hardly a poet whose greeting would be more radiant and inspiriting. He is the poet of courage; but of the kind of courage which is inseparable from hope.

III

When one comes to think of his work as a whole, prose as well as poetry, courage seems his favourite virtue. It is the quality he relishes so immensely in his amazing and often preposterous

aristocrats; it is what he praised, to the astonishment of the
Victorian world, above tenderness and self-sacrifice in women.
His laughter even is rather the shout of a victor over squeamish-
ness and vanity than the laughter of a humorist. Vanity, which
he often calls egotism, he detested, because he thought it
incompatible with any passion worthy of the Muse. Love had to
be noble strength on fire, or he tore it to pieces. As an amorist,
he detested those elements which most commonly and insidiously corrupt the passion he believed in – vanity and
sentimentality. It is against sentimental egotism in relation to
Nature and the order of the world as science reveals it, that
most of his didactic verse is directed. His attitude towards
Nature is one of acceptance and so far, it is religious. But in his
case, acceptance is not founded upon belief that *if* man understood, he would see that Nature satisfies his desires. On the
contrary –

He may entreat, aspire,
He may despair, and she will never heed.
She drinking his warm sweat will soothe his need,
Not his desire.

Meredith was the first Victorian poet to assimilate into his
poetic conception of the world the idea that death and battle is
the law under which all living things exist and come to their
proper perfection; and by poetic assimilation, one means that
the beauty which he understood and expressed implied that
this was true. Other poets, Tennyson for example, glanced at
the conclusions of biologists; but, for their inspiration, they
turned always away to pre-Darwinian conceptions of the order
of Nature. Meredith was the first poet whose sense of beauty
sprang directly from the contemplation of Nature as 'red in
tooth and claw', and from an acceptance, not only of man's
mortality, but of the passing of all good things. His poetry is a
paean of affirmation in the face of these facts. In one of his

letters, when he was near upon eighty, he wrote: 'I can imagine that I shall retain my laugh in Death's ear, for that is what our Maker prizes in men.' And once Meredith had embraced this faith, vague enough in form, he kept his ear alert for every message or clue to practical conduct that his interpreting imagination might divine in Nature. It is this part of his work which is perishable stuff. In those poems he becomes too much the schoolmaster abroad, tagging instruction and exhortation on to every scene and incident. A thrush tapping a snail, a night of frost in May, a cutting wind, everything he perceives turns to homily. We may welcome this when we are young enough to be prodigiously interested in the improvement of our own characters: but it is the response of the poet rather than the hearty confidence of the moralist which, in the long run, affects us most. The moralist in Meredith cramped his receptivity; he was often insufficiently passive towards what he described to write his best. There is a monotony of strenuous zeal in his work. His aim is too often to strike some spark out of objects which might kindle a useful fire of enthusiasm, rather than to exhibit them in their beauty. But it is not for those on whom such sparks have fallen, even though they did no more than light a blaze of straw, to gird at him for that. And setting aside this didactic element in his work, he has written memorable things which we can quote,

> For proof that there, among earth's dumb
> A soul has passed and said our best.

His delight in physical vigour, his laughter which is 'a sudden glory', his preoccupation with the question – how fine characters are made? – his praise of courage, his abounding hope, his respect for thought, his delight in the passion of love, made him youth's poet. His very difficulty made his verse companionable to us; his hard sayings were good to ruminate, and as satisfying as a crust of good bread on a long day's walk. Meredith made a welcome third when two friends travelled on foot together. His thought bred discussion; they could unpack his phrases together; his words brought Nature nearer and companions closer, when –

> To either, then an untold tale
>   Was Life, and author, hero, we;
> The chapters holding peaks to scale,
>   Or depths to fathom, made our glee;
> For we were armed of inner fires,
> Unbled in us the ripe desires;
>   And Passion rolled a quiet sea,
> Whereon was Love the phantom sail.

IV

Meredith's poems attracted little notice, but brought him the acquaintance of Swinburne and Rossetti. Possessing the instincts of a novelist as well as the enthusiasm of a poet, it was natural that he should care more than either Rossetti or Swinburne for the contacts of Society, its elegancies, amenities and chicaneries so dear to the museful eye of the comic spirit; while as a poet, too, he felt far more than they the romance and interest of the big common world. He belongs to that small class of novelists (when we have mentioned his name, Emily Brontë, d'Annunzio, and perhaps, George Sand, we seem to have almost exhausted it) who may be described as poet-novelists; writers who strike one as being poets first and novelists afterwards. Meredith's most noticeable, his most distinctive characteristic as a novelist, is lyrical emotion. As a story-teller he is impatient of all episodes and incidents which do not lend themselves to transfiguration. As Henry James has said, 'He harnesses winged horses to the heavy car of fiction.' No better metaphor for him as a novelist can be found than that of a charioteer driving at the mercy of such a team; rejoicing in the sparks they strike from the high-road of narrative, wheeling round sharp corners with a masterful grasp on the reins; and gloriously confident and at ease only when at last he feels himself rising on the lift of wings. He is at his best when he attempts what only a poet can do. In giving us the sense of time and change, in the composition of a story, in allowing his characters freedom to show themselves, in producing the confidence that the events narrated, and no others, were inevitable, he is far from being a master; but at moments of tragic significance, of exultation, of profound happiness, he is supreme. Hardly any fine novelist has been so little of an *observer*. In conversation, he used to disparage characters in fiction constructed from the hoardings of observation. He took hints from the real world and created from them another which was a fit stage for men and women filled with the courage and beauty of life. He drew the children of leisure and pleasure not as they are, but as it delighted him to contemplate them, keeping in reserve a ray of derision to illuminate their capricious activities and fantastic dilemmas.

V

After his early poems followed the longest silence in his career as a writer; an interval which there is reason to think was the period of his 'ordeal'. At the end of five years, *The Shaving of Shagpat* appeared (written at Weybridge with duns at the door). As a boy, he had been devoted to *The Arabian Nights*, and the book is a fantasia on an Arabian theme. It is utterly un-Oriental, though 'perfumed with gums of Paradise and Eastern air'. It is not one of his fine books, but in Meredith's life it has the significance of *Sartor Resartus* in Carlyle's. Henceforward he too has his philosophy, the product of his imaginative reason. *Shagpat*, with its towerings of gaiety, its rollicking praise of thwacks, its confidence that salutary and saving grace is to be found in fortune's blows, marks the birth of his faith. Like *Sartor*, it records a conversion. He has got his courage, the ground of his optimism, the justification of his delight in life, the conviction that, to the brave life must be *good*, which he expresses again and again in verse and prose. Whatever else the world was to him, it was emphatically a place where courage was the most necessary virtue. 'The more I know of the world,' he said, 'the more clearly I perceive that its top and bottom sin is cowardice, physically and morally.' Henceforth he is free. What price he had paid for that freedom no one, of course, can know; but henceforward, pain, evil, and grief never appear in his work as utterly useless and meaningless. They have not a Boig-like quality. (You remember that ghastly and profound invention of Ibsen's in *Peer Gynt*, that shapeless, overwhelming, nightmarish *something* which confronts Peer and bids him 'go round' – and he can't?) Tragedy in Meredith never has that quality. The absence of it, as much as the keen auroral light in which his fortunate figures stand, gives to his work the colours of an indomitable optimism, of a victorious happiness which owes nothing to radiance borrowed from another world. It is noticeable that *Modern Love*, which was quarried out of the experience of those years before he had found his philosophy, is the saddest of his works. In *Modern Love* there is a sense of nothing having come from what once was much – of beauty destroyed. It is significant that it should be the poem, perhaps the only one of his poems, which finds favour with the young generation today. It is certainly free from that optimism, which they cannot help interpreting as an offensively artificial robustness. Meredith himself had no great liking for *Modern Love*, though it is certainly one of the finest things he wrote. He thought the poem morbid; he missed in it his own philosophy. He put 'The Day of the Daughter of Hades' at the head of all his poems, a judgement of his old age, only explicable when one remembers that this poem expresses directly his conception of the right attitude towards the brevity and tragedy of life.

VI

Meredith has more fault-finders among his critics than he ever had before. His drawing of character and his style can best be defended, it seems to me, on some such lines as these.

Every sentence he wrote, whether you like it or not, shows a love of his craft you must respect. How can one describe the general characteristics of this very personal style, in which many touches are there not so much to help you to realize the object as to put power into the form, a style in which 'reflection on a statement is its lightening in advance'? Firstly, it is the style of a poet, metaphorical, fearless and allusive. Nothing in Meredith is more remarkable than his power of swift allusion. To that gift he also owes his power of suggesting beauty and intensity of feeling in his characters. When we come to examine *how* we have been brought to realize so unforgettably his men and women, the impression they have made upon us seems due, not, as in the case of the creations of other novelists to our having known them intimately, but chiefly to this poetic gift of allusion. In describing them he 'shoots at nature' and at what is most beautiful in nature. To him (for Nature to him is alive and divine) these allusions are no mere metaphors, they are almost revelations of the one truth. If I did not believe that a man's philosophy sprung from his feelings and not his feelings from his philosophy, I would say that his philosophy was the origin of his power of convincing us of the beauty of which human nature is capable. Here is an instance of his power of describing human emotion in terms of nature, which will recall many others: 'Rapidly she underwent her transformation from doubt-fully-minded woman to woman awakening clear-eyed, with new sweet shivers in her temperate blood, like the tremulous light seen running to the morn upon a quiet sea.'

And if our sense of the beauty of character, and the impress-iveness of his men and women are due to his drawing upon what is beautiful in nature to express what he feels about them, how much too is our retention of the most moving scenes in his stories due to his having created a romantic harmony between the passions described and surrounding nature; a harmony so complete that in memory both rise up together. We remember Clara Middleton, because, besides being an extremely sensible, quick-witted young lady, she has reminded us of so many beautiful things, of summer beechwoods with brown leaves underfoot, of mountain echoes and torrents with their ravishing gleams of emerald at the fall; and how closely involved, also, are such scenes as Diana's early morning walk on the slopes above Lugano with her character. Through the description of the scene we understand her feelings, so that, like her lover Dacier, we also know her best when we remember the rolling grass meadows and pale purple crocuses, the rocky pool beneath the icy cascade. Sandra herself, waiting, with the patience of passion under the cedars in the yellowish hazy moonlight, is indistinguishable from that scene, and our comprehension of Beauchamp's eagerness, travelling to obey the sudden summons of Renée, is one with the sight of the Normandy coast, 'dashed in rain-lines across a weed-strewn sea'. How distinctly too Richard's desolate convalescence is stamped upon the country the train passes as it carries him away from his love, the pine hills, and the last rosy streak in the sky! But most wonderful of all for harmony between nature without and emotion within, is the chapter in *Richard Feverel* called 'Nature Speaks'. The chapter in which, after hearing that Lucy has borne him a son, he walks rapidly into the woods, and a storm breaks over him. Every detail of the storm, the oppressive slumber of the air, the crash and quiver of the heavens, the cool steady drench of rain, seem in turn to express better than direct description the feelings which take him back to her at last.

It is this poetic power, *not* Meredith's power of analysis, which makes us feel afterwards that we have lived in his characters. In tracing a train of internal reflection, in following the thoughts which were those of that particular person and no other, he is not an equal of such writers as Tolstoy or Henry James. He may surprise in a flash sentiment at its source, but it is much truer to say of him than of them, that when he is no longer writing as a poet, he *dissects* his characters. He does not, like Henry James, turn and return with intricate delay, till by almost abstaining from touching the subtle thing he conveys it at last to you living and complete. In *Sandra Belloni* he says of the Pole family that they all had a kind of dim faculty of imagination. One sees how true that might be of them; but when he handles the three sisters ('the three fine shades and the nicer feelings', as he calls them), it vanishes. He knows the quality is there; he tells us it is there. But in their talk – for their thoughts he makes no attempt to follow – it does not appear. He is no artist in psychology.

Again, what lapses of credibility occur in his plots! No novelist who was a thorough artist in his craft would have ever left unexplained, or so little explained, such a number of important occurrences. How did Diana come to marry Mr Warwick? Meredith makes some casual attempts long afterwards to make it credible, but he avoided the scene. Why did Nesta engage herself to Sowerby? It is not explained. Then there is the case of Richard Feverel. After he had yielded to the 'enchantress' and rushed abroad, he destroyed unread letter after letter from his wife. Accept the fact that he did so. Would not the first time that he handled an envelope with Lucy's writing on it have been a moment in his 'ordeal' worthy of the novelist's art? We are only told that he had gone on destroying unread letter after letter. There are instances of this kind in almost every novel. Meredith's admirers must admit that, when he is not writing as a poet, he often fails to handle the novel like an artist; that he often does not go thoroughly into his theme, nor treat it with an artist's respect. But he was a poet, and he did the best things in his novels best.

SAMUEL BUTLER

Samuel Butler played a not unimportant part in my own
education (I made his acquaintance when I was ten years old),
and later my work as a journalist and critic was often concerned
with his books. In 1909 I edited a periodical called the *New
Quarterly*, and Festing Jones gave me for it extracts from Samuel
Butler's *Note Books*. Butler was not yet famous. When he died, in
June 1902, the measure of his reputation was given by an article
in *The Times*, regretting that so talented a man had not done
more. That estimate seemed later beside and far below the
mark. Samuel Butler was one of those rare, incontestable
personalities in literature, who affect permanently the thought
and temper of all predisposed to their influence; indeed, the first
impression made on anyone reading his *Note Books*, which date
from the 'sixties, may well be that many of Butler's ideas are
those which are at the present moment 'in the air', and by 'in
the air', of course, people mean in the papers of other men's
books.

Later, Bernard Shaw pointed out his own debt to him in his
Preface to *Major Barbara*, which was one of the earliest and most
effective statements of Butler's claim to wider recognition. In

this Preface, Mr Shaw insisted that Butler 'in his own depart-
ment was one of the greatest writers of the nineteenth century'.

As a moralist, Butler was a confirmed hedonist and Laodi-
cean; *surtout point de zèle*, he believed was the finest motto ever
coined for humanity. He really and utterly believed that compromise was the guide to life; he saw compromise written over
the face of all creation. And not only in action, but in thought,
right behaviour and truth were best obtained by combining the
conflicting reports of faith and reason. The blend was only
perfectly satisfactory when the balance was reached unconsciously; every philosophy was nonsense when ridden home,
and every moral ideal which outsoared the practice of averagely
good men was suspect. Scattered up and down his books are
aphorisms to the effect that a man whose mind is of the right
temper must be certain in spite of uncertainty, and uncertain in
spite of certainty, which in practice comes to something like
having a sense of humour, for it is characteristic of humour to
hold together, at the same moment, the profound and the
superficial, the doubtful and the obvious, the serious and the
indifferent aspects of things. The favourite virtue of the humorist is always toleration: it was Butler's favourite virtue, too.

The most comprehensive description of Samuel Butler as a
writer is, then, that he was a humorous philosopher. The
interdependence of his philosophy and his humour is, indeed,
often so complete that it is puzzling to decide whether he was a
philosopher who chanced upon explanations which would
justify humour, or a born humorist who set out in search of a
philosophy to explain the way things naturally struck him.
Both processes had a share in his work. He saw jokes where no
one else saw them, because, sceptical and curious, he looked at
everything in his own way; and things would occur to him first
as jokes which afterwards impressed him as perfectly true.
Butler's sense of humour often performed the service for him
that the dove did for Noah in the ark. It flew out into the
unknown, bringing back to him an indication that he would

soon find solid ground beneath his feet. The humorous philosopher is rare, but when he does appear his influence quickly spreads. We laugh with him, not taking him seriously, and lo! we have already caught his way of thinking.

I made Butler's acquaintance at an hotel in the valley of the Saas in Switzerland, where I was staying with my parents. Opposite us at *table d'hôte* sat an elderly man with very bushy black eyebrows, and with him, from time to time, they interchanged a few cheerful polite remarks. A day or two later I happened to feel an extreme reluctance to notice the bell which announced the midday meal, and instead of going in I continued to clamber about the valley rocks. After a short interval I saw what I knew I should see next, my mother appearing at the door of the hotel frantically waving her parasol. This was a signal which could not be ignored like the bell. She had evidently waited until lunch had well begun, and then, losing patience, come out to fetch me. I was not surprised. What did surprise me was that she was presently followed by the old gentleman with the thick eyebrows. As we all three entered the hotel together he whispered: 'I thought I'd better come, with a stranger Mama couldn't be quite so angry.' It was only long afterwards that I realized how it was kind of an elderly gentleman to jump up from his midday meal and hurry out into the blazing sun to protect a small boy from a scolding; but when I did, I realized also that it was thoroughly characteristic of him to suppose that *every* child was likely to be bullied by its parents. (Readers of *The Way of All Flesh* will understand.) After that, I used often to go sketching with him. No doubt while he sketched and I lay beside his easel he talked wisely, but I heeded him not. I cannot remember a scrap of our conversations. But I do remember that on Sunday mornings at breakfast he used to say: 'Do you think Mr Selwyn would mind (Mr Selwyn was the chaplain, and in those days every hotel haunted by the British had its chaplain), do you think Mr Selwyn would forgive us if we did *not* go to church?' (He had been pleased to find that my favourite text was 'And now to God the Father, God the Son, etc.') And off we would go together. If our acquaintance had ended there I should have little to tell, but later, when I was in London, I used sometimes to go and see him in his rooms in Clifford's Inn. I was dimly aware that he was a remarkable man – but that was not the sort of fact which interested me. I only divined it from the interest my father took in his conversation, while I ate nuts and apples and listened. Mr Butler would sometimes give me one of his books, always with strict injunctions not to attempt to read it.

As I grew older I began to go and see him by myself. He often talked in a way which both puzzled and amused me, giving me advice of which I could make nothing at the time, advice which did not agree at all with that of my masters and pastors. For instance, he would say, looking at me gravely: 'As long as you tell no lies to yourself and are kind, you may lie and lie and lie and yet not be untrue to any man.' Once I remember giving up the last two hours of the Eton and Harrow match – it's true the result was a foregone conclusion – in order to go and see him. Instead of sitting and keeping the bowling averages, I went off to listen to his talk, which, I take it, is one of the greatest compliments ever paid to a philosopher in England. I must have been seventeen then, I was beginning to understand him.

In stature he was a small man, but you hardly noticed that. His slightly built frame was disguised in clothes of enviable bagginess and of a clumsy conventional cut, and he wore prodigiously roomy boots. But it was the hirsute, masculine vigour of his head which prevented you from thinking him a small man. Indeed, it was a surprise to me to hear afterwards that he had coxed at Cambridge the St John's boat: I had remembered him, it seemed, as even rather a heavy man. His company manner was that of a kind old gentleman, prepared to be a little shocked by any disregard of the proprieties; the sort of old gentleman who is very mild in reproof, but whose quiet insistence that everybody should behave properly is most soothing to elderly ladies of limited means. He spoke softly and slowly, often with his head a little down, looking gravely over his spectacles and pouting his lips, and with a deliberate demureness so disarming that he was able to utter the most subversive sentiments without exciting more than a moment's astonishment. The next, his companion was completely reassured. 'No, Mr Butler could not have meant that. I wasn't quite quick enough. Mr Butler is such an *original* man.' Such was the impression he made on circumspect, humdrum people. It was comic to anyone who knew what a bull in a china shop he really was. And though he was a great adept at poking gentle fun at people, he never snubbed them or scored off them. In fact, he had a strong abhorrence to anything of that kind. I think he enjoyed, a little, the irony which resides in perfect politeness, but politeness was not in the least a pose on his part. It sprang from his dislike of overbearingness. To take advantage of superiority of intellect, or any other kind of superiority, moral force, knowledge of the world, reputation, wealth, social position, a fine manner, and to use it to browbeat a helpless person, was in his eyes a revolting, unpardonable offence. I often heard him use the word 'caddish', and it always stigmatized that kind of behaviour. If I were to mention the names of those he called 'cads' the list would cause great surprise. Besides, he liked mediocre, humdrum people; they were at any rate freer from this odious sin than the intellectual and successful.

I asked him once if he were any relation to the late Master of Trinity, Dr Butler. 'What!' he exclaimed with soft and gentle emphasis, '*that* beastly cad!' It took me a moment or two to rearrange my ideas – on the Master, caddishness, Samuel Butler himself! Then I guessed: Dr Butler's eighteenth-century suavity might easily strike his namesake as coming suspiciously near an attempt to play him off the social stage, though in the Master's case it was nothing of the kind. Perhaps – I knew they had met after Samuel Butler's *Authoress of the Odyssey* had appeared – the Master had asked him, accidentally and sweetly, some question about Nausicaa equivalent in its effect to his famous invitation at a Trinity Lodge musical party, 'So pleased you have come. Won't you take a back seat?'

The last time I saw him was at a dinner at the Albemarle Club, given more or less in his honour. It was in the winter before he died, and he was already very tired. He made, I remember, a little fun of an intense lady who declared that Art was more to her than Nature. He was not always very quick to see the point when others poked fun at him. I remember his coming back from a visit to Lady Ritchie, who was as good a hand as he at gentle irony, and telling me with amazement that she had said: 'Mr Butler, I will tell you my theory about the sonnets (Butler had just published his *Authoress of the Odyssey*, and was about to publish his book on the Sonnets): I believe they were written to Shakespeare by Anne Hathaway.' 'Poor lady,' Butler went on, 'that *was* a stupid thing to say!'

HARDY

Seventy years have passed since Thomas Hardy wrote his first novel – years that have brought more changes into the world and our way of living than any other stretch of time of the same length. So Hardy, as a novelist, belongs to a different epoch, but his verse had affinities with later times – with poetry we label modern. The slow rhythm of old country life in England, the seclusion in which people lived, seeing only neighbours, are reflected in his leisurely stories. Nor were his characters pelted day in, day out, with scraps of miscellaneous knowledge; it was easier perhaps for those who were not foolish to be wise. All this gives an old-fashioned air to his fiction, refreshing to the reader, once the slowness of his story-telling and his simplification of character and motive are accepted.

He came of peasant stock, but his people, though from the squire's point of view villagers, were of that standing from which it is fairly easy for a clever son to rise in the world. His father was a builder; he worked with his own hands, but he was also an employer of labour. Hardy received a good education. He read good books as a child, learnt some Latin and a little Greek. His parents could, I think, have just afforded to send him to the University, say with the help of a small scholarship. But instead he was trained as an architect. In leisure hours he took to writing poetry. From poetry he turned to novel-writing, and after the publication of *Jude the Obscure* in 1896 (*Jude* was abused and the abuse disgusted and hurt him), he took to expressing himself only in verse, though he published one more novel which he had written earlier.

I remember his saying that it was the desire to make a little money that first made him turn to fiction. He had heard that Meredith, whom he knew as reader for Chapman and Hall, had made a hundred pounds by a novel – and he thought he would try to do the same. The result was *Desperate Remedies*, 1871. I should be surprised to hear that it earned that, but those with eyes might have seen in it (I don't think anybody did) that here was a writer who might learn to handle words so as to convey a new beauty and his own sense of life; who, to use his own words, was born 'to intensify the expression of things'. His second novel, *Under the Greenwood Tree*, a beautiful humorous little story published the following year, brought him recognition from writers like Leslie Stephen, and two years afterwards, with *Far from the Madding Crowd*, he began to capture the wider public – you see, he did not write long in obscurity.

Like Meredith, his great contemporary, Hardy belongs to the class of poet-novelists. Meredith in his novels dealt with the sunny side of life; Hardy with its shadows. There was little humour in Meredith, but much wit; Hardy is the reverse of a *clever* writer – but there is much delightful humour. His country folk have been compared with Shakespeare's rustics; and, personally, I often prefer them. They seem in touch with life in a deeper way; and though their minds are slow and cumbrous, their sense of words is delightful. In their talk there are long pauses of silence when heads are shaken over life and tankards drained. They've a great appreciation of silence as well as savoury phrases. Here is a scrap of the conversation of the Melstock choir in *Under the Greenwood Tree*:

'Yes, Geoffrey is a clever man if ever there was one. Never says anything; not he.'

'Never.'

'You might live wi' that man, my sonnies, a hundred years – and never know there was anything in him.'

'Ay, one of these up-country London ink-bottle fellers would call Geoffrey a fool.'

'Ye would never find out what's in that man – never.'

'Silent? Ah, he is silent. He can keep silence well.'

'That man's silence is wonderful to listen to.'

Hardy's themes are generally sad, both as poet and novelist. There are green isles of peace and happiness in his stories, but a greyness beats upon them and the ominous murmur of it is heard in their most sheltered recesses. Is this* the moment then, you may ask, to turn to *Tess of the D'Urbervilles*, *The Woodlanders*, *The Mayor of Casterbridge*, *The Return of the Native*, *Jude the Obscure*? Yes, I think so – it is the function of tragic literature to dignify sorrow and disaster.

A good many years ago I had the pleasure of seeing Hardy sometimes, of talking with him, and sometimes bicycling with him. His simplicity of feeling was more impressive in him than anything he actually said. A few characteristic things, however, I remember him saying. He had been reading or rereading *Tom Jones* and referring to that character – the poor trollop in Tom Jones' village, Molly Seagrim, about whose humiliations there are many jokes – he said 'It's a most extraordinary thing but Fielding seems to have forgotten she was a woman.' I remember thinking at the time – 'There speaks a man to whom village life is real in a very different degree to which it is to a writer of the squire-class like Fielding; and how characteristic too of one who never in his work forgets the pain and seriousness of life.'

Once when we were passing the scene of some incident in

* 3rd June, 1940

[90]

Tess, he said to me, 'If I had thought that story was going to be such a success I'd have made it a *really good book*.'

One other trifle comes back to me. He was telling me about Andrew Lang to whom he had been reconciled (Lang had written a cutting review of *Tess of the D'Urbervilles*). 'Oh he *was* a clever man. I never talked to a cleverer man. I suppose it's living in towns and talking that makes one like that. Do you think if I lived in London, I would become clever too?' I remember saying 'Clever people are as common as blackberries – I'm a clever man myself; I don't think you need bother about cleverness' – and we looked at each other and smiled.

Hardy's appearance is familiar from photographs and pictures. Two of the best known of his portraits, Augustus John's portrait of him and Strang's etching, do not seem to me like him. I do not recognize in the John portrait that startled and supercilious stare. There is far too much vigour and not nearly enough delicacy in the face, and the same comment applies, in my opinion, to the etching. There was something far more odd, winning and somehow twisted both in his features and expression; something agelessly elfin in him which neither artist has caught, and a glint in his eye which one might have associated with slyness in a mindless and insensitive man. He was very small, very quiet, self-possessed and extraordinarily unassuming. I seem to remember that his laughter made no sound. As is usual with subtle people, his voice was never loud and a gentle eagerness which was very pleasing, showed in his manner when he wanted sympathy about some point. He would instantly recoil on being disappointed. I observed in him once or twice a look, a movement, too slight to be called a wince, but not unlike the almost imperceptible change one sees in a cat when a gesture has perturbed it.

Hardy the novelist and Hardy the poet are the same man, though people differ as to whether his verse excels his prose. Certainly as he grew older he himself came to prefer the condensation of verse, but he did not keep poetry to express only the more intense and rarer kinds of emotion. That's where he is akin to modern poets. Many of his poems were on subjects he might have treated in a story – that vivid and moving ballad 'A Tramp-Woman's Tragedy', for example. He constantly noted in verse the same kinds of incident he makes important in his novels. It is a dangerous thing for a poet to attempt, but Hardy could afford to because of the great seriousness of his attention. If his poetry was often that of a novelist, his novels were always those of a poet – put it like that, if you like. In both is the same profoundly tragic, wistful, watchful response to life. Much of his work is an austere but gentle descant upon the dust and ashes of things, of the fragility of love, and the perversities of fate. Unwelcome truths, but old truths, and Hardy presented them with a consciousness of their gravity. 'The solemnity of earth, its woods and fields, and lonely places, has passed into his work; and when he takes it in hand, to deal with the passions of men, that spirit guides and directs him.'

His work has weaknesses. His writing is sometimes clumsy and pedantic. He will say, for instance, 'every point in the milkmaid became a deep rose colour' when he meant that she blushed; or speak of 'atmospheric cutlery' instead of a sharp wind. He has written exquisite meditative lyrics, but also some which are more like tunes played on a snoring old 'cello.

If you listen to such criticism, and a true admirer always listens to the other side, don't forget that no fault-finding can reach that high simplicity which underlies Hardy's work, and is one of the marks of fine literature. It may sink into mere naïvety in places; that tragic sense may here and there sag into a too-easy and passive a melancholy, but it is there – this profound sense of man's destiny and of the turning of the wheel of fate.

MAX BEERBOHM

'I shan't offer you the slightest assistance,' he wrote, on hearing that the late Bohun Lynch intended to write a book about him. 'I won't read a single word until your book is published. Even if modesty didn't prevent me, worldly wisdom would. I remember several books about men, who, not yet dead, had blandly aided and abetted the author, and I remember what awful asses those men seemed to me thereby to have made of themselves. I, who am a hundred miles away from being great, cannot afford such luxuries. My gifts are small. I've used them very well, and discreetly, never straining them; and the result is that I've made a charming little reputation. But that reputation is a frail plant. Don't over attend to it, Gardener Lynch! Don't drench and deluge it! The contents of a quite *small* watering-can will be quite enough. . . . Oh, keep it little – in proportion to its theme.'

Bohun Lynch's book, alas, was not a good one. After that letter he doubtless did his best to find faults, but unfortunately those he discovered were not there. But that letter, will enable you to guess that Six Max Beerbohm is a most sensible man.

When in August 1942 a young admirer of his, Mr Alan Dent, founded a 'Maximillian Society' to celebrate his seventieth birthday, I had the privilege of taking the chair. We entertained him with old music-hall songs and turns such as he loves. They were interpreted by those brilliant artists of 'Late Joys', who helped to keep up our spirits during the first two years of the war. We also presented him with a small cellar of vintage wines. It was one of the few occasions on which I have enjoyed making a speech. I remember saying:

> We all, whatever the date of our birth, continue to be the children of that period when each of us came intellectually of age – I'm speaking of imaginatively receptive people. You, Max, and your oldest friends here, writers and painters, are children of the 'nineties. And one of the things for which your contemporaries are so grateful to you is that your skilled example as a writer has kept them aware that, in that respect, they were not unblessed. It was a period where it was easier than it became later to perceive that Art has some connection with beauty; that craftsmanship is as important in the arts as originality; and that in a writer humane detachment is possibly quite as valuable as a burning ethical or economic conviction.
>
> You have been most loyal to our period; you have shown us that in literature, even a shallow stream should be forded as if it might at any moment prove to be deep; that in prose as well as in poetry even a hair can throw a shadow. As a servant of the Comic Muse, you, like Sterne, have also known how to invest with a little loveliness – a joke. Of the 'nineties you were 'the wise youth'. The years have taught you very little –

(At this point, I remember, a slightly startled look replaced on Max's countenance that becoming expression of mingled incredulity and gratitude which we all endeavour to wear while listening in public to our own praises.)

> The years have taught you very little – you could not help being *then* almost as sensible as you are today.

(To my joy I thought I saw him give a little nod.)

Then, although every leader of taste admired your elegantly unspontaneous essays, there was already in them something disconcerting to the more luxuriously confident of nineteenth-century aesthetes. I wonder if a remark which Wilde made about you ever reached your ears: 'The gods', he said, 'bestowed on Max the gift of perpetual old age.' At the time, in your twenties, this jibe might possibly have made you a little uneasy – for a little while.

The explanation of it is that you could not be silly even about Art – or Oscar. Now the chief – perhaps the only – distinctive virtue of old age is an inclination towards tolerance; when that inclination is combined with the fastidiousness of youth – well, then we get a 'Max'.

I cannot say that I knew 'Max' as he has drawn himself at the age of nineteen. It must have been some eight years later that I first met him, though I already knew him by sight. I remember walking one night down Piccadilly behind that high-hat with its deep mourning-band which he has recorded. It was then perched above a very long dark top-coat with an astrakhan collar. I like to think I followed their wearer with something of his own interest in 'types'. In a gloved hand this figure held an ebony stick with an ivory knob which, wonderful to say, has not yet been lost. I remember noting also the little black curl on the nape of his neck like a drake's tail. His walk was slow and tranquil, such as one could hardly imagine ever breaking into a run.

But it was at the house of Mabel Beardsley, Aubrey Beardsley's sister, that I first met him . . . and oh! I was never going to let him go. He had replaced Shaw as dramatic critic on the *Saturday Review*, and he was living with his charming eager old mother and two of his sisters in a little house in Upper Brook Street. There I often visited him. Only on the very day when his copy was due was he invisible; for like myself, who had by then also become a dramatic critic, he needed the spur of dire compulsion to exchange the pleasures of thought for the pains of composition. He seemed to feel as I did that there was not very often anything much better to do with Time than to waste it rather fastidiously. His books are those of one who has always insisted on having leisure to observe. I put him right at the top of modern essayists.

The essays of Chesterton and Belloc are often like gusts of wind blowing off the hills of poetry, but my own kite will not always fly in that wind; it is liable to flutter, slant, and drop. In the hands of 'Max' I know it will be gently lifted and sail steadily for a while, pulling gently, with the scraps of criticism, ingenious comments on life and manners, tied to its tail, against a sky of calm contemplation. This is the function of the essayist. Or put it this way: he should find for us some inconspicuous turning which leads from the thoroughfare of every day into the garden of fancy or philosophy. He need not stop there; if he peeps in it is enough. Different he from the poets who with rhymes and rhythms, and extraordinary devices, peremptorily bid us put off our ordinary mood if we are to accompany them; and against whom we feel in consequence no little resentment should they afterwards neither astound nor delight us. The transition from humour to serious reflection is always deftly managed by 'Max'; nor could anything in sentimental fiction be more finely touched than that scene in his story of 'William and Mary', where the story-teller pulls the bell of their empty house, tugs at it again and again, that he may hear repeatedly that quick sequence of notes, faint, far off, but so clear – and so like the dead woman's laughter.

It is the business of the artist in caricature to record what is comically characteristic and be true to his vision. He must have strong sympathies and antipathies and no respect for persons. 'Max's' own talent for caricature is the most intellectual in the history of English caricature. Compare it with the work of

Gillray or of Rowlandson in the gross Flemish style of Jan
Steen. The range of these old masters, however pretty in colour
and animated in line, stretched little beyond the mere deform-
ities of excessive fatness or emaciation; a guffaw at swollen
thighs, exuberant bosoms, lantern-jaws, and round haggard
eyes peering over a steaming dish – such was their stock-in-
trade. The din, the racket, the monotony of such laughter! They
set up to be satirists, but their own sense of the comic was itself
that guzzling, roaring, man-and-woman-baiting kind of fun
they satirized. Nevertheless they had the verve, skill, and
thoroughness of artists; and when the horse-laugh dies out of
English caricature, something vital and important dies with
it. Caricature becomes half-hearted till it revives once more
in Pellegrini and then in the implacable levity and literary
subtlety of 'Max'.

Turn over one of his volumes of caricatures. How many are
really literary or psychological *criticisms* presented in a visible
dramatic form? They remind us that 'Max' is also one of the
most accomplished of literary parodists. The parodies collected
in 'A Christmas Garland' used to appear about Christmastime
every year in the *Saturday Review*. I remember two of his victims
confessing (they were Henry James and Arthur Benson), that
after reading his devastating exaggerations of their respective
mannerisms, they had been inhibited when they next sat down
to write. 'Max' would have been almost more distressed than
flattered to hear that his parody of Henry James had embarrassed for a week a writer whom he so much admired; but
that he might have temporarily impeded the placid flow of
commonplace from the gentle pen of Benson would have
given him no pain.

To visit one of his exhibitions during his early period as a
caricaturist was to gaze upon well-known figures at various
stages of transformation towards the mechanical and grotesque; dandies dancing on their toes like puppets, or petrifying in
starched shirts and resolutely buttoned coats; venerable states-

men appearing like creatures which loom for a moment through the green dusk of aquarium tanks; aesthetes drooping like tallow candles in too-hot air. As time went on, however, his methods changed, swerving in the direction of a comic portraiture, nearly wholly sympathetic in spirit, and away from pure caricature. Subjects in which his line was guided by aversion became rarer and rarer. His dislike of the hard vulgarity of Edwardian Society, typified often in the person of the monarch himself; his hostility towards noisy British Imperialism which was most intense during the Boer War, and was always visible in his caricatures (merciless) of Kipling, gradually changed to a more philosophic criticism of his age; a change which culminates in such a series of cartoons as those personifying the three centuries; wherein first the supercilious, clever eighteenth century is seen taking a pinch of snuff as he contemplates his stout, innocently-gaping successor, dressed in a chapel-going manufacturer's frock-coat; while he, in his turn, gazes in utter bewilderment upon his own offspring – a leather-clad, be-goggled robot, racing with incredible speed into the unforeseen.

Yes, incredible as it might seem that anyone as mellow as young 'Max' should become mellower, as a caricaturist he certainly did.

In a caricature by Osbert Lancaster published in the *Strand Magazine* for December 1946, 'Max' appears at a window. Osbert Lancaster has caught a characteristic attitude. He has duly exaggerated the lucid regard of those large grey heavy-lidded eyes. Here, decidedly is an old dandy, whom the young can regard as out-moded, though they had better beware of his mild scrutiny and the formidable civility of his wit. No doubt he 'dates'; of that he is proud. He looks easy to fluster, but he is really 'unusual calm'. Can you divine beneath the old pink and white face at the window, the dark round countenance of a rather melancholy Pierrot? It once was his. You will, I think, have no difficulty in attributing to the old gentleman a soft deliberate utterance, an almost soundless chuckle, and a manner quiet, though a shade more gesticulatory than is common. (Remember his half-brother was that imaginatively exuberant actor, Sir Herbert Tree.) But you cannot guess that all his life he has also been fond of a hoax, and ingenious in devising them. I am hoping that he will soon add to his delightful but too infrequent 'Talks', one of the art of hoaxing. I will not describe a little trap he once laid for me and into which, to his joy, I tumbled headlong.

But to suggest his impromptu gifts in that direction, let me recall one winter morning, when I was staying with him in lodgings at the seaside, and how he overcame my reluctance to rise. My bed was in a corner of the room, and you must imagine 'Max' standing at the window in his long white dressing gown, while I enjoy snuggling down under the blankets as we talk. Suddenly a remark of mine meets with no response; I notice on his face a look of grave delight. I repeat it, but he is silent. Then slowly, and in that literal tone with which we speak when really moved, I hear him say: 'That light! That grey and silver on the sea!' In an instant I am beside him and find myself face to face with a brick wall: *he had got me out of bed.*

His conversation, like his prose, is full of slight surprises. As a talker he belongs to more leisurely days, when the tempo of conversation permitted people to express themselves, and hosts did not prefer emphatic jawing guests, who shift their topic every moment. The art of conversation has passed away. In London to tell a story well is now impossible, for it may take more than two minutes; Oscar Wilde would be voted a bore, and neighbours at dinner would begin talking to each other after his third sentence.

'Max', it will not surprise you to hear, is, too, within a limited range, an excellent mimic, and not only of real people: he is also an impersonator. I have sometimes found I was no longer in *his* company, but in that of a dramatic critic whose accent was unrefined and whose mind was coarse, but who invariably contrived (confound him!) to hit nails on the head. I regret to say 'Max' always enjoyed my exasperation. . . . But I have told you enough about the old gentleman who stares so gravely from his window.

ASQUITH

I

When I had finished Lord Oxford's *Memoirs and Reflections* I, too, began remembering and reflecting. . . .

I am back in the narrow white dining-room of The Wharf, with its two garden windows. Sunday luncheon is in progress; and, as is often the case in that room, there are more guests than you might think it could accommodate, and more talk in the air than you would expect even so many to produce. The atmospherics are terrific. Neighbour is not necessarily talking to neighbour, nor, except at brief intervals, is the conversation what is called 'general', that is to say three or four people talking and the rest listening. The conversation resembles rather a sort of wild game of pool in which everybody is playing his or her stroke at the same time. One is trying to send a remark into the top corner pocket farthest from her, where at the same moment another player is attempting a close-up shot at his own end; while anecdotes and comments whizz backwards and forwards, cannoning and clashing as they cross the table. Sometimes a remark leaps right off it at somebody helping himself at the sideboard, who with back still turned, raises his voice to reply. And not only are half a dozen different discussions taking place simultaneously, but the guests are at different stages of the meal. Some have already reached coffee, others are not yet near the sweet; for everyone gets up and helps himself as he finishes a course. Now to get full enjoyment out of these surroundings it was necessary to acquire the knack of carrying on at least two conversations at once while lending an ear to a few others; not so difficult to acquire as perhaps your first visit might have led you to expect. On one such occasion I happened to be shouting about autobiography: 'Yes, there are only three motives for writing it, though of course they may be mixed; St Augustine's, Casanova's, Rousseau's. A man may write his autobiography because he thinks he has found "The Way" and wishes others to follow, or to tell us what a splendid time he has had and enjoy it again by describing it, or to show – well, that he was a much better fellow than the world supposed.' 'I'm glad to hear you say that,' said a voice behind me. I turned my head; Mr Asquith was cutting himself a slice of ham. 'That', he added, before carrying back his plate to his seat, 'is just what I'm now trying to do.'

I knew that he was at work on this book, *Memoirs and Reflections*, 1852–1927. So it was to be more personal than his *Fifty Years of Parliament*. Would it prove to be anything as unlike him as a piece of intimate self-justification? That it would be in the least like Rousseau's *Confessions* was out of the question; but he might be going to tell us not only what he had thought, but what he had *felt*, during that long career in the course of which he had borne the heaviest responsibilities and later, without complaint, humiliations and gross misrepresentation. In the garden after luncheon, before the cars came round to whirl us in different directions, I asked myself these questions. I did not put them to him, for although he was not formidable, one felt reluctant to push past his reserve. This inhibition did not seem due so much to fear of being snubbed as to a natural unwillingness to drive so sensitive a man to an evasion which might be interpreted as a denial of his friendship. Reticent on any subject about which he had not already made up his mind, he was extremely reserved when it also touched him personally. He loved above all things the comfort of spontaneous communications; and that comfort is, as everybody knows, most easily obtained by keeping to the surface in talk. As a rule he did so.

II

Now the book is in my hands. It is a remarkable one, for it reflects his mind and character but it is *not* a piece of self-portraiture. He tells us in it from time to time what he thought of his colleagues. Passages are even 'indiscreet', and the book has faults which he deplored in the books of others. It was written hastily when he was tired; it is botched together. Part of it is hardly more than the rough material he would have used. He never saw it through the press. It had to be enlarged at the last moment to meet the exigencies of the market, and he had no time to weld together or mould the material then thrown in. We may however be thankful that financial pressure compelled him to write it; for it is doubtful if he would have written at all without that spur – and it is a remarkable book. Indirectly it is a self-revealing book. One caution, however, to those who are either about to read it, or having read it, have formed hasty impressions: except for very brief and intermittent periods he never kept a diary. The extracts embodying his passing comments on events as they occurred during the War, are mostly taken from letters written at the time. This accounts in many cases for their tone. When complete distraction was impossible, he would obtain some relief from anxiety by writing confidentially to someone about the lighter side of events, in a way which would at once amuse his correspondent and refresh the sense of intimacy between them. As is not unusual in the case of men actively engaged in momentous affairs whose habits of thought are markedly independent, that correspondent was always a woman. It was not counsel he sought, but comfort, communication and relief. It is noticeable that there is not a line in this book which expresses perplexity or hesitation; not a page in which we can watch him making up his mind. It has been always made up when he puts pen to paper. He explains his motives and reasons for having acted in such and such a manner, but we are given the results, not the processes of deliberation. This is profoundly characteristic of him; so is the absence from it of all mention of feelings, whether of elation, disappointment, disillusion, resentment or satisfaction. Yet that he was a man of feeling could not escape the notice of anyone who saw him from a short distance. It is chiefly to bring out these characteristics which everyone could perceive at close quarters, that I am now 'reviewing' this book. Many who have discussed and described Lord Oxford have not seen his main characteristic.

In all the appreciations written after his death his 'impersonal' attitude was made a subject of comment; but amid the praise lavished upon him there was a suggestion that his master faculties were perhaps, after all, those of the judge or possibly the historian or scholar. That he was extraordinarily impartial, that he was a scholar and would have made an admirable historian was clear to everyone, but that he was a scholar, or historian, pitchforked into active life is, I believe, an utterly false reading of him. I knew him during twelve years, and for a considerable part of them I was on terms of affectionate familiarity with him, though never on those of intimacy. This was at any rate sufficient to enable me to form a positive opinion about his nature, and my conclusion was that the cast of his intellect and imagination was essentially that of a man of action. Being of a literary turn of mind myself, it was perhaps easier for me to detect the essential difference. Literature also requires 'detachment', but the sense of proportion in the man of action is different from that of the man of letters. In the born

master of affairs imagination is neither 'dreamful nor dramatic'. His observation is a process of direct calculation and
inference; he has not the habit 'of enacting in himself other
people's inward experience or dwelling on his own'. Lord
Oxford enjoyed the kind of talk which consists of drawing
picturesque and psychological portraits of people, but when it
came to practical affairs he took no interest in imaginative
interpretations of character. I remember this being brought
home to me when he asked me once to tell him about the Irish
leaders. I had been acting as correspondent of the *Manchester
Guardian* during part of the struggle between the Irish and the
Black and Tans, and I began to describe the Irish leaders in a
manner which I am quite sure, during dinner, would have won
his attention. But in the middle of adding a deft touch or two to
a character-portrait of Arthur Griffith, I looked up and saw on
my host's face a look of unmistakable, not to say stern, boredom. He did not want anything of that kind. What he wanted to
know was how Griffith, Michael Collins, and De Valera would
probably behave if Ireland were offered Dominion Home Rule
at once, and my opinion on that point with reasons for it. In
action, and in the calculations necessary to concluding rightly
with a view to action, personal emotions are mostly irrelevant.
Men of action also often surprise us by the dryness and curtness
of their comments. Their sayings may (*vide* the Duke of
Wellington) often appear humorous in their seeming neglect
of all aspects but one. This trait was very marked in Lord
Oxford.

To brush aside what was insignificant and only to attend to
the residue was an instinct in him. It may be illustrated by a
story of his first meeting during his Paisley campaign, though
the story also shows still more forcibly his attitude in the face of
silly misrepresentation. There was only a very narrow Liberal
majority and the election was a touch-and-go one. He had
barely got a hearing for his speech; there was a strong Labour
element in the audience, and interruptions had been fierce and

frequent. When questions were reached one man asked him why he had murdered those working men at Featherstone in 1892. His instant answer was: 'It was not in 'ninety-two, but 'ninety-three.' A small inaccuracy was the only thing worth correcting in such a charge. And his reply to an American, who, at the end of a somewhat lengthy preamble explaining how interested he was at last to meet him, 'after having heard President Wilson, Colonel House and your wife often talk about you' – 'What did my wife say?' is decidedly in the vein of the Duke of Wellington. But more apposite examples can be found in this book. He wrote on August 2nd, 1914:

> Happily I am quite clear in my mind as to what is right and wrong. 1. We have no obligation of any kind either to France or Russia to give them military or naval help. 2. The dispatch of the Expeditionary Force to help France at this moment is out of the question, and would serve no object. 3. We must not forget the ties created by our long-standing and intimate friendship with France. 4. It is against British interests that France should be wiped out as a Great Power. 5. We cannot allow Germany to use the Channel as a hostile base. 6. We have obligations to Belgium to prevent it being utilized and absorbed by Germany.

Such an entry is not at first sight impressive, but examined it will be found to contain a complete summary of facts relevant to a possible decision. Note the word 'happily' – decision in certain events would be justified.

During the Curragh row just before the war, I happened to be sitting one off him at dinner, and my neighbour was evidently anxious to make the most of her opportunities. She had never met him before. I heard her say, 'Do you *like* being Prime Minister?' This question only elicited a dubious rumble.

'Don't you enjoy having so much power?'

'Power, power? You may think you are going to get it, but you never do.'

'Oh, then what is it you enjoy most in your work?'

'Well . . . perhaps – hitting nails on the head.'

III

The more closely his career is examined in future, the more false the charge of 'indecision' is likely to appear. On the contrary, as when he peremptorily prevented General French from retiring behind the Seine, though the General declared the army to be in hopeless difficulties, or when he dealt with the Curragh complication, he will be seen to have exhibited at critical moments rapidity of resolution; and, still more often, that rare instinct for 'timing' a decisive action correctly so that it should occur at the most effective moment. That this involved sometimes delay incomprehensible to the public is of course true; but the art of statesmanship, and this is an important part of it, is incomprehensible to them.

His drawback as a leader during times of frenzied anxiety was a concomitant of his two strongest points: his immunity from the contagion of excitement, and his instinct to think things over by himself. There is a passage in one of his later letters in which he says there are three kinds of men: those who can think when they are by themselves – they are the salt of the earth; those who can only think when they are writing and talking; and those who cannot think at all – they of course are the majority. He was a man who did his thinking alone. To talk while he was still making up his mind was repugnant to him. In war, when the urgency of this or that measure is vividly brought home to those in immediate contact with one aspect of the situation, and everybody is seething with projects and suggestions, self-withdrawn composure is apt to be exasperating, and the habit of postponing discussion is apt to undermine confidence. Mr Winston Churchill, in his article on Lord Oxford, gave an example of the surprise it was to find, after imagining that Lord Oxford had dismissed some urgent matter from his mind, that he had all the time thought it over and reached a conclusion upon it. Conversation did not help him, but when he met others in council they found that he was prepared.

I associate this characteristic in affairs with two others observable in his private life, his strong inclination to sidetrack avoidable emotional complications, and his reluctance to express opinions on any subject upon which he did not know his own mind completely. For instance, in his youth he had been much interested in philosophy, and he still possessed that respect for thought which only those who have drunk a fair draught at the springs of thought retain. Yet because he did not think his opinion on such points instructed, he was unwilling to discuss the Universe or the life of man in its widest aspects. He would show you by a remark or two that he was even more aware than most people who are eager to discuss such problems, of the general philosophical bearings of any particular theory, but he did not want to go into it. He had a great aversion from stuffing the blanks in his convictions with provisional thinking. It was the same in literature. He discussed readily only those aspects of it of which he felt he had a thorough comprehension. And since human beings are endless subjects for discussion, and each one a forest in which it is only too easy to lose one's way, though he would listen with pleasure and amusement to ingenious interpretations, you felt they were far from impressing him deeply. He liked gossip and the quasi-intellectual discussion of character, but he himself rarely contributed to such discussions anything but the most obvious common sense.

His reluctance, in private as well as public, to discuss what was not yet clear to him seems to me to be the manifestation of a fundamental characteristic – one which I personally admire more than any other – a perfect integrity of mind. The foundation of his character was the adamant of intellectual integrity. It made magnanimity natural to him for, as he himself might have quoted in this connexion, *Infirmi est animi exiguique voluptas Ultio* (Revenge is the joy of a sick or puny soul). It made it easy for him to put aside personal considerations when the interests either of the nation or his party were concerned. At such junctures the very soul of his honour was at stake, and I do not believe that the historian will discover one instance in his long career in which he risked it. (The shameful jettisoning of Haldane was not his work, but was forced upon him by the then inevitable Coalition.)

IV

I have spoken of his mind as, in my judgement, essentially that of a man of action. Such intellectual integrity is necessary to a man of action who can be trusted to be effective not merely once or twice, but continuously. Yet it also prevented him from touching some of those levers which circumstances may compel a man of action to pull. He could not make an unfair appeal. In the War he lost the confidence of the mob. The change from the Asquith to the Lloyd George régime was a change to an appeal to the subconscious and usually the baser side of it, both in the public and in those actively concerned in carrying on the War administratively. Asquith knew all about such appeals, but he could not bring himself to make them. He was out of touch, therefore, with what is instinctive and emotional in human nature, which is so much to the fore at such times. In private and in administrative life he shrank from using authority or personal appeal as a weapon to produce conviction, and it was acute pain to himself to speak words which might give pain. After he had indicated the reasonable course he could not bring himself to do more; it seemed to him, I expect, like an insult – a disloyalty – to use irrelevant means of persuasion – something certainly quite impossible in relations where affection or trust already existed. His opinion of human nature struck me as being neither high nor low. Where colleagues were concerned it might seem to have often been too high, in this sense, that he did not see that there was much difference between mediocrities; A was practically as good a man as B, though B was abler.

I was an 'Asquith man' long before I knew him; and I remember, on his appointment to the Premiership, when the papers were discussing as his 'one defect', a lack of magnetism, that it was precisely that defect that attracted *me*. I have no confidence in the steady sagacity of the so-called magnetic. And when I came to know him, the absence of either magnetism or any desire to impress, grew beautiful to me.

As a member of the public, I felt he sought our solid advantage and not our ridiculous patronage; and as a friend, that there was in him that integrity of feeling and thought which is a permanent guarantee of right action.

His talk was that of a man who had more faith in facts than theories, more interest in records than conjectures – unless those were fantastic, when he could be amused by the ingenuity and recklessness of other people's opinions. I soon noticed that though he enjoyed cleverness, he never missed it in a companion whom he liked. He seemed to get more and more fond of people he was used to, and to suffer comparatively little from boredom, that common scourge of uncommon men. It did not matter to him if his friends were always the same. In fact, he seemed to like them to be so; just as he never got tired of either the books, or the places, or the jokes, or the anecdotes which had once pleased him. He was even like a child in the pleasure he took in having something 'over again'. This characteristic and the absolute self-sufficiency of his mind (not his heart) struck one. When he *was* bored, however, it appeared to be an unusually acute form of discomfort. Over the wine, after dinner, and under the spell of an unduly explanatory or pretentious talker, sounds which at first resembled considerate murmurs of assent, would gradually prolong themselves into unmistakable moans, terminating at last in a flurried gesture of hospitality and a sudden rise from the table. Complacent long-windedness or attempts to draw him out were apt to produce these symptoms. At dinner, when in danger of being thus submerged, he would catch eagerly at any lifebelt of a remark thrown him by one of his children. That he should have enjoyed Society, and frequented it so much during his life may seem incongruous in him, until we realize that he took it as a rest: amiable people, pretty women, bright lights, friendly festivity and remarks flying about which he could catch and reply to by employing an eighth of his intellect, afforded distraction. It was a refreshment. Henry James, coming back once from a luncheon party at Downing Street during the War, remarked on 'the extraordinary, the admirable, the rigid intellectual economy' which the Prime Minister practised on such occasions.

V

Lady Oxford, in her preface to *Memoirs and Reflections*, draws attention to an important fact which is not generally understood: he was an emotional man and a very sensitive one. Signs of that sensitiveness were his inability to ask for fairer treatment for himself, or to take any step to further the interests of his children. He could not bring himself to do such things. The strength of the emotional side of his nature is known to those he loved. He covered his humiliations with silence, both in public and private. But after his fall in 1916, though apparently bearing it with the greatest equanimity, the shock produced an attack which, for a few hours, was taken for paralysis: when his own followers did not take him at his word that it was impossible to work any longer with Mr Lloyd George, the disappointment struck him down physically. Some time afterwards – I noted it, because it was a rare gleam of self-disclosure – he said, in dating some event: 'Ah, that was while I was recovering from my wound.' And once I remember, after he lost his seat – the conversation had been about the difference between metaphor and comparisons – he said to me: 'I will show you a *comparison* in poetry which moves me.' He took down a Coleridge and pointed to the lines

> Like an Arab old and blind
> Some caravan has left behind

and then rather hurriedly left the room. But despair, whether about himself or public affairs, was to him mere weak-mindedness. He never indulged in pessimism, there again showing one of the traits of the man of action. Whether or not he thought of himself as a great man I could never discover. He probably would have said the term was an exceedingly vague one, and he would certainly not have trusted the reports of introspection on such a point.

VI

Before he had published any books, we knew from his speeches he wrote well. I was amused when *The Times* reviewer referred to aid 'from the practised hand of Mr Gosse', as though Lord Oxford were not himself a practised and even voluminous writer. Many men's writing is the spoken word on paper, merely titivated conversation. But he actually spoke the language of the pen. His oratory was a broad continuance of statement, reasoning and reflection, with no hazy, no preparatory interludes. What collected vigour of mind that famous concision required, can be measured best by those who often take ten minutes to knock two sentences into one. He drove a Roman road through every subject.

I became his admirer many years ago, when I discovered in him a completely intelligible politician whose principles were generous and steadfast, whose judgement never seemed to fail him, who let the calm of the intellect into discussion, and never saw an enemy except the enemies of his country. It is much to claim for any leader; but his speeches bear it out.

His diction is plain yet ornate, very accurate, succinct yet full and rounded. As in all oratorical styles, heed is paid to a simple sonority and easiness of cadence. It is formal and traditional rather than personal. It reflects not passing moods, but habits of thought and feeling. The senses have contributed nothing to its vigour, which is intellectual; nor is it at all indebted to random meditations for richness – the laden camels of such dreaming moments have never brought to it their far-fetched consignments of spices and dyes. It aims at definition rather than suggestion. The emotions it expresses best are those of the intellectual or the moral life. Its most obvious merits are those of order, brevity, clearness and good manners. It is a mode of addressing us that takes for granted that we ourselves are not restless, tired, craving for sympathy or distraction; not unbuttoned, but on the contrary, well pulled-together and alert. It leaves the reader nothing to do but to understand, and when so many writers of talent 'put deliberate fog on paper' that is refreshing. The pitfall of such a style is the too frequent use of clichés of good pedigree; its advantage that it almost automatically excludes trivial egotism and exterminates misrelated ingenuities.

VII

Had he been a scholar or historian by profession he would have written books thorough and of trenchant classic economy; works which, like Sir Henry Maine's, would have tempted even those not really interested in the subject to read on. In a scholar's life (this is a deduction the reader of his *Occasional Addresses* cannot fail to draw) he would have found great satisfaction and content. When a peculiar fervour spreads through a passage, it is often one in which there is perceptible a feeling akin to homesickness for that world in which questions are not settled by votes or irrelevant adroitness, and where to be impartial is itself the condition of success. Of course the other side of the road in life generally looks the most attractive; but even allowing for the undue fascination which the careers of men of thought have for men of action, and vice versa, it would be a mistake, in the light of such passages, to read his references to the atmosphere of contention from which he emerges with relief to address his audiences upon such still-life subjects as Biography and Criticism, as merely the courteous phrases of an eminent man, intended for those who might be feeling, at the moment and in comparison, a little unenviable and dull. It is certain in the light of those passages that they are sincere. His Glasgow and Aberdeen Rectorial addresses are in the main panegyrics, defiant and triumphant, of Ancient Universities; that is to say, of the education which has classical literature for its main foundation, and philosophy as its apex. Here for once his enthusiasm is untempered. He scorns to defend that tradition as a means of training the memory or the taste. It is an end in itself – a life; and much depends upon its being enjoyed and remembered afterwards at its true value.

> For the moment you are here and can concentrate on the things of the mind, installed as you are in the citadel of knowledge. But after these student years are over, the lives of most of us are doomed to be immersed in matter. If the best gift which our University can give us is not to be slowly stifled, we must see to it that we keep the windows of the mind, and of the soul also, open to the light and the air.

'For the moment,' he says to these young men, 'you are here.'

And he goes on to 'compare the noble optimism which in spite of all disappointments and misgivings holds fast to the faith in what man can do for man', and 'the noble pessimism which turns in relief from the apparent futility of all such labour to a keener study and a fuller understanding of the works of God'. The peroration is fervid, idealistic and strong. The Aberdeen address closes upon the same theme. Both are fine specimens of that lofty and formal oratory into which, down the ages from Classic times, so much emotion, natural and histrionic, has poured. Indeed, I doubt if since Gladstone's day you could find better. Yet quote them I cannot; so distasteful to me has all eloquence of an idealistic strain become since the war. And I cannot but believe that the feeling is shared by those readers to whom it is the critic's chief pleasure to fancy he is showing what he has found; and that to quote such eloquence here would have the same effect as if I had promised you the sight of a beautiful living man, and then brought you to where he lay on a slab, waxy and yellowing and cold, with that grimace of meaningless energy so often seen upon the masks of the dead.

VIII

The sentence I have just written would have been condemned by Lord Oxford, apart from its general significance which would have been repellent to him. There is a comment upon De Quincey in his lecture on Criticism, which might make a good many critics when they write such sentences, uneasy. It runs as follows:

De Quincey, with all his powers, has in him more than a little of the literary coxcomb. Whatever may be the work of the author that for the time being occupies his pen, he never ceases to be self-conscious; he rarely fails to remind the reader of his own experiences, tastes, eruditions, accomplishments; and, whether he praises or blames, admires or disparages, you never feel that he has lost himself in the subject, but always that he wishes to interest you in the subject because it interests himself.

Yes, it is difficult for a critic not to believe sometimes that his own mind and his own feelings are more interesting to the reader than his subject, and on occasion it may even be true; but certainly if that is his constant persuasion he can be no critic – an essayist perhaps, but not a critic. This passage is also interesting, because it illustrates Lord Oxford's preference for the impersonal. I do not suppose he would have assented to the proposition that *le moi est haissable*; but he would certainly have said that it was very apt to be trivial, and generally an impertinence in literature as well as in politics. I note that in his address on Biography (a lecture as light, by-the-by, as any dilettante could make it, and as solid as an essay by Leslie Stephen), the only writer to whom he is downright unsympathetic, is Rousseau. The qualities of his own style have their counterpart in his scale of values and the range of his interests, which shows that though his style is traditional it is also his very own. It was not a Roman toga put on for the sake of its seemliness and its air of dignified reserve, though the folds of it were arranged with a view to deliberate effect. It was his natural garb, and few other men could have worn it without looking as grotesque as the statue of Canning in Parliament Square.

DISRAELI

I

The statues in Parliament Square are ridiculous; there is no doubt about that. Next time you are passing just look at Lord Palmerston with his coat over his arm, stretching out his hand for his hat to an invisible lavatory attendant; glance at the legs of Sir Robert Peel or turn your eyes to the figure of Mr Canning habited as a Roman, with, perhaps, a pigeon perched on his black bald head, and you will be amazed and tempted to murmur: 'There is no other country that can show anything like this!' The only statesman on that celebrated spot who does not appear a figure of fun is Disraeli. I have thought, as I passed that slightly stooping figure in Garter robes, with head decorously inclined and a long hand laid a trifle coyly on the Order of St George, 'O Dizzy! Dizzy! Your lucky star! You made fools of men when you were alive, and when dead even an official sculptor could not make a fool of you!'

II

Men love ritual, and modern life starves their appetite for it. They will seize upon the most incongruous opportunities of satisfying their craving. Once every spring the woods and hedgerows are robbed of their little pale flowers in order to lay a heaped tribute at the feet of – Disraeli. And what absurd inscriptions accompany these tributes! One huge wreath composed of hundreds of packed flowers was labelled: 'To a great Englishman!' I recalled Carlyle's indignant query: 'How long will John Bull allow this Jew to dance on his belly?' The answer is – many a long year yet.

In Mr Buckle's last volume of his life of Disraeli we have the full story of the origin of this custom. It was started by Queen Victoria, and we know the tone of Disraeli's response. He regarded primroses as 'the gems and jewels of Nature,' as 'the ambassadors of spring'; and in using these phrases he was bestowing on their beauty the highest praise, the most extravagant praise he knew how to give, for nothing on earth was so beautiful to him as objects possessing a high prestige value, such as gems and ambassadors. My thoughts began to turn in the direction of prestige: how prestige was deserting the holders of high offices of State and public life, and how, after all, it was the faculty of creating 'prestige' for himself and for others which had been the master gift of this old comedian, half popular tribune, half courtier, whose bronze effigy seemed now to be bowing discreetly and ironically over the wreaths at his feet.

III

I do not often wish I was older, but I sometimes regret that I am not old enough to have seen Dizzy making his way very slowly up the celebrated slope of St James on the arm of Montagu

Corry. Happily however he is so picturesque that he is easy to see in imagination.

Once I was present at a discussion between two men, both so famous in their own day and in their own way, that it was natural that they should wonder, perhaps a little wistfully sometimes, how long they would be talked about after they were dead. Ingratiating little books, such as pass during a celebrity's lifetime for biographies, had been written about both of them. The man of letters argued that writers were remembered most clearly; the statesman, that the surest fame was linked to important events in history. And as I listened to instances that each in turn brought forward in support of his view, the idea occurred to me that, as far as this kind of personal fame was concerned, it was not *in proportion* to the importance either of a man's deeds or his books that he became the object of it, but rather according to the degree in which he appealed himself to the imaginations of those who live after him. I instanced small authors who were thought about more often than the great ones. And, if it came to men of action, was not Sir Robert Peel probably the greatest Prime Minister of the nineteenth century? Yet how seldom we recalled him. The suggestion had the effect of changing the conversation, for neither of the two candidates for fame present was, as a human being, likely himself to excite much posthumous curiosity. Now, the peculiarity of Disraeli was that he possessed in an unusual degree that qualification for fame.

One of the scenes in which he figures most often before me in the theatre beneath my hat, is a scene very near the drop of the curtain: a carriage is drawn up at the front door of Hughenden; a bent old man, with glistening raven locks, befurred and befrogged, and of a somnolent saturnine countenance, is already seated within it, and already, it seems, asleep; a footman comes running down the steps carrying one of those circular air-cushions on which lean invalids delight to sit; a flicker animates for a moment the extinct heavy face; the old man waves gently the back of his hand and murmurs, 'Take away that emblem of mortality.' All that I like best in Dizzy is in that story. His unconquerable hatred of the ugly prosaic; his readiness to accept anything at the hands of life except humiliation; his quick fantastic imagination which made him recognize instantly in that india-rubber object an emblem of mortality more sinister than a skull.

One more scene. This time the background is the House of Commons, and the principal figure would hardly be recognized as the same. Two traits the young Disraeli has, however, in common with the old – coal-black glossy ringlets, and a face which at this moment also is an immovable mask. Although his dress is altogether different from that of the befrogged old man in the carriage, it, too, has an extravagance which announces to all beholders that 'good taste' is a quality which the owner of such clothes either despises, or has failed altogether to understand. The impassive young man who is addressing a simmering House (for this is not his first attack upon his respected leader) is as exotic and noticeable as a flamingo in a farm-yard. He would strike one as rather ridiculous, if his affected coolness did not set off a deadly animosity. A few days before he had been apparently rolled out flat by this same respected and respect-worthy chief on whom all eyes are now turned; he had been crushed, demolished, as might be expected when practical Integrity deigns at last to turn on a venomous Theatricality. Peel had quoted Canning's lines a few days before; Canning, who had once been Peel's own friend and whom, so Peel's enemies delighted to think, he had afterwards badgered to death. The quotation was apt enough, for Disraeli had kept up hitherto a pretence of being Peel's friendly critic:

Give me the avowed, erect and manly foe;
Firm I can meet, perhaps return the blow;
But of all plagues, good Heaven, thy wrath can send,
Save me, oh, save me from the candid friend.

One can imagine the effect: the clear, ringing tones with which Peel delivered those lines; the slight emphasis with which such a practised orator would linger on the word 'manly'; his smooth triumphant air. Now listen to Disraeli's reply: 'If the right honourable gentleman may find it sometimes convenient to reprove a supporter on his right flank, perhaps we deserve it. I, for one, am quite prepared to bow to the rod; but really, if the right honourable gentleman, instead of having recourse to obloquy, would only stick to quotation, he may rely upon it – it would be a safer weapon. It is one he always wields with the hand of a master; and when he does appeal to any authority, in prose or verse, he is sure to be successful, partly because he seldom quotes a passage that has not previously received the meed of Parliamentary approbation, and partly and principally because his quotations are so – happy. The right honourable gentleman knows what the introduction of a great name does in debate – how important is its effect, and occasionally how electrical. He never refers to any author who is not great, and sometimes who is not loved – Canning, for example. That is a name never to be mentioned, I am sure, in the House of Commons without emotion. We all admire his genius; we all – at least most of us – deplore his untimely end; and we all sympathize with him in his fierce struggle with supreme prejudice and sublime mediocrity, with inveterate foes, and with "candid" friends. The right honourable gentleman may be sure that a quotation from such an authority will always tell – some lines, for example, upon friendship, written by Mr Canning, and quoted by the right honourable gentleman. The theme – the poet – the speaker: what a felicitous combination! Its effect in debate must be overwhelming; and I am sure, were it addressed to me, all that would remain for me would be thus publicly to congratulate the right honourable gentleman, not only on his ready memory, but on his courageous conscience.'

One more peep through the peep-show. This time, let us use

Mr Asquith's eyes. The scene is now laid in the autumn of 1864. Disraeli, then leader of the Opposition in the House of Commons, had attended a clerical meeting at Oxford, where Bishop Wilberforce was in the chair: 'The appointed day (it was in the month of November) arrived; the theatre was packed; the Bishop was in the chair. Mr Disraeli, attired, we are told, in a black velvet jacket and a light-coloured waistcoat, with a billy-cock hat in his hands, sauntered in, as if he were paying a surprise visit to a farmers' ordinary. At the request of the Chairman, he got to his feet, and proceeded to deliver, with that superb nonchalance in which he was unrivalled among the orators of the day, one of his most carefully prepared and most effective speeches. Indeed, among all his speeches, leaving aside his prolonged duel with Sir Robert Peel in the 'forties, I myself should select it as the one which best displays his characteristic powers, and their equally effective characteristic limitations: irony, invective, boundless audacity of thought and phrase, the thrill of the shock when least expected, a brooding impression of something which is neither exactly sentiment nor exactly imagination, but has a touch of both, a glittering rhetoric, constantly hovering over the thin boundary line which divides eloquence and bombast. First he pulverized, to the complete satisfaction of the supporters of better endowed small livings, the Broad Church party of the day and its leaders – Stanley, Jowett, Maurice, and the rest. Then came the magniloquent epigram: "Man, my lord, is a being born to believe." And, finally, he proceeded to dispose of Darwin and his school. "What", he asked, "is the question now being placed before society with glib assurance the most astounding? The question is this: Is man an ape or an angel? My lord, I am on the side of the angels." There was nothing more to be said. The meeting broke up, their faith reassured, their enthusiasm unrestrained. There had been no victory so complete since "Coxcombs vanquished Berkeley with a grin".'

IV

'A brooding impression of something which is neither exactly sentiment nor exactly imagination, but has touch of both, a glittering rhetoric, constantly hovering over the thin boundary line which divides eloquence and bombast' – how admirably that describes Dizzy's style at its best! His writing – I am thinking of his novels – is often so grossly lush and vamped that no writing could possibly be worse. Bret Harte's parody is only a shade more absurd than what it ridicules: 'This simple, yet first-class conversation existed in the morning-room of Plusham, where the mistress of the palatial mansion sat involved in the sacred privacy of a circle of her married daughters. . . . Beautiful forms leaned over frames glowing with embroidery, and beautiful frames leaned over forms inlaid with mother-of-pearl.'

There was a time when the novels themselves were considered, in spite of being crammed with intellect, gaudy and vulgar. Lush in language, unduly profuse in description, often absurd in sentiment they certainly are; yet though Disraeli wrote of splendours and fashion with the gusto of a Ouida he somehow combined with it something not unlike the detachment of a Diogenes. He loved pyramids of strawberries on golden dishes; he revelled in what he was capable of calling 'palatial saloons'; in balustrades, proud profiles, terraces, fountains, marble, tapestries, feasts, and precious stones. ('Good things', by the bye, 'like the wind on the heath, brother.') His taste was not refined, his sense of beauty deeply committed to prestige values; but how much that is ridiculous and over-rich in his writing is redeemed by the vitality of his preferences and the fearless candour of his romantic buoyancy. 'Think of me', he wrote after the smashing fiasco of his *Revolutionary Epic*, 'as of some exotic bird which for a moment lost its way in thy cold heaven, but has now regained its course and wings its flight to a more brilliant earth and a brighter sky.' I am afraid, however, when he soars, whether in prose or verse, the effects attained correspond too closely to that unfortunate definition of poetry itself in *Contarini Fleming*, 'The art of poetry is to express natural feelings in unnatural language.' Yet how genuinely romantic he was; and his style even at its worst is a style. The words and sentences, however gaudy and ludicrous – and they often are both, whenever he rhapsodizes or attempts to convey his sense of beauty or of what is noble – do bear a genuine relation to what the writer has really felt. This is also most certainly true of the stories themselves with all their exaggerations and absurdities. It is most perplexing and intriguing. One moment you find yourself exclaiming – 'This is the most impudent paste that ever pretended to be precious,' and the next – 'This is the writing of a man singularly direct, no writer could be more free from the disgusting fear-of-giving-himself-away disease which corrupts insidiously so many imaginations.' One moment he seems like a man who apparently does not know that there is such a thing as ridicule in the world; the next, one discovers that he is not only the greatest master of ridicule himself, but is under no delusion whatever respecting the private opinions which people hold about the pretensions even of their friends – in short, that he is the last man to live in a fool's paradise.

And as a public figure and a politician he perplexes and intrigues us in the same way. Compare him with his great rival Gladstone. At first glance no one can hesitate in deciding which of the two is genuine. Gladstone is in an incandescent state of conviction; whereas Dizzy has charlatan written all over him – 'Peace with Honour', 'Our Young Queen and our old institutions', 'I am on the side of the angels', etc. He makes no concealment of his intention to feed people on phrases; it is the only diet they can digest. Think, too, of the coolness of his retort to Sir Charles Wood, who had made some unanswerable criticisms upon his ridiculous budget, 'I am not a born Chancellor of the Exchequer'. And again, who, Gladstone or Disraeli, treated Queen Victoria with the more genuine respect –

there is no doubt which of the two she imagined did so? Gladstone, with all the force of his natural veneration, pleading, expostulating before her in the politest of long sentences, or Disraeli, who said of his relations with 'The Fairy', as he called her, 'I never contradict, but I sometimes forget'; who after the publication of *Leaves from my Journal in the Highlands*, referred to 'we authors'; whose dictum on flattery was that it could hardly ever be over-done, and in the case of Royalty must be laid on with a trowel? Do you remember that story of his encounter with a simple conscientious, high-Tory magnate, whom it was necessary to propitiate? Afterwards the magnate confided to another that though he did not think Mr Disraeli was a very clever man, he was certainly a very good one! I think it was Browning who told Gladstone the story of Dizzy saying at a private view of the Academy that what struck him most, when he looked round, was the appalling absence of imagination, and declaring that very evening in his speech at the Academy dinner that what had impressed him was the imagination shown in the pictures. The story was not a success. The G.O.M. glared at the teller as though he had been the hero of it himself, 'Do you call that funny? I call it *devilish*.' Dizzy was constantly doing 'devilish' things – and with relish. It would be ludicrous to describe him as 'honest'.

And yet when you look deeper into the two men a doubt creeps over you whether after all Disraeli's sincerity was not of a finer, purer quality. Sincerity is a vague word; it means different things in different connections. The sincerity in which Disraeli excelled was the kind which is all important in an artist and in intimate personal relations. Part of that sincerity consists of a natural incapacity for telling lies to yourself, at any rate gross ones; part of it is courage to refrain, when truth is really essential, from telling lies to other people, and part of it is the power of self-orientation. It is extremely difficult to discover what one really loves and understands best. Human nature is so impressible and imitative. We meet people, read books, and unconsciously propose to ourselves to like what they like, feel as they feel. Many do not discover to their dying day even what gives them pleasure. Dizzy knew himself extremely well. Gladstone's enemies professed to be astounded at his powers of self-deception, and even his admirers were inclined to admit that it was his danger; Labouchere said he did not mind the G.O.M. keeping a card up his sleeve, but he did object to his always believing that the Almighty had put it there. With regard to sincerity in personal relations, Disraeli's marriage is at once proof of its supreme importance and the fact that he possessed that virtue. When Mrs Disraeli was an old lady she once triumphantly exclaimed, 'My Dizzy married me for my money, but I am certain that he would marry me *now* without it.' His marriage had in the course of years turned at last into a perfect relation. It would have been a shabby enough marriage had he told lies to himself and to her. And again, Dizzy never scrupled to admit either to himself or the world that he was actuated by intense personal ambition. In his early books, *Vivian Grey* and *Contarini Fleming*, ambition is the one passion which finds really passionate expression. When he wants to convey a young man's love he instantly compares it with ambition: 'We feel', he exclaims, 'our flaunty ambition fade away like a shrivelled gourd before her vision.' He cannot conceive any stronger way of asserting the power of love than to say that it triumphed for a moment over ambition. His early books are full of genuine groans and ecstasies, but these do not spring from love. The groans and cries in *Henrietta Temple*, his only love story, are hollow and falsetto. On the other hand, Vivian's exclamation: 'Curse my lot! that the want of a few rascal counters, and the possession of a little rascal blood, should mar my fortunes,' rings true. So does this: 'View the obscure Napoleon starving in the streets of Paris! What was St Helena to the bitterness of such existence? The visions of past glory might illumine even that dark imprisonment; but to be conscious that his supernatural energies might die away without creating their miracles: can the wheel or the rack rival the torture of such a suspicion?'

V

Personal ambition is not the noblest motive which can actuate a public man, but it is usually one of them, and it is a source of strength to recognize it in oneself and others. I always enjoy, when I think of it, the picture of Dizzy helping Bright on with his coat in the lobby after one of the latter's lofty orations, and whispering as he did so, 'We both know that what brings us here is – ambition.'

Lastly, with regard to that power of self-orientation, which is the power of instantly recognizing how things subtend towards what we value most; in that faculty (it is a part of sincerity) I am inclined to think he was Gladstone's superior. It was often as hard for Gladstone himself as it was for others to discover whether his sympathies were with the old order or not. Disraeli knew with the certainty of an artist what kind of a world he was fighting for. It was one in which the imaginative adventurers would be at home. There must be inequality or there would be no joy – man being a competitive, admiring animal. There must be variety and colour, institutions and customs linking the present with the past, and prizes for youth to struggle for. It must be a world with heaps of luck in it (never mind the injustice, think of the fun), and one which would stimulate dreams and dreamers. A vague ideal for a statesman? Yes, certainly – and much too vague. It was streaked, too, with a fantastic, materialistic, not over-refined, Solomon-in-all-his-glory, messianic mysticism. Certainly it was much too vague a faith for a statesman. But it is almost impossible for a reader of political history to think Disraeli a great practical statesman. He was an imaginative man, an artist. He thought imagination was the greatest power in the world, and he believed that it was only through their imaginations that men could be ruled and guided – and, for matter of that, made happy. It is not the whole truth; but his own career shows how much truth there is in it. 'Even Mormon counts more votaries than Bentham' – that reflection did not fill him with misgivings; on the contrary, it was his supreme consolation.

VI

And it is the old Disraeli who fascinates the imagination most. We have plenty of disillusioned romantics, and we are sick of listening to their wailings. Give us a still blazing fire, though the wind is howling dismally in the chimney!

He despised those who had no sense of the romance of their own lives. No wonder he detested the Whig noblemen, apart from their exclusiveness, who merely used their position as a practical asset; no wonder he adored the young who, having the adventure of an uncommitted life before them, are apt to be most conscious of that romance.

GOETHE*

It is odd that Carlyle should have been the first exponent of Goethe in England, Carlyle, who lived by the light of passion, who made hatred of the Devil first test of intelligence, and, while shouting for deeds not words, treated every contemporary reformer as a contented imbecile. It was indeed strange that he should have devoted arduous admiration to a sage whose fascination lay in self-possession, who made poetry the connecting link between faith and science, and attained through that means a rarefied serenity without definite beliefs, who lived moreover on particularly good terms with the Devil – indignation and fear of evil seeming to him childish emotions.

Yet it was due to Carlyle that younger men, such as George Lewes, Matthew Arnold and Edward Hutton afterwards expounded Goethe to us, and it is perhaps still mainly due to Carlyle that the sound of Goethe's name carries to English ears suggestions of grandeur and mastery. Few of us read German, and even literary England mostly takes *Faust* on trust. 'Close your Byron, open your Goethe,' was good advice in its day; and

* Review of a biography by Emil Ludwig.

although my own acquaintance with Goethe's works does not warrant the assertion, Ludwig's life of Goethe has suggested to me that it might possibly repay some to close, for a while, even their Tolstoy, Dostoevsky, Ibsen, Shaw, Wells, Proust, Gide and D. H. Lawrence to study this great poet-sage. Doubtless we shall not do so, for we leave German to scientists and researchers, and, with the exception of Carlyle's masterly *Wilhelm Meister* and Shelley's fragment from the prologue of *Faust*, there are few English translations of Goethe which do not hopelessly blur the original.

Moreover, Goethe cannot reach many; he is too interested in truth to be afraid of being dull. Even when, in spite of his having sympathized more with Napoleon than with his fellow-countrymen during the struggle, liberated Germany turned him into a national idol, he had no illusions on that point: 'When they applauded me I was not so vain as to take it as a tribute; no, they expected some modest phrase of self-depreciation. But as I was strong-minded enough to show exactly what I felt, they called me arrogant. . . . And of my lyrics which survive? One or another may be sung now and again by a pretty girl at her piano, but for the real public, they are as dead as mutton. . . . I'll tell you a secret – my things could never be popular . . . they are only for the few who desire and look out for that kind of thing, and are doing something like it themselves.'

Who, then, are those who are 'on the look-out for that kind of thing'? The poets and writers who have found it impossible to reconcile intellectual scepticism with a creative emotional attitude towards life, and to maintain the detachment of an artist while living in touch with modern life round them. They are not uncommon. The extravagant subjectivism of much modern art, its avoidance of the simple and its pursuit of the idiosyncratic, its distrust of big common themes and its interest in small subtleties, are solutions by flight of the very predicament from which Goethe extracted himself in a lifelong struggle. Only the truths which a man finds on his own path can be of much service to him, but he may get hints from following the footsteps of another; especially of an artist whose work, poetry, and prose, was a search for spiritual liberation; one for whom that search itself was a frequent theme, whose nature comprised a mass of contradictory sympathies, interests and impulses, and to whom the lopping or starving of even one of them seemed a confession of failure.

No one ever found himself more difficult to deal with than Goethe found himself, and no one could have found his own times more perplexing; yet the fascination which he exercised was that of one who has attained a mysterious self-mastery and clarity. He was born a lyrical and passionate amorist, yet the peace and finality of domesticity appealed intimately to his sense of beauty; the urge within him to live by impulse was tremendous, yet to catch the joy as it flies was not more essential to him than to make a pattern of his life and to subordinate experience to an end. He could not be happy unless he was practical, acting on others and the world, yet he was driven to contemplation; he expanded naturally in society, yet solitude was an absolute necessity to him (that was one of the easiest of his contradictions to solve, for he soon learnt how to carry with him into company a little bit of solitude); he could never tell whether in pursuing knowledge or poetry he was really following his deepest impulse. He was emotionally romantic, and he adored the simplifications of classic form. Anatomy, painting, botany, physics, drama, poetry, politics, love (miscellaneous and perpetual), geology, business, farming, family life, philosophy, archaeology, connoisseurship, worldly success, retirement, history – he felt passionately certain that he was fitted for them all; and not merely felt it as an average man, who is also a miscellany of fickle tastes and leanings, but with the ardour of the poet who understands the charm of each pursuit or condition of being, and with the confidence of the man of thought who has justified them severally to himself. His longing for universal knowledge was only equalled by his passion for thoroughness. Both the artist and the practical self in him kept calling out, 'In limitation alone lies mastery'; and yet those voices were not louder within him than another which was ever urging him to refuse nothing, to experience all.

What a difficult team of horses to drive – at a time, too, when the highways were broken and the waters were out! In childhood his native city was invaded; twice Napoleon's soldiers were quartered on him; the little Dukedom he had helped to govern was turned into a battlefield, and on one occasion he was within an ace of being murdered by Alsatian soldiers in his bed. Nor does the metaphor apply less to the world of changing ideas and violent emotions into which he was born. The times were not more propitious then than now for a man set upon calmly 'building the pyramid of his own existence'. Yet that pyramid got itself built.

How it was done it is for the biographer of Goethe to show. It is the test of his success, and a very big undertaking. Herr Ludwig's book is not the one we wanted. It is a contribution and one of considerable interest, yet it cannot supersede the tedious but thorough work of Bielschowsky, or compare in various important respects with Lewes's *Life of Goethe*. It is impossible to follow satisfactorily the life of a great representative man apart from the history of his times. Herr Ludwig shirks this, as he did in the case of Napoleon; he dwells exclusively upon those psychological aspects of his subject which interest him.

Unfortunately, what interests him even in psychology is what is popular rather than what is permanent in biography. Everybody is immediately interested in love affairs, fewer in the intellectual development of a great man's mind or his art – yet those aspects alone make such a biography worth while. The reader of Herr Ludwig's *Goethe* might be almost excused for concluding that the determining influence upon Goethe's art at every turn in his career was invariably love for a woman. I cannot suggest more quickly his lack of proportion than by saying that Spinoza, whose thought had such an enormous influence upon Goethe's view of life, is never once mentioned by Herr Ludwig; while every woman, except (I think) a little French dancing-mistress at Strasburg, is recorded as bringing her stone to the pyramid. There would be no distortion of truth in mentioning their contributions, if the biographer had not ignored the great procession of tugging camels and straining horses, the huge fragments of old temples and blocks of philosophy and science which also contributed to the making of it.

It would be a mistake to conclude that all Goethe had had to do to become himself was to fall constantly in love on that limited liability system at which he became early adept; yet against such a howler the critic is bound to caution Herr Ludwig's reader. The effects of Goethe's emotional life on his work are excellently traced in these pages; the effects of his intellect upon his emotions (in his case supremely important) most inadequately. Heaven forbid that we should underrate the power and stimulus upon a poet of the *mater saeva cupidinum* or even of lighter loves; but though it is important that the biographer of Goethe should do justice to the influence of Kätchen, Fredericka, Lili, Lotte, Charlotte, Christiane, Minna, Ulrike, etc., etc., Goethe's relation to his thinking contemporaries and the great men of the past, his indebtedness to Germany, England, France, Italy, Greece, Rome, also demand attention, if we are to measure the diameter of his mind or understand the quality of his work. Much fuel chokes a little fire, but makes a big one blaze. It was not only the mass of experience which Goethe's art consumed that was so astonishing, but the mass of learning and reflection; and what makes him almost unique among artists is that at the same time he made a good work of art of life itself.

His practical plastic power Herr Ludwig does succeed in bringing out, especially in the second volume; but from his first volume no one could guess that the influence upon Goethe of Oesler and Lessing (Herr Ludwig does mention Herder), of Wieland, of Dodd's *Beauties of Shakespeare*, of Sterne and *The Vicar of Wakefield*, of Strasburg Cathedral and German ballads, even of the Lisbon earthquake, were as great in their several ways as that of Kätchen or Lili. However, let us take the book as what it is – suggestive, but incomplete; a study of entertaining acuteness, chiefly concerned with Goethe's love-life, and here and there showing original insight.

The book does convey what it is conceivable some may have forgotten – that a man cannot be a world-poet without possessing a temperament of extreme sensibility, not to say a violent one. Herr Ludwig does that most effectively. His account, too, of the years of bourgeois placidity which followed Goethe's open adoption of Christiane as his mistress is new and convincing. His championship of his subsequent marriage to her, which more idealistic and staid biographers have treated as a sad affair, and his explanation of the failure in comparison of Goethe's lofty relation with Frau von Stein, which they have exalted, are also real contributions to the subject. For an inquisitive psychologist, however, he fails in making as clear to us as we might hope what peculiar quality it was in Goethe himself that made him in his love-affairs invariably save himself in time. Herr Ludwig calls it his 'genius'; and Goethe's contrary impulse to fling himself again and again into life, to adore, to yield, to lose himself, he calls his 'daemon'.

This really does not get us much further. Goethe himself was fond of the word 'daemonic'. He endeavoured at different times to explain what he meant by it; but it seems that since this divine or diabolical factor cannot be grasped by the reason or understanding, he could not express clearly what he meant by it. He felt it too in inanimate things. This much however is certain, that he held it to be, in the case of man, a mysterious power which fills him with boundless confidence in himself and makes him capable of enormous and successful undertakings, but also betrays him to disaster. He says it was not part of his own nature, and that he had been under its sway.

'His love affairs', says Mr Santayana, 'were means to fuller realization of himself. They were not sensual, nor were his infidelities callous – far from it – they stirred him deeply and loosened the springs of poetry in his heart. That was precisely their function. But he must press on. The claims of his own spiritual growth compelled him to sacrifice the object of his passion and his own lacerated feelings on the altar of duty to himself.' This is much better put than Herr Ludwig succeeds in putting it. Goethe was far from being ruthless, far from being a Don Juan. On the contrary, he was often an unsuccessful lover, nearly always a prostrate one – till the moment of escape. He suffered agonies of sympathetic pain in departing, and never forgot his loves. His old loves remained till death in his memory on the tenderest terms; he never tried to keep, but he never lost, one really dear to him. He did not abandon Fredericka or Lili, as Herr Ludwig once suggests, because he wanted a wife and they would not do. It was something subtler and more general than that.

In the story *Die Neue Melusine* a man falls in love with a lovely creature of the dwarf kingdom; he can only remain with her by becoming as small as she, and when she puts a ring on his finger he too becomes a dwarf. At first he is blissfully happy, but soon he remembers his former condition. 'Now I understood for the first time what the philosophers meant by their ideals, by which men are said to be tormented. I possessed an ideal self, and often in my dreams seemed to myself like a giant.' In his misery he files the ring in two and regains his natural stature. This is what happened time after time in these love stories which Herr Ludwig tells, and that allegory is the plot of them all. True, in the end, Goethe married a little dwarf, but not one who belonged to the magic kingdom. There was something deep down in his nature which enabled him to lend himself un-reservedly in imagination, not only to his loves, but to philosophies, religions and ideas, and yet to attain peace of heart without espousing one of them. He could combine Christianity, Paganism, Sensuality, without becoming a Christian, Pagan, or a Sensualist; thus many conflicting currents of the times met and mingled in him. The gift which saved him was poetry.

As I have said, it is surprising that Carlyle should have chosen Goethe as a favourite hero. One would have expected that the grand, bland, Olympian calm of the sage of Weimar would have exasperated the flaming sage of Chelsea, who spent some time trying to inspire Emerson with an agitated horror of the Devil. (It is said that he took him to a House of Commons debate with that purpose, turning on him fiercely with 'Will ye believe, mon; in the Deil *noo*?') The serenity of Goethe seems to me to lie in his temperament rather than in his philosophy, and therefore, alas, cannot be transferable. His contemporaries were amazed, and many of them shocked by his indifference during those years when his country was being broken up and overrun by the French. While patriots were in despair, he wrote poetry; nor did the confusion round him reflect itself in a word he wrote. On the day of the battle of Leipzig he wrote an epilogue to his tragedy of *Essex* for his favourite actress. He followed everything with his mind, but he let nothing upset him emotionally. He allowed his love affairs to go further than most things in that direction, but he always just managed to extricate himself – intact. It is this mixture of extreme sensibility with detachment which makes him unique. His sensibility was great enough to make it almost impossible to tell him bad news, and he put off to the last moment facing anything disagreeable; yet his detachment was so complete that men thought him unfeeling. His constant effort was to keep himself always in a frame of mind to make the most of the alleviating occupations of the present. Of all the stories told of him, the one which seems to illustrate best this temperament is the account of an incident which occurred on his voyage from Sicily to Naples. The ship was in great danger of being driven on the rocks and the deck was crowded with terrified Italian peasants. To Goethe the ignoble uproar was more detestable than death; he delivered a little speech and told them to trust in the Mother of God. It had a calming effect. 'They were so near the rocks that some sailors had seized beams to stave the ship off'; Goethe then went down to the cabin, lay on his back, and called up before his mind's eye a picture in Merian's illustrated Bible.

BOSWELL

I used to think that when the Great Book was opened in the Valley of Jehoshaphat, it would be the entries under the head 'Byron' which would contain fewest surprises for us, but apparently it is Boswell who after all has succeeded best in anticipating the Day of Judgment. These volumes* promise to be the complete revelation of 'a man', or at any rate as complete as words can achieve. Of a normal man? Yes and no: normal in the sense that the man revealed is 'human, all too human' and at the same time queer (for seen close we are all queer), but emphatically not normal in the intensity of his curiosity, his complete transparency, and his unflagging aspiration after virtues which any one day of his life might have taught him he would never attain. 'My warm imagination', he once wrote when comparatively young to Temple, 'looks forward with great complacency in the sobriety, the healthfulness, and worth of my future life.' He continued to look forward in vain.

American scholars have made a corner in Boswell, and they are dealing with him with Germanic thoroughness. It was an

* *The Boswell Papers*, Isham Collection.

American, Mr Tinker, who edited the most complete, though still very incomplete, edition of Boswell's letters; and now comes, from America, an edition of *The Hypochondriack* – seventy essays contributed by Boswell to the *London Magazine* from November 1777 to August 1783, and reprinted for the first time in two volumes. The book is even more of a literary curiosity than a contribution to literature, although the essays are good eighteenth-century essays and worth reprinting. Yet one tends to peep and peck about in them for information on Boswell's life and character, rather than to read them for their own sakes. One does not read, say, Boswell 'On Death', though it is a laudable essay, in order to learn more about death, but more about Boswell, to see how far he will exhibit his own engaging, humble, fatuous, flighty character in treating that grave theme, and how far he will pull himself together and reflect the meditations and opinions of the great man, his friend, or of others. The editor comes to our rescue by giving us the necessary references at every point where our memories are likely to fail us.

One question she discusses is the question why Boswell wrote these essays. She concludes that the primary motive was self-discipline. She says – and it is true – that 'Boswell's biographers have overlooked the fact that whatever he desired for himself – fame, distinction, success – his most constant wish was to be a good man, and that he was conscious how much his unsettled physical and mental habits contributed to his failure in that respect. In his youth he tried to acquire "an even external tenor", to have a "settled serenity". His friendships with men much older than himself, and his desire to meet great men, were largely caused by his hope of finding an inspiration to lead a sober, righteous, and godly life; his fidelity to Dr Johnson and General Paoli came from his certainty that these were the most elevating characters he knew. He went to Europe in his early twenties with the hope that he could attain a "serene contentment", and "so much taste as never to be idle for want of elegant occupation" – or, as he told Rousseau, with "*un véritable désir de me perfectionner*". Disappointed in the effect of Europe, he wrote to Wilkes in 1765, "In the course of our correspondence, you shall have the various schemes which I form for getting tolerably through this strange existence." Of these the most important seems to have been a resort to his love of writing. Certainly it was in this year, 1765, that he formed his plan of writing *The Hypochondriack* – the idea, perhaps, occurring to him as a result of the "*ébauche de ma vie*" which he had sent to Rousseau at the end of 1764.'

Now, from Macaulay onwards, all the robust commentators upon Boswell's character, Leslie Stephen and Carlyle for example, have interpreted his pursuit of great men as a delight in basking in reflected glory, and have treated him with smiling patronage as a comic snob. There is certainly some truth in this point of view. But it was for another and deeper reason that Boswell flew like a moth to the light towards any example of shining excellence. No man was ever more acutely conscious of himself than Boswell, and therefore more painfully aware of being a bundle of confused and contradictory impulses. His will was naturally weak (at the end of his life, after the deaths of Johnson and Mrs Boswell, it became completely dilapidated), and he longed passionately to pull himself together. Men who had nobly succeeded had an irresistible attraction for him. With them for a while his better self was uppermost, with them his fluttering aspirations could take wing again in spite of ever-repeated falls, with them he could luxuriate in that glow of self-satisfaction which was such a relief from the torture of bewilderment and self-disgust that was his fundamentally persistent mood. Drink, frivolity and the companionship of the great and good were his means of escape from that misery. It is his great merit that he passionately preferred the last expedient, though he could not do without the others. It is this preference which helped to make him so representative of average men; for without aspirations, however futile, no one is very interesting to his fellow-men or representative of them. It is however a fact of great significance that he should have signed these essays 'The Hypochondriack'.

I do not know the medical definition of hypochondria, but it cannot be far from this: an affliction of those who are too acutely and perpetually conscious of the state of either their bodies or their minds, and in whom awareness reveals most constantly what is painful in those conditions. It is a malady most incident to men of genius, many of whom spend their lives in watching the stream of consciousness in the hope of mastering and understanding it. Leslie Stephen has laughed at Boswell for 'emulating the profound melancholy of his hero'. 'He seems', he says, 'to have taken a pride in his sufferings from hypochondria; though, in truth, his melancholy diverges from Johnson's by as great a difference as that which divides any two varieties of Jacques's classification. Boswell's was the melancholy of a man who spends too much, drinks too much, falls in love too often, and is forced to live in the country and dependence upon a stern old parent, when he is longing for a jovial life in London taverns. Still, he was excusably vexed when Johnson refused to believe in the reality of his complaints, and showed scant sympathy to his noisy would-be fellow-sufferer.' This comment is only partly true.

When *The Boswell Papers* are given to the world, it will be seen that Boswell's sufferings were at least as genuine as those of the Sage, who in strength of mind was so vastly superior, but whose lapses from the better life were not quite so unlike Boswell's own or quite so infrequent as his moral grandeur has led the world to suppose. All through Johnson's life there runs a tragic tension, which found expression in sudden profound groans and beatings of the breast, a tension due to a discord between his public role of moralist and his way of living. We tend naturally to attribute this to a superior tenderness of conscience; yet the profoundly honest spirit of Johnson would contemptuously scout such a flattering interpretation. 'When I say I am a miserable sinner,' he would roar, 'I mean it.' But he did not think it good for the cause of virtue that men should know too particularly the frailties of those to whom they already look up. This was an ethical point in which Boswell was deeply interested.

I am told that in *The Boswell Papers* there is a record of a conversation between Hawkins and Boswell, in which the former says he is very sorry that he ever read Johnson's private diary, now destroyed. The implication is that it was not unlike that, let us say, of Tolstoy, which is a record of unceasing aspirations, lapses, and self-reproach. Perhaps the greatest difference of all between the two friends lay in the extent to which each allowed himself to reveal his own weaknesses. 'One day', says Boswell in the *Life*, 'I owned to Johnson that I was occasionally troubled with a fit of narrowness.' 'Why, sir,' said he, 'so am I, *but I do not tell it.*' Boswell, and it is his supreme service to mankind, always 'told'.

Boswell was born with the great gift of admiration, and it was so instinctive in him that it exterminated completely that fear-of-giving-oneself-away disease to which all are prone – especially authors. That authors should be so unfortunately prone to this malady is inevitable, since one of the strongest impulses which drive men into writing is vanity. It is inevitable therefore that the author, when he is conscious of the figure he is cutting in print, should trim, alter, ennoble and strengthen the thoughts and impressions he transmits, otherwise he would be defeating what is really one of his principal aims in writing – to impress others. The result of this editing is that his work is often far less intelligent and original than it might have been. We are all, not only authors, more intelligent than we appear to be. But we do not dare to risk looking like fools, and very foolish we feel when someone, who did take that risk of expressing what we knew all along ourselves (like the child in the fairy story, who cried out, 'But the King is naked!'), is hailed in consequence as a genius. Boswell was a rare mixture of humility and self-complacency; his weakness and his prime virtue played up to each other, making him what every man of pen and ink should hope to be, the transparently honest man.

HERBERT SPENCER

Herbert Spencer's *Autobiography* is one of the most transparently honest books ever written.

Men have often tried to describe themselves, but vanity or desire for sympathy, or the penitent instinct are the strongest motives which usually prompt them, and these are insidiously distorting influences. To achieve truthful self-portraiture a man must be both self-complacent and detached. Self-complacency by itself may produce a memorable but not a truthful book. The *Life of Lord Herbert of Cherbury* and Benvenuto Cellini's *Autobiography* are excellent reading, but pinches of salt must be taken with every paragraph. Such excessively self-satisfied men are out to make a definite impression. Again, complete detachment probably prevents a man from writing about himself at all. Those, therefore, who have written about themselves most truthfully are men who have taken their work so seriously that it seemed natural that the world should want to know about them, and yet at the same time have been so satisfied with what they have done, so convinced of its importance, that they do not care a rap what others think about them. Of such was Herbert Spencer.

A happy blend in him of self-complacency and detachment has produced a book of unrivalled honesty and tepidity. Gibbon, it has been said, wrote about himself in the same tone as he wrote about the Roman Empire; Herbert Spencer wrote about himself in exactly the same tone as he wrote about the Universe. He was not afraid of making the Universe dull, and he was quite indifferent to our opinion if we thought him uninteresting. His aim in both cases was to generalize and correlate phenomena.

Many men have screwed themselves up to confessing humbly that they were wicked or did mean things; but then, as in Rousseau's case, pride usually peeps out in an assertion that other men conceal what they confess. They turn out after all to be proud when they compare themselves with others. Many have written themselves down as rascals, or as asses of the gay and freely kicking kind; but very few men have carefully depicted themselves, full length, as dull. Such an achievement is beyond the reach of humility. It can only be accomplished by one who, like Herbert Spencer, is self-satisfied *and* only interested in facts.

The result is fascinating. Perhaps when the *Synthetic Philosophy* is never read – that row of stout volumes bound in the philosopher's favourite colour, 'an impure purple' – its author may be still remembered as a perfect specimen of a human type. There is no name for this type, but we have a name for his opposite, whom we call the Humorist. Not that Herbert Spencer was an antigelast; so far from looking forward to the day of the last joke, he was pathetically appreciative of jokes, seeking them himself with care and hope. But his mind was precisely the kind in which humour does not flourish. The jokes he made, or appreciated, were small; he never saw a big one. He tells us how a brief access of good health once enabled him to make a joke in the Isle of Wight. He was on holiday there with G. H. Lewes, George Eliot's husband, and at lunch he remarked that the chops were very big for so small an island.

Now, Herbert Spencer had a deep and hearty laugh, and his chuckles when this jest occurred to him must have been extremely funny. We can reconstruct the scene: Lewes, after gazing for a moment at the delighted countenance of the philosopher, would start laughing himself, and his laughter would be echoed by still deeper guffaws from the begetter of the joke, which, in their turn, would provoke redoubled peals from Lewes, till between them a climax would be reached memorable after forty years. Then, as he himself has told us, the philosopher recovered his balance and gravely commented on the causal connection between humour and improved health.

Describing his descent from the summit of Ben Nevis, he says in the *Autobiography*: 'I found myself possessed of a quite unusual amount of agility; being able to leap from rock to rock with rapidity, ease and safety; so that I quite astonished myself. There was evidently an exaltation of the perceptive and motor powers. . . . Long continued exertion having caused an unusually great action of the lungs, the exaltation produced by the stimulation of the brain was not cancelled by the diminished oxygenation of the blood. The oxygenation had been so much in excess, that deduction from it did not appreciably diminish the vital activities.' What on earth, you ask, is all this about? Well, on the summit of the mountain the philosopher had taken a pull of whisky on top of wine, and this is Herbert Spencer's description of descending Ben Nevis charioted by Bacchus and his pards.

His attention habitually dwelt on the causes of things to the exclusion of all other aspects of them. At the Athenæum complaints of the toughness of the meat came before the kitchen committee, of which he was a member. It was agreed that the butcher should be interviewed. But Herbert Spencer would not hear of his being admitted until the nature of the complaint had been better defined; it was unfair, he said, to assert vaguely that his meat was tough. After a discussion, the butcher was sent for and the philosopher informed him that his joints 'had too much connective tissue in them'.

Now this habit of mind, though it occasions humour in others, is unfavourable to the production of it; and this is shown by the specimens of Spencer's humour, given in *Home Life with Herbert Spencer*. It is an amusing book, written by two young ladies who kept house for him for eight years. One example will suffice. The ladies were dissatisfied with a photograph which had been taken of him: 'It gives', they said, 'neither your serious nor your frivolous expression! We don't like it at all. . . .' 'About ten minutes or a quarter of an hour afterwards, we were astounded to see the philosopher in his shirt-sleeves standing at the dining-room door tying his neck-tie. The intensely amused expression on his face showed he was quite alive to the surprise he would occasion. Without any apology for his deshabille he laughingly remarked: "I have come down to fire off a joke before I forget it! Your criticisms of my photograph – which you expect to be grave and gay at the same time – remind me of the farmers, who are never contented unless simultaneously it is raining on the turnips while the sun shines on the corn." And with an audible chuckle he hurried back to complete his toilet.'

But it is a severe test to be described in intimacy by two superficially reverential, but unconsciously frivolous young women. Herbert Spencer with his foibles, his ear-stoppers, his valetudinarianism, his habit of giving to everything – potatoes, religion, salt-cellars the same quality of attention, was at the mercy of such observers; while the enormously wide sweep of his intellectual curiosity was only paralleled by the narrowness of his emotional responses.

He was a man who could not attend to anything he did not think of the utmost importance, and he was driven by his temperament to attending to trifles. He thought that complete rejection of tradition was as important in deciding how a bed should be made, or how thick socks should be (it was illogical that the foot should be less clad than the rest of the body), as in setting out to investigate the problems of physics; and while he was making an heroic lifelong effort to cram every branch of experience into a world-formula, he was agitated by a smut on a potato. What a victim for the feminine eye!

The authoresses say that on finding them ignorant of some fact, he was in the habit of exclaiming, 'Dear me, how innocent you are!' But the reader is much more inclined to apply that adjective to him. Indeed, it is Herbert Spencer's innocence which after all saves his dignity. When they suggested that the next time a rather overtalkative visitor came, they should *all* wear 'earstoppers', he entered into the project without a notion that it contained any reflection upon his favourite method of guarding against too much conversation; and he proceeded to superintend enthusiastically the melting off the rims of old saucepan lids, to make the curved springs, which held the pads tightly over both ears.

He was unable to believe that the application of reason to any matter could ever lead to ludicrous results. That is why he is the opposite type to the humorist, who is ever conscious of the double aspects of things. The contradiction observed may lie between feeling and thought, or reason and convention, or the contrast may be between the seriousness with which something is felt and its trifling nature, or between its importance and the lightness with which men take it. If the unreasonableness of convention strikes one humorist, another laughs from the point of view of use and wont at the absurdity of result reached by reason; if one finds jokes in the ease with which tragedies are born, another will find them in the seriousness with which trifles are taken. Humorists take sides on all sorts of questions, but they are essentially men who feel, whatever they may think, that there *are* two or even more sides to them.

SWINBURNE

There are few experiences which I envy more than that of having heard Swinburne recite his own poetry, say such a poem as 'The Triumph of Time'. Sometimes, in reading, we are told, he lost control of his emotions and 'he would dance about the room, the paper fluttering from his finger-tips like a pennon in a gale of wind'; but at others, though surpassingly strange, it was – and without the least tincture of affectation – a transfiguration, an ecstasy, 'a case of poetic "possession" pure and simple'.

'On these occasions', wrote Sir Edmund Gosse, 'his voice took on strange and fife-like notes, extremely moving and disconcerting, since he was visibly moved himself. The sound of Swinburne wailing forth in his thrilling semi-tones such stanzas as that addressed to the Sea:

> I shall sleep, and move with the moving ships,
> Change as the winds change, veer in the tide;
> My lips will feast on the foam of thy lips,
> I shall rise with thy rising, with thee subside;
> Sleep, and not know if she be, if she were,
> Filled full with life to the eyes and hair,

> As a rose is fulfilled to the roseleaf tips
> With splendid summer and perfume and pride.

is something which will not fade out of memory as long as life lasts; and, perhaps, most of all, in the recitation of the last four of the following very wonderful lines:

> I shall go my ways, tread out my measure,
> Fill the days of my daily breath
> With fugitive things not good to treasure,
> Do as the world doth, say as it saith;
> But if we had loved each other – O sweet,
> Had you felt, lying under the palms of your feet,
> The heart of my heart, beating harder with pleasure
> To feel you tread it to dust and death –

'The Triumph of Time', one of the few of Swinburne's poems which can be traced to a powerful emotion (in this case a love-disappointment) which had its origin in life, not in his imagination; it runs on for more than fifty stanzas, each of which seems in turn to reach the acme of emotion. There is nothing in the experience of a poetry-reader quite like reading Swinburne. True, he is a poet who lends himself rather ill to cool, detached admiration. You must allow yourself to be carried away to enjoy him. And having yielded, you may then find yourself stunned in the cataract of his surging energy, or that your mind is lulled to sleep by his strong monotonous melodies. The poet himself is often swept past the subject which he set himself. His command of means is so great, his mastery over metre and rhythm so astounding, that he often loses sight of his end. His great defect is one to which all eloquent writers are liable – he could not stop. It was the defect also of Victor Hugo, whom he admired so much. I am not musical, but I sometimes guess that Wagner suffered from it. There is a too-muchness about them all. Their Niagaras go on pouring down long after our little cups are full. They pursue the unending crescendo. We are at first exhilarated and then fatigued by this miracle of inexhaustible eloquence. At first it seems a marvel that they can go on so long; presently, that they should ever come to an end. We await nervously the absolutely last chord of the apparently interminable pianoforte-player. But how magnificent the performance has been! And if one has kept one's intelligence alert in spite of the overpowering swing of Swinburne's verses, one is often surprised at the sublety and coherence of the poet's thought. It is impossible to find a phrase to describe him completely, but perhaps when one calls him the Rhapsodist of Freedom one comes nearest to hinting at what most distinguished him. Freedom is a vague word. That vague but real thing the brotherhood of man, the wind, the sea, the life of a seabird (these are symbols of liberty) – aroused in him a boundless exultation which he expressed better than any other poet. Even his sensuality is transformed into a mystical passion for release; while his political poems gain intensity – however misplaced and excessive his particular admirations and hatreds – from the idea of liberty itself: Freedom, the mother and the bride of man's soul, his implacable goddess too, demanding bitter sacrifices.

There is in modern poetry a tendency to discard formal metres altogether, and to rely instead upon changing rhythms imposed by the subject. Consequently, Swinburne is held in small honour by the new poets. But since down the ages formal metres have been found most potent aids to inducing that state of mind in which poetic intuitions become transferable, it is certain that his fame is safe.

I myself enjoy Swinburne's prose very much, but this is so exceptional a taste that I have been tempted to insert an Agony Column advertisement: 'Lonely literary man of moderate means wishes to meet friend: must appreciate Swinburne's prose.' That would tell me much about him. An anthology of Swinburne's critical writings would prove him a critic of rare excellence, and that as a prose-writer he had been unduly depreciated.

He possessed, in a degree never excelled, the great gift of praise, a lyric faculty of unbounded despairing admiration. 'I shrieked and clasped my hands in ecstasy' – Shelley's line will stand as a general description of this aspect of his criticism; though he could also suggest the beauty and excellence peculiar to this or that writer with the lucidity of a man of genius. Gratitude for gifts of imagination was in him equivalent to worship. When he wrote, he set up an altar festooned with alliterative sentences, looped about with garlands of fruits and flowers gathered from every clime and period of literature. Then, before the kindled fire of his own enthusiasm, he celebrated rites so exuberant and sonorous that they resembled a grand choral celebration. At such rites the bodies of bludgeoned victims were also not out of place; scalps and corpses were laid at the feet of the deity, and among them were sometimes former occupants of pedestals. Thus, at the feet of Dickens, he throws the body of Matthew Arnold, whose poems he had declared to be 'in the highest tone of Wordsworth's, as clear and grave as his best, as close and full and majestic'. Arnold did not admire Dickens; and his indifference, since it is now Dickens who is enthroned, must be explained to the greater honour of the creator of Mrs Gamp. Therefore, Arnold is described as 'a man whose main achievement in creative literature was to make himself by painful painstaking into a sort of pseudo-Wordsworth'.

Swinburne wrote his essays in the spirit in which he wrote his sonnets and odes to great men. For the time being their country was his country, their gods his gods, their enemies his enemies. It is one method of legitimate criticism. The critic's functions are by no means limited to comparison, analysis, and judgement: he may simply make us feel what he has felt. Swinburne was the most magnificent sounding-board for rapturous admiration.

I can pardon all Swinburne's critical excesses. When he says things like, 'History will forget the name of Bonaparte before humanity forgets the name of Rathbert' (perhaps I had better mention that this is a character in one of Victor Hugo's minor works), it does not prevent me from appreciating his splendid imaginative insight. I love him, too, for the same sort of reason that men of science love Darwin – for being an example of complete and pure devotion to a pursuit. To Swinburne literature was everything; literature and art, not life, inspired him. That is his peculiarity and his glory. I know it is not quite sane to be like that; I know it implies enormous limitations, but – how thankful we should be that a Swinburne has existed.

KIPLING

When Kipling died my mind went back to 1898, when he was lying so gravely ill in New York that there seemed small chance of his recovery: to the public anxiety, and the bulletins, posted up two or three times a day, so urgent was the demand for news. 1898 marked the highest point of his popular renown in England and America. To English-speaking peoples, he then seemed to represent in literature deep instincts of their race. How young he was and yet how much he had achieved! But after the Boer War, Kipling never again stood in quite the same relation to his country; the heyday of British Imperialism was over, and the national spirit was too divided to find complete expression in his work, though he remained the mouthpiece of a very large section of the public. Those were the days when a Frenchman could actually write a book called *A quoi tient la supériorité des Anglo-Saxons?* and the Continent was searching Kipling's works for the answer. But all this is unimportant today to those who are endeavouring to make up their minds about Kipling's permanent *place* among English writers.

Let us run over what are the most obvious things to say about him; they are not all of them of the first importance, but together they make an imposing impression. He was a genius, there's no doubt about that. He was a most conscientious and able craftsman. He stood for a number of years in a symbolic relation to the spirit of his times. He was recognized as a master of the short story and he was *the bard* of the British Empire. I don't propose to say anything about him as the poet of Imperialism, but to recall certain of his characteristics as a craftsman, as a writer, as a teller of tales.

First, however, one other thing must be said. However much opinions may differ about his work, Rudyard Kipling has been the most wide-flung combustion in the sky of English letters since Byron and Dickens. This, no doubt, was partly due, as it was with Byron, to the representative and political character of his work, but it was by no means due entirely to that. Let's consider for a moment other causes of the astonishing width of his appeal. Although his style possessed one of the most important qualifications for immense popularity, namely, un-flagging vigour, it displayed at the same time an unpopular quality: extreme virtuosity. In his later work especially his prose was marked by an acrobatic verbal ingenuity hardly exceeded by Meredith. It seems on the face of it strange that an author who is so tremendously concentrated and latterly ellip-tical should have continued to appeal to *non-literary* readers. Kipling is a writer whose phrases must be allowed to soak a moment in the mind before they expand, like those little Japanese pellets which blossom into flower only when they have lain awhile on the surface of a cup of water. Yet with all his ostentatious word-craft, he remained a favourite author of thousands upon thousands of readers who are ordinarily impa-tient of that kind of writing. No author, too, had a more various audience of admirers, while, oddly enough, it was among *literary* people, among literary artists and critics, that this master craftsman was apt to meet with grudging appreciation. We admitted his genius, his power, but we often wrote and talked as though we were sorry we had to.

What then were the qualities which made him admired by
millions and yet often abused by those who loved, as he did, the
painful art of writing? Of course, many of those who criticized
him coolly or adversely were those who also hated his politics
and his morals. These pervade his work. They are as tribal as a
Prussian historian's, or a schoolboy's. Even when addressing
children, the savour of them was pervasive, and because it was
Kipling who was writing, their savour was invariably pungent.
That important fact, however, is not the most interesting one.
His style, while loved by the unliterary, often irritated the
literary because the aim of his virtuosity was always a *violent
precision*. His adjectives and phrases start from the page. He
forced you first and foremost to see, to hear, to touch and to
smell – above all to see and smell as vividly as words can be
made to compass those ends. In Kipling, when the greatest
vividness was inconsistent with an aesthetic impression – well,
that kind of beauty went by the board. His metaphors and
comparisons are apt to be chosen (and like all vivid writers he
used them continually) with complete indifference to associations and overtones, and with a single aim – vividness. To take
an example from his *Letters of Travel*: 'There was never a cloud in
the sky, that rested upon the snowline of the horizon as a
sapphire on white velvet.' Now we have all seen a sapphire on
white velvet in a jeweller's window, and it calls up vividly the
intense blue of dark sky above a snowfield, but that comparison
does not bring out, it even destroys the beauty of the picture
itself. Of course, this is not true of all his comparisons and
metaphors. Some had poetry and depth. What fine phrases and
sentences he found to describe the sea in *Captains Courageous*; for
instance, the sleek swell before storms, 'grey, formless, enormous and growing', or 'the heave and the halt and the howl and
the crash of the comber wind-hounded'. Think, too, of the
scenes that rose before our minds while reading *Kim*! No writer
triumphed more completely in combining the arresting detail
and wide horizons (so hard to do) into one picture. But this

trend of his style towards perpetual vividness, to which beauty was often sacrificed, alienated the more aesthetic type of reader. None of his contemporaries could condense more into a brief description. I cannot resist giving one more example. Here is the opening of one of his later stories about a break-down of a motor on the Great North Road. The story resolves itself into a fantastic discourse by an American on the ruinous effects of Prohibition – a linguistic feast, but empty of lasting interest. Listen:

> By the time we had found the trouble, night shut down on us. A rounded pile of woods ahead took one sudden star to its forehead and faded out; the way-waste melted into the darker velvet of the hedge, another star reflected itself in the glassy black of the bitumened road; and a weak moon struggled up out of a mist-patch from a valley. *Our lights painted the grass unearthly greens, and the tree-boles bone-white.* A church clock struck eleven, as I curled up in the front seat and waited the progress of Time and Things, with some notion of picking up a tow towards morning.

But now let's turn to the *other* sources of his immense popularity. Everyone likes a good story, and Kipling was an admirable story-teller. But it was not only that. The short-story-teller is more dependent than any other kind of literary artist upon lucky choice in his subject. If one looks through the works of the world's famous short-story writers – Maupassant, Chekhov, Henry James, Kipling himself, Ambrose Bierce, and today Mr Somerset Maugham – one sees that it is only when the writer has hit upon a story *good in itself* that he has written memorably. His other stories, though they may be as skilfully told and presented, do not make a deep impression. In the short-story the theme is all important. It is only from time to time in an author's career that a good theme comes to hand. Master as Kipling was of description, of recording distinctive speech (a gift so necessary where there is no space to expound character), his fine stories might all be comprised in a single volume. It was not only his skill in description, not even his power of heightening characteristics by intensifying modes of speech (we all remember his soldiers' talk and that of the enormous variety of men and women who figure in his pages), but an interest more fundamental which took the world by storm. He made every character in his stories an artist in his own lingo: the schoolboy, the engineer, the soldier, the bagman – even, by a stretch of the imagination, different kinds of animals, in the *Jungle Books*. But the most significant thing of all about him as a story-teller was that he put these gifts at the service *not* of the love-story, not of some adventure in sensibility, not of worldly success, but for the first time at the service of a man's *relation to his work*, whether that work was departmental, military, journalistic; whether it was medical, building a bridge, running an engine or stopping a famine or commanding a ship; whether it was a common job or a unique one.

Instantly, all over the world the sympathy of all sorts and conditions of readers went out to hug an author whose theme was a man's relation to his work; how a man could stick to it even when sickened by it, see it through in spite of defeat, loneliness and weakness. This is a more pervasive characteristic of Kipling's work than what sometimes seemed most prominent – its connection with militarism and Empire building. He idealized for an enormous variety of men their relation to their work: and such stories were a 'felt want', as they say in the advertising world, they satisfied a stronger thirst than that for exotic colour and adventure, though Kipling also provided that.

Connected with this sense of a man's relation to his job was his strong sense of group loyalty – the herd instinct, whether it took the form of patriotism, or schoolhouse against school, or school against the world, or regiment against War Office. The romance and meaning of life lay according to Kipling in the bee's devotion to the hive. Kipling was the poet of the herd instinct, and to such a writer independence of thought presents itself as the most insidious enemy. The diameter of his mind was not wide. He distrusted 'thought', knowing that it separates men, or rather unites them only on a plane of which he had little cognizance and seen from which group-emotions and group-morale appear narrow. Hence the permanent quarrel between him and the thinking sort, whether they were artists themselves, or people preoccupied with things of the mind. Put yourself in the heart and mind of a young aesthetic intellectual at the beginning of the century and you will feel Kipling to be your *enemy*, an honourable and strong enemy; but an enemy, and thank goodness an enemy who was *afraid of you* – or rather of thought. I say independence of thought was Kipling's enemy, not independence of action. In nothing was he more representative of the Anglo-Saxon character, American as well as English, than in his admiration, his demand, for individual responsibility in decision. M. André Chevrillon, his brilliant translator, has analysed well this combination in Kipling's work between emotional herd-loyalty and the necessity of being able to act on personal initiative. This conception of duty as something ultimately *self*-imposed, not commanded from without, is the moral soul of Protestantism. And it is the final test Rudyard Kipling applied to men.

In later years he treated new subjects. His style lost some of its early violent vitality and became more elaborate. But the main difference between his earlier and his later phase was that latterly he used his gifts for vivid presentation more often upon things dreamt through than lived through. His extraordinary avidity of attention to the actual lost something of its bite. *Puck of Pook's Hill, Rewards and Fairies* were inspired by his love of a *past* England. On the other hand, to sit loosely in the saddle of life, to roam, rough it, listen to travellers' yarns and to the talk of workers in all parts of the earth, had been more likely to bring him the short-story-teller's lucky finds. As a Sussex squire he continued to travel, but chiefly in the past; his creative work was fed henceforth mostly by books and dreams.

Was Kipling a great poet? He was not a minor poet, that is certain – as certain as that Byron was not a minor poet. But when I ask myself that question, I cannot remember anything of his to put beside the finest poetry. Nevertheless he lifted into the middle realm of poetry more moods and enthusiasms characteristic of active men than any of his contemporaries; and not one poet among them made so spirited, so sincere, so unselfconscious an attempt to handle in verse the romance of modern invention, or to celebrate the new opportunities for adventure and sensation opened up by modern life. He wrote poems about what a farmer felt watching his fat cattle go through a gate, what an ex-soldier thought while mowing the vicar's lawn, what an engineer felt about his engine. He wrote poems not only about love and death – the eternal themes – but what the average man felt to be romantic in his daily life.

There is a feeling abroad that it is time the Muse ceased to repeat her ancient divinations and that she dealt with *everyday* emotions, with *common* not *rare*, experiences. Who else has made, anything like so spirited, so sincere, so unselfconscious an effort to do so?

UNITY OF EFFECT

Anyone in search of an example in the art of conducting a story to its proper and foreseen close could not do better than study the construction of *Persuasion*, though such unity of effect presupposes something else not necessarily within the reach of other writers, however eager they may be to profit by Jane Austen's example. The consistency and confidence of her attitude towards every character, every event and every detail in her stories, cannot be imitated. Moreover such confidence must ever be as much the product of a period as of individual effort. It is the fruit of corroboration. Private conviction does not produce an equal stability, for human beings cannot possess the unselfconscious calm of complete assurance unless their judgements are confirmed by others. Here and there some passionate solitary may succeed in asserting consistently his own sense of proportion in the face of surrounding dissent, but inevitably in doing so he will feel a need to defend his views. He will be explanatory, and, almost inevitably, explanatory with that over-insistence which is liable to upset at any moment the subtle spiritual balance upon which so much depends in art. How distressing – and in the end how unconvincing – it is to find oneself catching continually the compelling but strained glance of the novelist's eye as one turns his pages! How blest, on the other hand, the writer of fiction who, if his reader should stop to ask, What is your point of view? can reply with mild surprise, 'Why, of course, that of all sensible men!' But it stands to reason that such writers can only exist when sensible people do as a matter of fact agree; and it follows that works which possess the solid, restful quality of Jane Austen's must be the product, in a sense, of many minds and not of one. *Daphnis and Chloe* could only have been written at a time when all sensible men conceived the pleasures of sensuality to be one of the blessings of life; when they felt no need to dress up or disguise young desire to make it charming. But when, in an age in which all sensible people are not agreed on this point, Mr George Moore, for instance, attempts to write in the same vein, consciousness of being naughty or daring inevitably creeps into his work. The benign and careful lubricity of Anatole France is not free from a taint of malicious awareness; he may have been sure that he was right to be on the side of Venus, but he was all too conscious that there was another. *Securus judicat orbis terrarum*; and it is a huge help to the artist to feel that 'the verdict of the world is conclusive' – and on his side. It is hard for a rebel to attain the peace of assurance.

This complete harmony and confidence contributes enormously to our pleasure in reading Jane Austen; but since it comes by grace and fortune, let us consider her imitable qualities. *Persuasion* is, in my opinion, the most perfectly constructed of her novels. The theme is definite, and limited with great discretion: it is the story of the re-engagement of two lovers after a parting which took place seven years before. The reader anticipates their reunion and there are no external obstacles to it: Captain Wentworth is still unmarried – even heart-free; and he is now well-off; Anne still loves him, and she has no obligations of loyalty or duty eleswhere which could prevent her from becoming his wife. In the heart of such a straightforward situation, how then does the author manage to create the suspense and complication so important in exciting intense interest in the happy ending to a love story? She does so by telling it from the point of view of the one who is compelled to be entirely passive throughout, partly owing to her sex, but above all, owing to her previous conduct. It was Anne who broke off the engagement. It is only Anne's feelings that we follow; every other character is seen from outside. We watch Wentworth only through her eyes (he is never on the scene unless she is there), and his behaviour in her presence, until near the end, is so adjusted to the purpose of creating suspense that it never conveys more than that his resentment may possibly be changing into temperate good will. Anne cannot hope for more than that. The reader is made to identify himself entirely with Anne, so far as Wentworth's behaviour is concerned, and to her each stage in their relations is full of pain, perplexity, and suspense, which the reader shares.

Henry James had a theory that it was necessary to get rid of the omniscient observer; that everything recounted in a novel should be seen through the eyes of some character in it; not necessarily the same, and perhaps through one character after another. *The Golden Bowl* was written on these lines. It seems to me a fallacious general principle. Let us test it by seeing what we should have lost had *Persuasion* been constructed in obedience to it. Let us suppose that everything, all the incidents, all the characters, Sir Walter Elliot, the Musgroves, Admiral Croft and his wife and Wentworth had been seen through Anne's eyes alone. Well, either Jane Austen's own delightful view of them would have been lost to us, or Anne would have become Jane Austen herself, with her intellect, irony and critical detachment; in which case we could never have felt the same poignant sympathy for Anne and her predicament. Suppose, on the other hand, that the business of reporting had been transferred later on to the brain of Wentworth; we should then have known every stage of his affections, and consequently followed Anne's misreading of them with indifference. Henry James would probably have then turned, say, Lady Russell and Charles Musgrove into a pair of gossips of genius who would, by exhibiting at once an extraordinary clairvoyance and an odd blindness to obvious probabilities, have complicated considerably the situation. But what a loss such a transfiguration would have been! Charles Musgrove, while doubtless keeping his gun, his riding-breeches and his good temper, would have been endowed with his creator's restless analytical curiosity – in short, have become unrecognizable as a normal young English squire. Here lies the fatal flaw in Henry James's theory. If the narrator is abolished, the characters who narrate in his place become inevitably endowed with the novelist's own peculiar faculties and intellectual temper. This happened in his own later novels, in which the characters were often so steeped in the colours of their creator's mind, that their individual tints barely showed through the permeating dye.

Contrast this method with the instinctive tact of Jane Austen in such matters. Her characters are introduced briefly and objectively. At first her heroine is a mere background figure, a member of the Elliot family: 'Anne Elliot had been a very pretty girl, but her bloom had vanished early'; that is all we hear about her in the first chapter, which is devoted to exposing so amusingly the vanity of her father and sister, and those financial family embarrassments, incidentally the initial causes of bringing Anne and Wentworth together again. How quietly and inevitably it is done! The letting of Kellynch Hall is the first step in the love-story, yet we are not aware of it as such, but only as part of the comedy of Sir Walter. This is the art of construction. Gradually Anne comes to the front as the most sensible and honourable member of the family. The novelist continues to present scenes, to describe thoughts, and feelings, and characters objectively. She uses the privilege of omniscience only in the case of Anne's emotions; and that these are centred upon her old lover gives him a special prominence in the eyes also of the reader. Although Wentworth says and does very little, that little has peculiar weight because it reaches us through Anne's feelings about it. He alone is seen subjectively, emotionally; and this gives him a unique position among the other characters. Thus he need not do much or say much to make an impression on us; he is a man who is loved, moving among other men and women who are observed. This gives an intensity to all the scenes in which Wentworth appears which links them together in the reader's mind, so that the surrounding comedy never for a moment destroys, though it may suspend, the continuity of the love-interest.

GERTRUDE STEIN

I

Our period – I am speaking of a short stretch of time which, in the history of literature, will shrink to nothing – looks to me like a period in which small things are done well, valuable experiments are tried, and muddles are exploited without being cleared up. It seems to me rather a silly period. Enterprising writers, who are also self-critical, seem more than usually doubtful whether they are pioneers or will-o'-the-wisps – and chance it. Certainly more downright nonsense will pass as wonderful today than ever before. Respect for the unintelligible in prose and verse inhibits readers who, in other matters, show unmistakable signs of intelligence, from recognizing rubbish when they see it. The 'dread of offending against the Unknown Beauty' has never exercised a more paralysing effect on criticism.

Among the Second Series of the Hogarth Press Essays you will find one by Miss Gertrude Stein. It bears the title *Composition as Explanation*; but if the word 'explanation' raises hopes, you will be disappointed. The first part of the pamphlet is a lecture on her own work, which Miss Stein delivered at Oxford and other places; the latter half contains four specimen compositions of her own, bearing the titles, 'Preciosilla', 'A Saint in Seven' (not in 'Heaven' but in 'Seven', which has the advantage of meaning nothing), 'Sitwell Edith Sitwell', 'Jean Cocteau', 'G. Stein'. You must not think, nor must Miss Gertrude Stein, that she is alone in producing this kind of composition. I happened to pick up a book the other day, and on page 6 I read the following passage:

> A jagged hedge ahead led Jill aside. She likes a side saddle; he is laid aside; he is laid aside; he is laid aside; he is laid aside; he has skill; he has skill; she is less agile; she is less agile; she is less agile; a seal likes fish; a seal likes fish; he sighs as if he is half dead; she said she had a legal lease; she said she had a lease; she asked if he liked a fiddle; she asked if he fiddled; she is glad she filed a deed; all lads like hill-sides.'

I turned the page and read, 'The quay was gaily arrayed with flags the quack had qualms, but made no reply. Pick a quantity of walnuts for pickling.' These passages possess unmistakably the same literary quality as, 'Paul makes honey and orange-trees. Michael makes coal and celery. Louise makes rugs and reasonably long. Heloise makes the sea and she settles well away from it,' which occurs in 'A Saint in Seven'.

I am sure it will not detract from the pleasure admirers of Miss Stein's work must take in these quotations to discover that they have been written by a less conscious artist in prose. The wind of inspiration bloweth where it listeth; and the fact that these passages are from Exercises 5 and 7 in *Pitman's Commercial Typewriting Manual* cannot rob this other artist of his meed of fame. That even when intent upon an end so remote from art as exercising a typist's fingers, we may produce the kind of 'modern composition' destined, according to Miss Stein, to become classical, should be a matter of rejoicing. Personally, I prefer Miss Stein in her less austere, less repetitive moods. For instance, in a little piece called 'Tails', which opens with a word suggested, as often happens in her writings, by rhyme: 'Tails: Cold pails, cold with joy no joy. A tiny seat that means meadows and a lapse of cuddles with cheese and nearly bats, all this went messed. The post placed a loud loose sprain. A rest is no better. It is better yet. All the time.' I cannot help preferring this to her austerer later work (*Useful Knowledge*, 1929), in which the words 'and one' are repeated a hundred times on a page, and 'yes and yes' considerably more than a hundred times on another.

'Are There Six or Another Question?' she asks in a title to a poem in that book:

One – Are there six?
Two – Or another question?
One – Are there six?
Two – Or another question?
Two – Are there six?
One – Or another question?
Two – Are there six?
Two – Or another question?

This is the first poem I have ever read which consisted entirely of the repetition of its title.

I may be misjudging the labour of the artist, but it looks as though it would be easy to write like this if one abandoned one's mind to it. I hope I shall never be tempted to make fun of Miss Stein; I would far rather make fun of those who encourage her to write.

Miss Stein is not to be blamed for indulging in automatic writing. I remember once composing a piece of prose under the influence of gas, which struck me as singularly beautiful. Alas, only the last cadences could be recaptured on waking: 'I prefer snails. Long may they continue, those black, blithering and blasted animals, to salt the rainy ground of virtue.' However, even as I remembered those words, they seemed to lose their magic significance. I was not to blame for having composed them, but if my friends had persuaded me to mesmerize myself back into the state in which that sort of stuff is produced, and if, when I wrote a thousand pages of it down, they persuaded me that I was doing service to art by publishing it, they would be very much to blame indeed.

'I created then', she says in her lecture, 'a prolonged present naturally I knew nothing of a continuous present but it came naturally to me to make one, it was simple it was clear to me and nobody knew why it was done like that, I did not myself although naturally to me it was natural.' This is one of the more lucid passages in her 'explanation', an explanation which is, unfortunately, itself too much of a 'composition' to be clear. She begins by saying that 'it is very likely that nearly everyone has been very nearly certain that something that is interesting is interesting them. Can they and do they.' There is no need here for so much caution. We may take it as true that some people have found some things interesting. 'Can they and do they' is otiose. Then Miss Stein asserts that 'nothing changes from generation to generation except the thing seen and that makes a composition'. This is not a happy way of saying what is familiar, namely, that different generations have different points of view which determine the kind of art which interests them. She continues: 'Those who are creating the modern composition authentically are naturally only of importance when they are dead, because by that time the modern composition having become past is classified and the description of it is classical.' This is very ill-expressed: the meaning is that new art is only recognized as 'classical' after its own period has passed away.

So far, her lecture has consisted of three commonplaces obscurely expressed; finally she reaches her own work. 'A continuous present is a continuous present. I made almost a thousand pages of continuous present. Continuous present is one thing and beginning again and again is another thing. These are both things. And then there is using everything.' She began by 'groping for a continuous present and for using everything by beginning again and again. . . . Having naturally done this I naturally was a little troubled with it when I read it,' she confesses. But she persevered. 'I did not begin again. I just began,' she says, which means that she went on in the same manner:

> In this beginning naturally since I at once went on and on very soon there were pages and pages and pages more and more elaborated making a more and more continuous present including more and more using of everything and continuing more and more beginning and beginning and beginning.

This is a very candid description of her method. We seem to be listening to a little girl who has been taught that she was a genius, and encouraged to talk about 'grown-up things'. We can almost see her fumbling with her frock and fixing her candid eyes upon her admiring parents. Of course 'very soon there were pages and pages of it'.

> It was all so nearly alike it must be different and it is different, it is natural that if everything is used and there is a continuous present and a beginning again and again if it is all so alike it must be simply different and everything simply different was the natural way of creating it then.

Alas, the stuff *was* all 'so nearly alike'. Alas, the idea that the repetition of the same words *must* be different, and that beginning the same sentence again and again led anywhere, was her fatal delusion. It is either very malicious or very asinine of other people to encourage her in it. She confesses that 'the quality in the creation of expression the quality in a composition that makes it go dead just after it has been made is very trouble-some'. So I found when my laughing-gas essay 'went dead' on me after I woke up. You see, if people did not encourage her she might lose confidence in her piffle.

The only significant statement in her lecture is that her work would have been 'outlawed' in any other generation than this post-war one. That is horribly true, and in that fact alone resides the importance of Miss Gertrude Stein.

II

I was once reproached for allowing commas to be inserted in the passage from Miss Gertrude Stein's writings. They are said to have destroyed its delicate organic beauty. Well, the harm has been done, so I will quote another passage to show her quality. The two commas in it are in the text:

> November the fifteenth and simply so that simply so that simply in that simply in that simply so that in that simply in that simply in that simple way simply so that simply so that in that way simply in that way, simply in that way so that simply so that simply so that simply simply in that, simply in that so that simply so that simply so that simply in that, so that simply in that way.
>
> Actually the fifteenth of November.
>
> Played and plays and says and access, Plays and played and access and impress, etc. etc.

How, one asks in amazement, can anyone suppose this sort of writing to have any value? It is that fact, not Miss Gertrude Stein's work, which is interesting.

She wrote a good many years ago, a good many, many, many, a good many, a good many ago, she, she wrote a good many years ago, a little book called *Tender Buttons*, and more recently a much larger book. I have lost my *Tender Buttons*, and into her last book I only glanced, seeing it was in the same form and only cut up into different lengths. Of course, if you start with a form which can convey no meaning, which ignores syntax, and consists in repeating either the same word or the next that suggests itself while the intelligence is completely in abeyance, it is impossible to develop; and her work has shown no development. Miss Stein sprang, fully armed like Minerva, from that part of the human brain which is usually inaudible in waking life, yet can sometimes be overheard jabbering nonsense to itself. Medical psychologists have discovered recently that this jabbering may have a value in diagnosing mental troubles, but that it could have any other, only a generation which theorized itself silly could suspect. Yet Mr T. S. Eliot has printed her in the *New Criterion* (in good company), and Miss Edith Sitwell once praised her as only fine writers are praised who run some danger of being misunderstood. I fear I shall not get to the bottom of this puzzle; but it is possible to indicate some of the proceedings by which people manœuvre themselves into positions from which rubbish in art appears worthy of respect. The inquiry is of wider application.

The door of welcome is first left ajar by some experimenter in a new art-form. Then the art-snobs (those whose desire to be the first to understand what others do not, is stronger than their power of enjoying or understanding anything), lean their backs against the door and push till it is wide enough to admit any enormity. The experimenters cannot then shut the door without leaving themselves on the wrong side of it. The solidarity of all rebels is the first thing to take account of in studying art movements. Whether they are genuine discoverers or humbugs, these rebels all stand in the same relation to current convention in taste; they are in the same boat, and the same charges are levelled against them all. Mr Eliot is an obscure poet; incomprehensible to many himself; he cannot object to

Miss Stein's writings on the score of their impenetrability, or to Mr Joyce's, who has also taken to writing intricate pitch-dark rigmaroles. Secondly, all new movements are defended by aesthetic theories. Alas, if these do not prove as much as is wanted, they can be easily made to do so by the application of a little logic. For instance, the recent movement in painting originally had for its defence the reasonable theory that the merit of a picture does not depend upon its subject: that seemed safe and sensible. We assented. But if the subject was indifferent, why need it be recognizable when painted? We were reminded that pots and carpets could undoubtedly be beautiful, and that they conveyed no information about reality. Why then should pictures? And we were presently given portraits in which the moustache of the sitter was discernible in one corner of the picture and one eye in another, while the rest had no resemblance to anything at all. Logically, we could not complain. We could only murmur that we missed badly something which was to be found in pictures which the ages had agreed in enjoying and the innovators themselves still admired. We were reluctant to say with the Rev. Dr Opimian, 'I must take pleasure in the thing represented before I can derive any from the representation,' so we were next asked to accept the dogma that as far as aesthetic emotion is concerned drawing and painting have nothing to do with representation. The same thing happened with regard to literature. Our attention was drawn to the fact that the aesthetic value of a poem, or of a piece of prose, had no fixed ratio to the value of the thought it expressed. We were next asked to admire arrangements of words which had no meaning at all. Beauty in words, like beauty in pictorial art, was to reside in pattern.

Miss Sitwell puts the matter clearly in her essay, *Poetry and Criticism*:

What may appear difficult (*i.e.* in modern poetry) is the habit of forming abstract patterns in words. We have long been accustomed to abstract patterns in pictorial art, and to the idea that music is an abstract art, but nobody to my knowledge has ever gone so far in making abstract patterns in words as the modernist poet has. The nearest approach known to me is Beddoes'

> Adam, that old carrion-crow
> The old crow of Cairo.

There is, of necessity, a connecting thread running through each pattern, otherwise it would not be a pattern. . . .

How slender this thread, presumably of sense, may be, we have seen.

She then praises Miss Stein 'for bringing back life to our language . . . by breaking down predestined groups of words, their sleepy family habits . . . and rebuilding them into new and vital shapes.' . . . 'The question', she continues, 'of the making of abstract patterns is far more important at this time than any question of whether free verse is on as high a level as other forms of verse.' I agree; it is much more important. The idea that the stuff of literature is a mass of words which can be arranged like coloured pebbles to make a pattern, undercuts almost the whole conception of what makes it valuable to man. It is not what modernists are up to that is difficult to see, but the value of what they produce.

What Miss Sitwell means by 'breaking down predestined groups of words, their sleepy family habits' is simply (to employ a word which Miss Stein in the passage quoted on page 171 has roused from its sleep) using them regardless of their sense, which Miss Sitwell herself does frequently, and Miss Stein habitually. The small basis of truth upon which they have raised this theory of literature is the fact of the aesthetic quality in the sound of vowels, consonants and rhymes in relation to rhythms, images, and sense. But what we mean by 'word-music' is not the mere sound of words. 'Cancer' is a word with an agreeable sound, and 'cellar-door' is magnificent, yet they cannot be used as notes in chords apart from their sense.

Such are the logical processes which have pushed open the door of welcome to much rubbish; but it would not have been kept open so long but for a threat.

III

The threat is a potent one. All dissidents or doubtfuls are warned that if they are not duly respectful towards the new enormities, they will find themselves numbered among the philistines who, in the past, derided and rejected 'the unknown beauty'. Modernist poets are never tired of pointing out that Coleridge and Keats were once jeered at; the supporters of cubist art continually remind the public that it once heaped abuse upon the now respected Impressionists. Indeed, the threat is in constant use, and it has an alarming effect upon people in whom the desire to be right about art is rather stronger than their power to enjoy it.

In its subtler forms this threat reduces the diffident to aspen-hearted acquiescence. One way is to write in an airy confident tone as though only fools, of course, and block-heads were conscious of those misgivings which are internally gnawing the would-be proselyte, and at the same time to remind him, perhaps, in the words of the Goncourts, 'The Beautiful is what seems abominable to uneducated eyes. The beautiful is what your mistress or your cook instinctively finds hideous.' If, at the moment of reading, the poor art-snob has any misgivings about either his cook or his mistress, such a quotation will at once open his eyes to the merits of the poet or painter in question. But, failing that, such a quotation as *'L'art n'est pas chose populaire, encore moins "poule de luxe"* . . . *L'art est d'essence hautaine'* will surely bring him to heel.

Note the flattery implicit in it. He will henceforth feel lifted above his fellows proportionally as they disagree with him, and also be able to pass through the houses of the rich and the galleries of collectors with pleasant, supercilious equanimity. Moreover, there is something besides flattery – there is also truth – in that statement. Art, like physics, politics or tennis, *is* best understood by a few, and those few are not necessarily to be found among the rich, who are particularly apt to confuse (though we are all liable to do so) prestige values with beauty. And it is precisely the blend of flattery and truth in this statement which makes it so persuasive. What, however, we are right to resent is a truth of such very general import being used to push us into admiring any particular book or work of art. Those who put their faith in the verdicts of the few often present a comic spectacle when the many come round to their opinion. While watching the ups and downs of reputations, I have often found myself exclaiming, 'Ah! The rats are leaving the floating ship.'

In reading criticism it is always well to keep a sharp look-out for flattery or intimidation; unless controversy is running high, these are generally the methods of imperfectly convinced critics.

Now with regard to that formidable threat, there are several considerations which may help us to bear up under it. In the first place, those who use the argument that the majority have been always unintelligent in the past omit to mention that they themselves often despise the same works which the majority once abused. *Hernani* was defended against mockery by a band of brothers whose smallness and compactness left nothing to be desired. Yet that Hugo's play was fustian the modernist poet would be the first to assert. The Pre-Raphaelites and Impressionists were not in favour with the very painters who recently called out loudest. 'You are abusing us as you once abused Whistler and Rossetti whom you now admire.' It was a good retort, but a trifle disingenuous, for they despised both artists themselves. The public is undoubtedly an ass, but not uncommonly in criticism we find the elect and progressive of a later date echoing that ass's ancient bray. And what is one to think then? Secondly, though it is lamentably true that Coleridge and Wordsworth were ridiculed, so was Mr Bowles. Comforting thought that some poet whom we find it impossible to admire, in spite of the threat that we are offending against 'the unknown beauty', may be a Bowles! Lastly, there is nothing to be ashamed of in not surrendering quickly to what is new, or in retracting opposition afterwards. In short, it is equally unsafe to despise a particular work because the many admire it, and to admire it because it is only understood or liked by a few. Even when minorities and majorities agree the corroboration may be valueless, for a work of art may be enjoyed at different levels – Hamlet, for example.

There is a passage in Mr Santayana's *Life of Reason* which throws light on the nature of all 'new' ways of writing; it justifies a stiff attitude towards them:

Pure poetry [he writes] is pure experiment; and it is not strange that nine-tenths of it should be pure failure. For it matters little what unutterable things may have originally gone together with a phrase in the dreamer's mind; if they were not uttered and the phrase cannot call them back, this verbal relic is none the richer for the high company it may once have kept. Expressiveness is a most accidental matter. What a line suggests at one reading, it may never suggest again even to the same person. For this reason, among others, poets are partial to their own compositions; they truly discover there depths of meaning which exist for nobody else. Those readers who appropriate a poet and make him their own fall into a similar illusion; they attribute to him what they themselves supply, and whatever he reels out, lost in his own personal revery, seems to them, like *sortes Biblicae*, written to fit their own case. . . .

THE IDEAL
SPECTATOR

I have been a dramatic critic (on and off) for over twenty-five years. I have had therefore to attend to the drama and make myself as far as possible into an ideal spectator. Who then is the Ideal Spectator? Well, of course, he must be one who is naturally preoccupied with human nature, since human nature is the stuff out of which drama is made. In the second place he must grasp the peculiar advantages and limitations which stage representation imposes on the treatment of any subject. And lastly, he must (this applies, however, equally to the critic of literature) take into account the aim in any particular case of the dramatist, not only in relation to his subject but in relation to his audience. What the phrase 'in relation to his audience' means may not be at once clear. What it means is that it is not only unfair to a play, but also silly from the point of view of our own pleasure to ask from it something which its author never intended it to provide. It is silly, for example, to crab your own enjoyment of a comedy because it is intended merely to amuse. The genuine dramatic critic is the spectator who gets most out of a play even if at the same time he notices its shortcomings, and the ideal audience is therefore an audience of dramatic critics. Now it may possibly help you to get all you can out of the theatre to describe briefly my own experience as a professional critic. Dramatic critics, owing to the various nature of the works upon which they must pronounce, learn, like very agreeable people of too wide acquaintance, to develop their multiple personalities. The same man no doubt writes the articles, but the same critic does not always attend the plays. In my case, D.M. No. 1, who is not easy to satisfy, and thinks nearly every play produced throughout the year practically negligible from the point of view of art (what else could he expect? Do master-pieces cluster every year?), seldom puts his nose into a theatre, or, if he does, the first act like a mesmeric pass, puts him asleep, and leaves D.M. No. 2 in control. He is, as a rule, a much more serviceable, generally useful, critic. The faculties of No. 1 need only be requisitioned when something exceptional comes along, or a cry of 'Lo Here!' arises over nothing in particular.

D.M. No. 2 has a natural taste for the theatre; the drop curtain fills him with agreeable expectations; he cries and laughs easily; a little common sense in a dramatist enraptures him; he feels all the time that it is very good of the management and actors to have taken such pains to get everything ship-shape; he has never been able to understand how people can begin fishing for their hats during the last five minutes of any play. He forgets there are such things as masterpieces; he really thinks (though it sounds stupid to say so) the author very clever to have written a play at all; though ways in which it might be improved may keep occurring to him, his comments are mostly made from the point of view of truth. 'Do I believe in these people? Why do they or don't they interest me?' Such is D.M. No. 2. Of course, the stage being what it is, the bulk of the work falls upon this good-natured and impressionable creature, and I have had all my life to make the best of such reports as he sends me. Now I expect nearly every thorough playgoer is conscious of two such critics in himself. There is, too, a D.M. No. 3, but I will not bore you with him.

Now sometimes it happens that the play is of such a kind that though D.M. No. 1 says, 'This is your job, No. 2,' he cannot get off to sleep; he is kept awake either because there is a broken frustrated, poetic force running through the play, or because it flies ambitiously high in its aim. And when No. 1 cannot efface himself and yet keeps grumbling, while No. 2 goes on picking holes from the point of view of matters of fact, the result must be an unfavourable notice.

Now, whether you recognize yourselves or not in this description, it contains a hint for you. If you judge every play from the point of view of that self which is only gratified by what is really excellent and significant, and without exaggeration can claim to be a work of art, then you will not only be very dissatisfied playgoers but unintelligent ones. The mind of the ideal spectator must, like a good motor-car, run on several gears; and from different plays you must ask not only different experiences, but be content with different qualities of enjoyment, sometimes with trivial ones.

But is there anything which you can demand from every play? I think there is: something must happen. The stage is particularly fitted to exhibit action. You can be immensely interested by a discussion on the stage as you might be in a debating hall or listening to the wireless, but since one of the essential advantages of the drama in contrast to all other forms is that you can *see*, with a vividness no description, however masterly, can achieve, something actually happening, not to use that advantage is to neglect the peculiar virtue of your medium. You can produce a highly instructive and enthralling entertainment without doing so – Mr Shaw has done it again and again – and one which is more worth attending than many plays which do exhibit something happening, but such a work can never rank among the world's first-rate plays. The best drama is that which incorporates its idea in action as well as in dialogue. Take Ibsen's *The Wild Duck*, for example. The theme of the wild duck – it is a tragic comedy, and this is the form of tragedy most acceptable to the modern mind – is that there are such things as vital lies, or illusions. In that play Ibsen faced the fact that it is not necessarily truth that saves men, that truth may, indeed, destroy them. *The Wild Duck* must have astonished his disciples when it first appeared; it looked like a satire on his own philosophy. It was an assault on 'Ibsenites', on men and women who think that to blurt out the truth, and destroy everything which has an alloy of compromise and sham in it, is the remedy for social and private evils. Nothing Ibsen has written makes us respect him more. He has always declared that, 'What is wanted is a revolution in the spirit of man'; in this play he faces the reformer's worst trial, recognition of the fundamental weakness of human nature. We are shown a group of dilapidated creatures, each of whom, maimed by life, has dived beneath its surface, as a wild duck dives after it has been mortally wounded. It is perhaps the most perfectly constructed of all Ibsen's plays. The idea of the play is audible when Relling, a rough, damaged, disappointed fellow himself, says that 'Life would be quite tolerable if only we could get rid of the confounded duns that keep on pestering us in our poverty with the claims of the ideal,' and that 'When a man has no hair of his own he must wear a wig, that is, find shelter for that necessary minimum of self-respect in some consoling illusion.' In the play the catastrophe is brought about, and the theme itself express-ed, by the tragic results of the well-meaning interference of a busy-body idealist. A terrible thing happens. It is a theme which would have also lent itself admirably to a stage discus-sion. The tipsy broken old hunter in the play could have expatiated on the happiness he found in shooting rabbits in a garret; the ridiculous Hialmer upon all that his 'invention' meant to him, and the protagonists, the realist Relling and the idealist Gregers, might in a hammer-and-tongs argument, ranging up and down the whole of experience, have thrashed out for us in the most exhilarating way the value of truth to humanity. Such a treatment of the theme might produce a stimulating entertainment, clarifying the minds of all who heard it, but, whatever its merits, it would be one which failed to take full advantage of the emphasis which the stage alone can supply. The triumph of the dramatist is to take advantage of this and to embody his idea in a story completely, as a sculptor expresses it in stone or bronze. Failing that, he may excite and instruct us through the clash of ideas and points of view – a great service, but one of less impressiveness than if he had incorporated those ideas in events.

If you examine the discussion plays of Bernard Shaw, *Getting Married*, *Misalliance*, *The Apple Cart*, you will notice that although the author has hardly attempted to do this, he has used to some extent the peculiar virtue of stage-representation. He has introduced events, which only aid discussion in an ancillary way: the crash of an aeroplane in *Misalliance*; in *Getting Married* the doubt – will a particular marriage after all take place?; and in *The Apple Cart* again suspense – will the king get the better of his ministers? Although Bernard Shaw ignored in these plays, to a large extent, the unique opportunities of the dramatist, he also recognized them for what they are. He has always been more interested in his ideas than in his genius. We have no reason to regret it, for we owe him too much; but posterity may think it was unfortunate.

The stage is almost fitted to exhibit action, but action without thought and feeling is comparatively uninteresting. The problem of the dramatist is, then, to choose a theme in which thought and feeling can be adequately expressed in action; that is what we mean by a dramatic theme. A conversation can, of course, be dramatic, but it is so in virtue of being part of a story. The most dramatic part of *St Joan* was the scene in which Warwick and Cauchon expounded their ideas in our hearing, but what made it so was not merely the interest of listening to those two men speaking out of themselves, but our knowing what hung upon their discussion, the bearing of their talk upon the fate of St Joan herself.

The same principle holds good of thoughts and feelings, of what we call psychological themes. The inner drama of thoughts and feelings can be as tremendous as any we can see translated in action before our eyes – consider the novels of Dostoevsky, or some of the short stories of Chekhov. But only some inner dramas gain more than they inevitably lose by being translated into dialogue and visible movement. Let me take an example.

It was, I think, in the year 1919 that I went to a performance of that excellent, but now defunct, society, the Pioneer Players. They were performing several short plays, and among them a stage version by Mr Miles Malleson of Chekhov's excellent story *The Artist*. It is a short story about a painter and two girls. The girls live with their mother in a country house, near which the artist is dawdling and painting. The play raised the question of the relation of psychology to the stage. It was Mr Malleson's object to tell in dialogue Chekhov's story of the love between the artist and the younger of these two girls. Their love-affair is stopped by the elder of the sisters, who is devoted to good works and regards the artist as a waster, which is partly true. He has no faith in himself. That his work is not more futile than other people's is about the limit of his faith in it; while he is convinced, seeing civilization is too rotten to be improved by piecemeal remedies, that public-spirited people are fools. Not unnaturally, he and the elder girl hate each other. She discovers her sister's infatuation for this ineligible loafer-artist, and, being ruler in the house, packs off her mother and sister that very night. When the artist returns, only the philanthropic sister is in the house. He hears her voice dictating to a small peasant child. She is teaching it to spell. He hears in the empty house her firm, monotonous voice repeating the sentence again and again, 'And God gave the crow a piece of cheese'. He never sees his love again. In the story the futility of his short romance, and the dreariness of the point of view which has destroyed it, find an echo in that meaningless, reiterated sentence. It is his state of mind, of course, that is the climax of the story; the sense of his own helplessness, the pain of having been pulled out of his faint-hearted loneliness only to be plunged into it again. Now the printed page can render that state of mind directly, and by describing surroundings reinforce it. But on the stage Mr Malleson was compelled to make the love-scene all important (for drama is dialogue), and to substitute for Chekhov's real climax a dumb scene in which Nicov was shown for a minute reading a letter which tells him his love has gone. That is to say, he was compelled to suggest instead of showing the heart of the theme. All he could get out of such a story on the stage was a clash of two points of view (the artist's and the philanthropist's) and a love-scene of no particular originality. What was most subtle and moving in Chekhov's story, therefore, inevitably evaporated on the stage. The drama is a medium of incomparable vividness, but of narrow scope compared with the novel.

Many changes within human beings, such as offer the most interesting themes, are inevitably hidden and silent, or too gradual for drama. 'To penetrate deeply into the human consciousness is the glory of the philosopher, the moralist, the novelist, and, to a certain degree, even of the lyric poet,' but the capacity to do so is not enough to make a dramatist. Whatever the temptation, he must not cease to show us something *happening* before our eyes. The stage demands action. When the curtain rises we cease to be possessed alone by a high curiosity. We become also spectators eager to see something happen. 'There are no words so profound or beautiful but they will soon weary us in the theatre if they leave a situation unchanged, if they produce no conflict, no definite solution.'

IBSEN

I

The Dramatist of the Future:
This article is about Ibsen and *Ghosts* – now running at the
Kingsway Theatre. I have put that heading at the top, hoping it
may seem provocative. There are many who think the world
has long ago absorbed as much 'Ibsen' as the system can stand,
and that, like a vaccinated person, it will not 'take' again; there
are others who regard him as a didactic and dingy playwright,
as an egotistic and elementary thinker, and some of the *jeunes
feroces*, I suspect, even suppose he was no artist. How natural it
is, however, that such false opinions should be current I shall at
once explain; and what follows is addressed to those who hold
them. To those who at the first night felt like boys again, and
glowed to find they had been no fools when they were young, I
can only offer the mild pleasure of reading what they already
believe, or, incidentally, perhaps the keener one of noting how
much better it might have been put.

Soon after returning from the first performance of *Ghosts* I
was rung up on the telephone.

Voice: 'What did you think of it?'

D.M.: 'Splendid play; poor performance.' (*The production and the acting have improved immensely since the first night.*)

Voice: 'What! Splendid? . . . Pastor Manders? . . . The whole thing? . . . It was like hunting down a mangy old stag let out of a box for the day.'

D.M. (*with the confidence of the critic whose ideas are as yet a rushing wind in his head, and seemingly irresistible*): 'You just wait till you've read my article.'

Voice (*expressing a mixture of patience, politeness, and scepticism*): 'Well, I know I'm . . .' (I caught a murmur, '. . . no artist and out of date'). 'Well, good-night.'

I felt every bit as polemical and confident as Mr Archer or Mr Shaw felt in the 'nineties. 'Ibsen', I said firmly, as I replaced the receiver, 'is among modern dramatists a sun among farthing dips.' Not Art, indeed! Out of date! The notion that there were intelligent people who could hold such views was disgusting to me. Now, too, of all times; precisely when there was more humbug about than ever before, more need of soul-searching, more need of the kind of clinical introspection that Ibsen stimulates; now, when people were forcing themselves all day long, on principle, to forget some things and take others for granted, to feel some things and not to feel others, to steer exclusively by ideals and yet keep one eye askew on the main chance. Out of date, indeed! No artist! After the Ibsen battle had been thoroughly fought out and won too! It was disgusting.

But then it occurred to me that it was also inevitable; it was always thus things happened in the history of thought. A great man appears, or a sense of the world is born which has implications of importance (evolution, for example), there is at once a prodigious shindy. All active minds start going for each other about it; while one writer sits forging arguments in its favour or against it, feeling he is giving his best to his generation, in the same street another is reading him and exclaiming:

'The fool, the animal, the jackass!' As long as this battle rages, everyone, even if ignorant, is still intensely aware of its importance (during this period the censorship of the press or drama can do enormous harm), and everyone feels how much hangs upon it. At last discussion becomes a bore; a lull occurs; both sides begin to count their dead, and one to retire ('voluntary evacuation') from positions which have become ridiculous and untenable; the tone adopted being, 'So that is what you meant? Why *we* drank in that with our mother's milk!' accompanied by a tacit resolve henceforth to kill only by kindness and silence.

But before this peace is patched up discussion will have raged up and down every sort of question which could possibly be connected with the new philosophy; and it is precisely over such remote practical implications that at this last stage of the controversy, discussion is likely to be fiercest and the loudest voices are likely to be raised. The consequences of this are serious. For the next generation remember consequently the artist or philosopher whose work has been alternately a weapon and a cockshy, as an *ad hoc* writer. They think of him inevitably as one whose work may once have been useful, but, since the shoe of social life pinches each generation in a slightly different place, must be now beside the point; and above all they come to regard him as a writer belonging to that inferior class of artists who find inspiration in the social problems of the moment. This has been the fate of Ibsen.

At the present moment many people actually think *Ghosts* a pamphlet it requires only a slight alteration in our laws to render nugatory. They think it is a play with disease for a theme; Oswald, they think, is the central figure. They are wrong. Ibsen was a profound and meditative mind. Whatever his story, his theme is always of lasting interest; it is, indeed, *the* supreme interest and attraction of the intellectual vision, the individual soul. It is Mrs Alving who is the central figure of the play; the revolution in her its theme. Miss Darragh depicted admirably Mrs Alving's sorrows and her tenderness; less adequately the rebel, who with a great price has won her freedom; ironically indulgent when let alone, but savage and shameless when conventions and traditions would push her again from the little bit of solid ground she has found at last in the quagmire of her life.

Ibsen's theatre is the theatre of the soul. Important as he was, and is, as a social reformer, it is that which makes him even more important as an artist. Society changes quickly; the soul hardly at all; it is that which makes his work permanent. It is that which makes his plays thrilling, gives them their curious intensity, enables him to mingle with a realism which sometimes has even a perverse kind of commonness, fantastic symbols – rat-wives, wild ducks, houses with lofty towers, and so to blend both together that the ordinary takes on a strange significance (a character in his plays can hardly thank for a match without seeming also to say something more), and the fantastically fanciful becomes in them oddly familiar. An architect who falls off his own scaffold because he would show off before a young lady; a sleek, shabby photographer addicted to noble poses and to shuffling away unpleasant thoughts by fooling with rabbits in a garret, like a child (a common type); a fraudulent financier, who after prison still hugs the dream of immense possibilities, and throws the cold shadow of his egotism across the lives of two devoted women; a successful sculptor who finds fame flat and is bored with his wife; smug and stuffy homes of all sorts, with here and there a character ugly or pathetic in his or her revolt against them; what dingy, mediocre events! And yet – what tragic plays! What insolent indifference to the surface value of materials; yet what profound intensity!

If one looked only at the sequence of events in Ibsen's dramas they would seem to have small value; the spell and the beauty lie within. He invented the realistic tragedy; but his successors have mostly not observed how he did it. A passage in one of his letters throws light:

Everything that I have written has the closest possible connection with what I have lived through, even if it has not been my own personal experience; in every new poem or play I have arrived at my own spiritual emancipation and purification – for a man shares the responsibility and the guilt of the society to which he belongs.

It is from his own dreaming, solitary mind they derive their intensity. There was always a connection, impossible perhaps to define, but there, between the nature of the theme he chose and the adventures of his soul. The base characters are not merely observed; they are known also by their kinship to the motives he has found in himself, squatting like toads in the marble virtues which his hammer has broken; the feeble are known as only a man who has lived a meticulously strenuous inner life himself can know weakness, its protean shapes and Boig-like quality; the strong are read in the light of his own strength; they carry about with them, too, the roughness and badgered impatience of a long struggle, and youth in his plays is the cry in himself of all he has ever given up. How he respects the aplomb of their selfishness and trusts the directness of their desires!

Ibsen is the out-and-out revolutionary. He is the militant poet of one side of man's nature, a one-sided poet therefore if you like, but by far the greatest spokesman of that side. His plays were a bag of dynamite into which any social reformer could dip, but it was not the fall of this or that institution or law that interested him. His scepticism regarding political reforms was well known; the words 'a committee has been appointed', when he read them in the papers, it is said, always made him laugh. There is a queer ironical poem of his, addressed to a revolutionary orator, in which he says: 'Go on, flood the world with your eloquence; let us have the deluge by all means, but then, please, allow me to torpedo the ark.' These are not the sentiments of a man who feels intensely that man is 'a political animal'; though that man is indeed such an animal was about the first truth he ever discovered about himself. Let it be admitted then: as a poet, Ibsen ignored that fact. He was the spokesman of the individualistic side of man's nature. If man is by nature one of a herd and nothing by himself, he is also conscious of being in himself the judge and dispenser of values, the end for which all traditions and customs exist. 'The State is the curse of the individual,' he wrote to Brandes; and it is not only the State, but all ideals, all aims, which ignore the simple, solid happiness of the individual and his right to it, that are also curses.

Men, according to Ibsen, are always being led by their idealistic noses away from the places where their welfare lies. His tragedies are stories of the sacrifice of natural good, of which the individual is the only judge, to some false ideal which has no instinctive root in human nature. Sometimes the ideal is a mean one as in *Ghosts* (respectability), sometimes heroic as in *Brand* ('all or nothing' religion), sometimes half-and-half as in *Gabriel Borkman* (ambition, at once beneficent and egotistic), sometimes, as in *The Wild Duck*, a craze for saving souls; but the clash and tragedy is the same. It is 'the joy of life', 'the love life in the individual' which it is 'the unpardonable sin' for any cause or reason to destroy. In his last play he turned on himself, on the artist; and in *When We Dead Awaken* he wrote a play inspired by the feeling that the disinterested artist was just as mad as the priest or the financier, the respectable citizen or the prig. Rubeck the sculptor is a man who has sacrificed his own and another's happiness to make out of it a symbol of the ideal. 'The love that belongs to the life of earth, the beautiful miraculous life of earth, the inscrutable life of earth – that is dead in both of us,' Rubeck says to Irene. The ruthless artist is also a traitor to the natural good.

But supposing everybody believed only in what was right in their own eyes? This is the question with which those who are most conscious of man as 'a political animal' pose the Ibsenites.

It can only be countered by another question just as disquieting: 'Suppose nobody did?' Upon what a wild, fantastic dance mankind would then be led, far from the natural goods on which his happiness (and therefore ultimately his integrity of feeling and thinking) must rest.

When I wrote *The Dramatist of the Future* at the head of this article I was thinking partly, too, that many people might well be feeling that men had been lately thinking of themselves too exclusively as 'political animals', and that a violent revulsion towards a philosophy which respects the individual and his happiness more might be near. There may or may not be a revolution in the streets, but in the minds of men the highways will be broken and the waters will be out. Then Ibsen will be our poet.

II

Rosmersholm is a magnificent play. Do not miss *Rosmersholm*. It will remind you how high dramatic art can rise, and how deeply intellectual courage can probe human nature.

We attend so many plays, we read so many books, of trifling, varying merit, that we are apt to lose our sense of real achievement. Some people hope by directing destructive sniffs at the small meritorious successes of little men to preserve that sense – usually in vain. The important thing is to respond to greatness when we meet it, and to deplore incessantly its absence does not increase our power of response.

Like nearly all fine plays, *Rosmersholm* has a vital moral interest. Ibsen's genius is inseparable from his conscience. He is, indeed, the dramatist of the Protestant Conscience ('Save his own soul he hath no star') at its highest pitch of searching intensity. For this reason his work is repellent to those who rest upon authority and to those who are bored with, or made uneasy by, moral questionings. To both these types his works must seem pernicious and even unintelligent. In so far as such people cannot escape being impressed by his power, they will attribute it to his amazing 'dramatic craftsmanship': a most incomplete analysis, a shocking-bad analysis, a shirking, loose analysis. I am sorry for those who hold the theory that morals have never anything to do with art, or conscience with creation, for Ibsen is a difficulty, and so is Tolstoy, and so are – well, no matter. It is impossible not to admire their works, and yet without their passionate preoccupation with moral values where would those artists be? True, it is possible, especially in the case of Tolstoy, to point to the interruptions of the moral theorizer as blemishes in his work. They often are. But that does not get us over the fact that his sense of life, which impresses by its beauty and startles by its reality, is saturated in conscience. In Ibsen's plays, too, it is the search for the right way of living which sharpens to penetration his eye for character and dramatic situations. To think that it is possible for anyone to bend upon life the intense attention which leads to discovery and creation, without something within him far more urgent than detached curiosity or a desire to write a good play, is to betray a colossal ignorance of psychology. It is the tension within – 'I must know, know or perish' – that is the driving force behind the creative faculty in these writers. And to know what? To know what is most important to man, how it can be obtained and kept. A poodle is the most teachable of dogs because it is the most greedy; Ibsen was the greatest of modern dramatists because he was the most hungry after truth.

The 'moral' of an Ibsen play is seldom the most important thing – indeed, usually it is not there, or discoverable only by ignoring part of the play. What, however, is always significant is the manner in which moral issues in his plays are juxtaposed and the tension between them exhibited. If you are rather clever you will probably think you have discovered 'a moral' in *Rosmersholm*; if you are clever you will probably not. When it was first performed the representatives of a Norwegian youth-movement wrote to Ibsen asking if the call to work for mankind were not the message of *Rosmersholm*. The hungry lambs looked up (you can see their faces); the shepherd, though he seemed so grim, was kind; he nodded a 'No doubt, no doubt'. 'But', he added, 'the play also deals with the war all serious people must wage with themselves to bring their lives into harmony with their convictions. Different spiritual functions do not develop evenly and abreast of each other in any one person. The intellect hurries on from victory to victory; the moral conscious-ness, what we call conscience, is, on the other hand, very conservative. It has its roots deep in tradition and the past. Hence the conflict.' Then he adds, and the sentence should be printed on the programmes of even the most apparently didac-tic of his plays: 'But the play is, of course, before everything a drama of human beings and human fate.'

Rebecca West is an embodiment of the vanguard intellect; 'Rosmersholm' of the moral consciousness, so slow to move, so hard to justify, so strangely authoritative.

And 'Rosmersholm' broke her. You remember her cry before she goes to her death. 'I am under the spell of the Rosmersholm view of life – *now*. I've sinned and must expiate it.' But was *that* the tragedy for Ibsen, that the self-confidence of an amoral young woman who had hitherto always made for what she wanted and grabbed it, who had slowly and slyly lured her benefactress to suicide in order to possess her husband, should have been sapped? Only that? To answer yes is to fail to measure the diameter of her creator's mind or the profundity of his doubts. Remember, that Rosmer has changed Rebecca. Her frantic passion for him has, under his influence, changed into love, bringing with it a new sense of values. She asserts this with all the energy of a woman ready to die to convince him of it. And it was true. We have watched on the stage altruism and delicacy of feeling begin to have a meaning for her. We have seen her change; seen her reject her adored one because the words in which he urges her to take him prove it cannot be a marriage of

true minds. We have heard her confess to him, in the presence
of her bitter enemy, his brother-in-law; a confession which
leaves not a rag to cover her hideousness in her lover's eyes, in
which she takes on herself the whole responsibility for Beata's
death, in order to enable him to live henceforth with self-
respect, as himself – not the man she once hoped to make him,
but as himself, with all his inborn moral scruples and aspirations. It is true, he has changed her. She has become an
'idealist', and presently she will die to prove it.

Disbelief in the possibility of that change from passion to
love, not to believe in love – however rare you may think it,
however common you may know its counterfeits to be – is the
sign of a vulgar soul – such scepticism is only pardonable in a
Democritus or two, and Ibsen was far from being either a
vulgar soul or a laughing philosopher. He is not 'on the side of'
the amoral egotism of the young Rebecca. Had he been, he
would have soon found rest, and we should have had from him,
instead of masterpieces, robust materialistic plays, with 'morals' attached as legible as posters; plays as cut-and-dried and
cooked as Brieux's stage-tracts for the times. Nor, either, is he
'on the side of' Rosmer with his fanatic's cry, 'There is no judge
over us; therefore we must do justice upon ourselves.' Yet it is
impossible to study Ibsen without feeling how *near* it comes to
being a cry also from his own heart. Ibsen was torn between two
ways of taking life.

Rosmersholm is a play which springs from the divided allegiance of the modern conscience to two different moralities;
both with their beauty, both seemingly fitted (and yet also
unfitted) to guide men. The tug of war between the ethics of the
will to power and Christianity, between the gospel of self-
assertion and of renunciation, had been a vital matter to Ibsen
as early as *The Vikings*. In *Emperor and Galilean* he had attempted
more, but only succeeded in depicting again their struggle, not
their reconciliation. 'Who shall conquer, the emperor or the
Galilean?' The answer was: 'He who shall swallow up both,'

but *he* does not appear, neither then nor at any time in Ibsen's work.

In *Rosmersholm* Ibsen transfers the same struggle into a psychological drama of modern life and then – watches what will happen. The rest is mutual laceration, not reconciliation – unless that climax-scene between Rebecca and Rosmer, that moment's marriage between them, is intended to be, not merely a Liebestod, an exalted crisis of erotomania, but a symbolic union of the forces each represents. The scene, immensely powerful to read when the imagination of the solitary reader is glowing and awake, is nearly impossible to act. The only fault Ibsen has as a stage-craftsman is that sometimes he will ask too much from actors. There are moments in his drama when the characters, whose motives and dispositions have been revealed with psychological exactness, suddenly become luminous and transparent; so that we are not so much aware of *them*, as of the forces they represent, and when the words they have to speak become expressive of their ambiguous condition. Sometimes, on the other hand, he frankly introduced a symbolic non-human figure to achieve this effect; the Rat-Wife, for example, who enters a solid suburban home. When these moments occur (they are frequent in the later drama, in *The Master Builder*, in *When we Dead Awaken*) it is important that the producer should explain to the actors that, however solidly real they have been till then, they are *now* also almost like figures in a symbolic drama. To modulate out of realistic psychological drama into poetic, symbolic drama puts an enormous strain upon both actors and producers; yet upon that successful modulation all depends. The beauty of Ibsen's work is at stake.

Such a moment is the suicide of the two main figures in *Rosmersholm*. There is another moment, just before it in the play, in which a minor figure – Brandel, a sort of little Peer Gynt – should appear with the effect almost of a phantom. He crosses the scene twice. The first time he is a megalomaniac day-dreamer, who is at last prepared to thunder out his message to the world, and give away his hoarded gold of thought. He acts for the moment as a stimulant to Rosmer's courage when meeting the harsh conventionalism of Kroll, utter sham though Brandel is. (Sham prophets often help a little while people more sincere than themselves.) The second time Brandel appears it is as a self-confessed bankrupt. On Rosmer he has now the effect of a shabby spectre of all idealistic aspiration.

CHEKHOV

I

Chekhov is among playwrights the master of dialogue in which characters give themselves away articulately without raising their voices above the pitch of ordinary talk. His people simply speak out of themselves. I propose to remind you first what sort of drama he wrote, that is to say, the kind of states of mind and the kind of emotions he reveals by means of dialogue.

Chekhov follows in the steps of Turgenev: his favourite theme is disillusionment, and above the kind of beauty he creates might well be written 'desolation is a delicate thing'. He is fond of the same kind of settings as Turgenev, too: summer woods, a country house full of cultivated people who talk and talk, in fact *une nichée des gentilhommes*. There you will find the idealist who melts over his own futility, the girl who clutches daily duties tighter in order to forget that youth is sliding away under her feet, the clever man turned maudlin-cynical after his failure to find a purpose in life, the old man who feels he has not yet begun to live, and the old woman who only wants things to go on quietly on humdrum lines. The current of their days is slow; the air they breathe is sultry with undischarged energy, and only broken by unrefreshing nerve storms. It is an atmosphere of sighs, yawns, self-reproaches, vodka, day-dreams, endless tea, endless discussion. These people are like those loosely agglutinated sticks and straws which revolve together slowly in a sluggish eddy. They long to be detached, and ride down the stream which they fancy is somewhere rushing past them. Some day – three hundred, five hundred years hence – perhaps life will be *life*. Ah! those fortunate heirs of the ages who will be alive then! But will they be grateful to their poor predecessors who after all made such glorious life possible? No: they will probably never think of them. That is another reason for self-pity. Stop! This is ridiculous, they argue. What are we doing for them? Nothing. What, indeed, can we do? Nothing, nothing, nothing. Such is the atmosphere in which Chekhov's characters live and move and have their being. It differs from that of Turgenev's generation in being a stuffier air, even less bracing to effort and to hope. There are no Bazarovs to break its spell and bring down the rains of violent tragedy. Tragedy is there, but it is tragedy in the form of a creeping mist which narrows the world to the garden gate. Sometimes the warm wet mist thins away, but it soon closes again, hiding the golden vista of hope for the race.

This is a generalized picture of Chekhov's world. What, you may ask, has it in common with us that it should move us so deeply? Well, I am not convinced that many of us have not after all more in common with these characters than at first sight seems probable. We have more self-control. It is true we are less hysterical, but do not the lives of many when examined resemble that of flies in a glue-pot? Yet it is not only upon this resemblance that the appeal of this drama rests. To watch a Chekhov play is to recapture one's youth; a most uncomfortable yet enviable time when there was intensity even in lassitude, when self-torture did not seem vain; when hope sometimes irradiated and sometimes took the shine out of the present, and when time seemed endless and impossible to fill. 'These people', the spectator at a Chekhov play finds himself exclaiming, 'are suffering from an unduly protracted youth!' In *Uncle Vanya*, Vanya's elderly passion for the self-centred Elena reflects something of the humiliation of young longing that expects everything and does not understand itself. To all of them, except the meaner, harder sort, it seems that life would be beautiful if, if, if . . . With *The Three Sisters* it is '*if* we could get to Moscow'; with the Baron, in that play, '*if* I could find my work'; with Vanya, '*if* only Elena loved me.' And to feel like that is to be, as far as it goes, young. It is, of course, young to want to prop your ladder against a horn of the moon, but it is also to be not quite an adult not to know that although we have immortal hunger in us, there are – a paradox thanks to which the world goes on – satisfying properties in a little real bread. Chekhov's characters have not learnt that. They have a wail in them responsive not only to their own particular frustrations, but to the inevitable disillusionments of life. This quality in Chekhov's work, though it is, as commentators point out, the product of a phase, of a particular period in Russian history, is also a quality which must keep it alive, though not always, of course, acutely interesting. The degree of contemporary interest depends on the degree of wistfulness there may be in the sensibility of any particular generation. But that general theme cannot grow incomprehensible, though it lies behind a picture of life which in many respects already 'dates'.

Chekhov is the artist of farewells; farewells to youth, to the past, to hopes, to loves. The climax of *The Cherry Orchard* is a farewell to an old home and all that such a home can mean to the middle-aged; at the end of *Uncle Vanya* the words 'They've gone' uttered by one character after another as they enter after seeing off the professor and his siren wife, are like the tolling of a bell for the burial of passion and excitement.

How does Chekhov get his effects? He has, of course, like all notable writers, an unerring gift of selecting significant detail.

One of the characters says enviously of the author Trigorin in *The Seagull*: 'With him the broken bottle-neck glitters on the dam and the mill-wheel casts a black shadow – and there you have the moonlight night.' That is a gift which cannot be analysed, cannot be taught. Let us take it for granted and pass on. He excels also in creating what is called atmosphere in dialogue. Atmosphere in description needs no definition, but atmosphere in dialogue means that when a group of people are talking together on the stage we are aware of the kind of chord which their separate moods or ideas are making, as though each speaker were a separate note. The mood of the moment, the composite mood of those particular people talking together, is vividly conveyed to us as well as what each speaker is feeling and thinking. When only two people are talking on the stage this is comparatively easy to achieve (in a love scene, for example), but when a number of characters are brought together, each sad or happy for different reasons, and each with different thoughts, who are nevertheless all involved in the same situation, it needs most delicate orchestration to give that moment itself a dramatic character of its own. Of this art Chekhov is a master. He is a master of the art of setting the mood of one person against that of another, so that the contrast makes the mood of each more poignant and interesting. Unfortunately for my purpose, this faculty can only be illustrated by quotations of considerable length; I will therefore go on to another characteristic, in Chekhov's case, closely connected with it.

I have already spoken of the pathetic childlike faith which his people have that the road on which they are *not* walking is the best; that somewhere the river of life is rushing sparkling by, though each feels himself or herself stagnating in a back-water. Let me take examples from *The Seagull*, though they might be found in every play Chekhov has written.

By means of subtle contrasts Chekhov shows in that play that what each character pines for makes no great difference to the happiness or unhappiness of another who does possess it. Trigorin's talent and adoration of Masha's love for him do not make him happy, though poor Konstantin shoots himself because he has neither her love nor her admiration; to be an actress and the mistress of a great writer bring only misery to Nina, though in prospect they seemed the gates of heaven to her. Though Madame Treplev, the successful actress, is blessed with a thicker skin, no one could call her a happy woman. Her jealousy of her son's new ideas, even of the young girl who might possibly win admiration on the stage by interpreting them, the frantic egotistic clutch with which she holds Trigorin to herself, her restlessness, stinginess and wild spoilt temper disprove it. Nor can you call the disillusioned resignation of Dr Dorn, the man who has, in the eyes of the dying Sorin, 'lived', happy either. He has about him just a sufficient touch of kindly stoicism to throw into relief the distress of the others, but that is all. Women adore him; they have been mad about him. But all his conquests mean to him is a succession of scenes and constant demands on his sympathy. Yet to old Sorin, who wanted love and wanted to write, but had to live alone and earn a living as a magistrate, it seems that Dr Dorn must be a satisfied man. 'It's all very well for you to argue, "You've lived your life"' [Dorn is much younger] 'but what about me? . . . You've had enough and you don't care, and so you talk like a philosopher but I want to live.' The pathos of this cry lies in his being so near the end of life himself.

Konstantin, again, would give anything for Trigorin's gift, and Nina imagines that to have Trigorin's fame must be the most ecstatic happiness. She is astounded to find that a famous actress should cry at not being able to use the horses one afternoon, and that 'a famous author [Trigorin] adored by the public, written about in all the papers, his photographs for sale, his works translated into foreign languages', should prefer to spend his time fishing, and be 'delighted at having caught two gudgeon'. When Trigorin shows her what a writer's life amounts to (one of the most interesting passages in the play) she cannot believe a word of it; to her, such life must be splendid.

It is true that a work of art to have any value must somewhere carry within it the suggestion of desirable life. Where then is that suggestion here? The answer is in the mind of Chekhov himself, in the infection we catch from the spirit of his plays; in the delicate, truthful, humorous, compassionate mind which observes, understands, and forgives.

These people, as I said, are revealing themselves every moment they open their mouths. They do so as completely as in plays old-fashioned in technique, in which the characters soliloquize. Yet Chekhov is a realist, and realistic not only in detail, which was the first form that realism took both in fiction and on the stage, but in his plots which resembled life. Above all, his dialogue resembles real life in its consequence.

This is Chekhov's favourite device for letting us into his character's inner feelings. They reply to each other, but they do not so much answer each other as soliloquize. Now, his habit of egotistic self-revelation is more characteristic of Russian than English character. Therefore English dramatists like Granville Barker, who are trying to write a dialogue which, while being as colloquial as Chekhov's, will be equally self-revealing, have a harder task.

II

The men of Leinster have a proverb, 'All the cows in Connaught have long horns,' and doubtless many who go to the Lyric Theatre, Hammersmith, to see *The Cherry Orchard* come away thinking that such characters are peculiar to Russia. Of course the 'atmosphere' is Russian, and this is one of the difficulties which, not unnaturally, the company failed to overcome. A Russian would no doubt smile at some of the scenes for being wrong as far as imponderables are concerned, just as an Englishman might smile at a performance of Galsworthy in Milan; but though the 'atmosphere' is Russian the human-nature in the play is universal. That is what makes it moving. Take Gaev, perhaps the most fantastic character in it, who, whenever a thought stabs him or he has to make a painful decision, whisks off his mind to his favourite game, billiards, and cries out, 'Cannon off the red and into the centre pocket.' How very Russian! exclaims the Englishman who takes refuge from worries in cricket scores, and in the middle of a quarrel with his wife will withdraw his mind and think of the approach shot he is going to make at the third hole next Saturday.

I have, I am glad to say, known a 'perpetual student'; and surely all have met an impulsive, hazy Madam Ranevsky (Lyubov), who gives largesse instead of paying bills, is a prey to any adventurer, and slowly, tender-heartedly resigns all she loves rather than stop muddling along. No; if you regard *The Cherry Orchard* as a study in national character you will miss its point, and, worse loss, you will not be touched, for nothing chills sympathy so much as consciousness of superiority. There is a difference, but it is not a deep one, between these characters and ourselves; the conventional façade of self-respect is not kept up between them; they would admit to being the childish creatures they are. This atmosphere of impulsive candour is intensified by Chekhov's method of making character reveal itself casually, irrelevantly. It is a method which requires the most careful minute acting. In acting Chekhov 'timing', the right pause before speaking, and the right change of tone are more than usually important, since it is not so much through literal meaning of remarks as through the attitude they betray in the speakers that we are conducted into the heart of the drama.

Take one instance: Trofimov, 'the perpetual student', 'the mouldy young man', who has been ten years taking his degree, ex-tutor to Lyubov's boy who was drowned, is obviously in

love, or about to be in love, with her daughter Anya. He has
been boasting (there is some truth in the boast too) that Lyubov
need not be afraid; he is above passion. He has been scolding
her, as the young will do, because she will not 'face facts' – the
fact that she must sell her home and look forward to a new life.
She has replied, as elderly people often reply, 'You settle every
problem so trenchantly! Dear boy, isn't that because you
haven't yet understood one of your own problems through
suffering? You look forward boldly. But isn't it because you
don't see and don't expect anything dreadful because life is still
hidden from your young eyes? You're braver, more honest,
deeper than we are; but think, be just a little magnanimous –
have pity on me. I was born here, you know, my father and
mother lived here, my grandfather lived here. I love this house.
I can't conceive life without the cherry orchard. If it really must
be sold – then sell me with the orchard. (She kisses him.) My
boy was drowned here. Pity me, be kind.'

'You know I feel for you with all my heart', says Trofimov.
And her reply shows how vital for the drama it is that there
should be coldness in his voice. 'Not like that' – she exclaims –
'you should say that so differently.' Then a wave of wide,
maternal tenderness sweeps over her: 'Don't be hard on me,
Petya – I love you as one of ourselves. I would gladly let you
marry Anya – I swear I would – only, dear boy,' (here the
practical mother speaks) 'you must take your degree. You do
nothing – you're just tossed by fate from place to place. – And'
(suddenly she sees him from outside, a poor, weedy, feckless
fellow) 'you must do something with your beard to make it
grow. (She laughs) You look so funny.' Trofimov answers
sullenly, 'I've no wish to be a beauty,' and picks up a telegram
which her lover has sent her from Paris.

The sight of it sets her off on wailing about the man whom she
still loves in spite of his abominable treatment of her; and
Trofimov, the remark about his beard rankling, blurts out
angrily the truth: that this fellow lives on her and that she is a

fool. As in real life, it is the feeling behind the words she answers. She, too, flares up. She sees again before her not the affectionate, high-minded Petya, but a weedy, presumptuous, pretentious weakling. 'You should be a man at your age – understand love.' Wounding words pour from her lips. He is a prude – a comic fool, a freak, a scrap of a man – 'At your age you haven't even a mistress.' 'You, *above* love! You're a –' and Trofimov in distracted agony, crying 'This is awful,' dashes from the room. There is a crash and the sound of laughter outside. He has fallen downstairs! Lyubov is now very repentant, and when he enters again presently (there is an untidy party going on) she insists on their dancing together. She, like a woman, is glib in asking to be forgiven; Petya is silent and still sore.

In almost every other modern play this scene would stand out as a moment of condensed emotion and revelation of character. In *The Cherry Orchard* it is only part of a consistent perfection. There is not five minutes space anywhere in the dialogue, which would not, like a drop beneath a microscope, be found swarming with life. I have translated it here into a sort of Braille, raised letters for the blind, because those bracketed comments, insulting to the intelligence of the sensitive, bring home the special importance of 'timing' and intonation in acting Chekhov. All depends upon the actors making pauses, pace, tone psychologically significant, so that we are made to feel the twists and turns of emotion within the speakers. If this is difficult in a dialogue, it is harder still when several people are speaking disjointedly and seemingly about indifferent matters. Even the poignancy of the departure of the family at the end of the last act depends on the way in which the interjected remarks, 'the things are all ready', 'Here are your goloshes', the hopeful cry of Anya, 'Good bye old home', the flourish of Trofimov, fall into a deep pool of still hopeless emotion, and make rings there.

What a master Chekhov is of farewells! Recall the last act of

The Three Sisters, when the regiment marches away, taking with
them the sisters' friends and their last hope, or the dim little
speech of Sonya at the close of *Uncle Vanya* – 'We must go on
living. We shall go on living, Uncle Vanya,' – a speech so
touching in the inadequacy of the comfort it can bring; and then
that sudden rush of emotion in this play, when brother and
sister fall on each other's necks; a desolation of spirit led up to
with such delicate art, interrupted so naturally, and heightened
so dramatically, by the constant intrusion of the commonplace.
Chekhov understood better than anyone that just as walking is
a perpetual falling so living is a perpetual series of good-byes,
and that courage lies not so much in the power of looking
forward to new things as in the power to break with the old.
These two hapless elderly people could not do that. The young
Anya and 'the perpetual student' had unsatisfied curiosity and
day-dreams to support them; the other two only their in-
corrigible fecklessness.

We get close to the spirit of Chekhov himself in these scenes of
farewells. He could not 'break the parting word into its two
significant halves adieu', though the tenderness of his indul-
gence sprang from seeing life as a constant slipping from one
good-bye into another. It is difficult to suggest a philosophy
which is never formulated. It is a feeling rather than a thought
which his work leaves behind, a feeling that though everything
is brief, precarious and empty, just because that *is* all, there is a
kind of sacredness about it which the angry cynic and impatient
moralist are too stupid to feel. Get rid of enormous hopes,
especially of exorbitant expectations regarding yourself and
others, and you will share an emotion towards mankind in
which irony and sympathy are so blended that it leads the
living, too, beyond 'a vale of tears'.

I will admit no writer to be a greater writer than Tolstoy, and
if as a reader of men and women I am about to compare him for
a moment with Chekhov to his disadvantage, I am not forget-
ting Tolstoy's superiority as a poet and a creator. With terrible

insight Tolstoy puts his finger on the very spot and tells us we
ail there and there. After that pitiless diagnosis, since he is wise,
he, too, forgives. But in Chekhov penetration and sympathy are
not successive movements of the mind, but simultaneous; a
single faculty, thanks to which no weakness escapes him or
remains unpardoned. It is a subtler justice.

Consciousness of the futility of men and the humiliating
brevity of their passions, tragedies and noble impulses, also
leaves behind a kind of phantom, first cousin to hope. It is a
very gentle irony which makes Chekhov put into the mouth of
the ineffectual Trofimov the expression of man's hopes – a
double irony, I think, which reflects as much on the practical
Lopahin as on the indolent 'perpetual student' himself.

In the dialogue between him and Lyubov observe how even
in two such affectionate and effusive people egotism keeps them
apart – to join, to part again, and so on inevitably for ever. One
source of the poignant impression Chekhov's picture of life
makes upon us is that justice is done in it to the isolation of
human beings. Each lives in his or her bubble of egotism; only
at moments do those bubbles break and join. The note is struck
at the very beginning of the play when the longed-for travellers
arrive.

> *Dunyasha*: We've been expecting you so long (*takes Anya's hat
> and coat*).
> *Anya*: I haven't slept for four nights on the journey. I feel
> dreadfully cold.
> *Dunyasha*: You set out in Lent, there was snow and frost, and
> now? My darling! (*laughs and kisses her*). I *have* missed you,
> my precious, my joy. I must tell you – I can't put it off a
> minute.
> *Anya* (*wearily*): What now?
> *Dunyasha*: Epihodov, the clerk, made me a proposal just
> after Easter.
> *Anya*: It's always the same thing with you . . . (*straightening

her hair). I've lost all my hairpins . . . (*she is staggering from exhaustion*).

This stress upon natural universal egotism takes sublimity from the sorrows of those we watch, but it adds to the moving reality of their sufferings.

III

Ivanoff is one of the least known of Chekhov's plays. It is not counted among his best, and yet how good it is! It was his first attempt at a big play, and it failed. Towards the end of his life he rewrote it and improved it immensely; it was played by the Moscow Art Theatre, and again it did not succeed. The reason of this second failure was (I have good authority for saying this) that the Moscow company did not bring out the comedy of the piece. They played it too tearfully, just as the English company the other day missed the rainbow effects, laughter through tears, in *The Cherry Orchard*. In *Ivanoff* the strain of comedy is far stronger, and it was clearly brought out in Mr Komisarjevsky's production.

Ivanoff is generally described as Chekhov's attempt to write a Russian *Hamlet*, and the description is a good one. Ivanoff, the principal figure, is a man whose will has been broken, and the line 'O what a rogue and peasant slave am I' runs like a refrain through all his speeches. He is sick with self-disgust. Before the curtain rises we are given to understand that he was a particularly fine specimen among Russian landowners, an active, aspiring, generous young man of high ability. He married for love a Jewess whose rich parents discarded her for making a 'mixed marriage'. You remember that in Hamlet's case, too, we must understand that the young Prince was full of promise. We catch through that play glimpses of the earlier Hamlet; in Chekhov's play (I think this a defect in it), there is only one flash of the hero's quondam spirit. It tells in his last cry, 'My youth has come back – the old Ivanoff is alive again' – uttered just before he shoots himself, but it occurs nowhere else.

During the rest of the play he is exhibited to us as helpless, morbid, vacillating, crushed by shame. Now it is exceedingly difficult to bring out the tragic quality of emotions which hearty, healthy people, let alone the medical profession, label as pathological. It is not easy to hold our sympathy in such a part as Ivanoff, and yet it is all important that we should distinguish between Ivanoff himself, who is a good man, and the view which all the characters save two, Sasha and her simple amiable old tippler of a father, take of his character. He brings misery into the lives of all near him; he fails to act consistently; his motives are open to misinterpretation by malicious gossips. His agent, Borkin, is responsible for this, but such gossip is also the result of Ivanoff's reckless self-depreciation. In a notable passage of self-condemnation Ivanoff compares himself to a vain young peasant who broke his back shouldering, out of swagger, a load far too heavy for him. What is the load Ivanoff has to carry?

Firstly, disappointment, and provincial life – its pettiness and dullness have proved stronger than his enthusiasms. Secondly, bankruptcy: and last, but not least, he has ceased to love his wife, his sick, beautiful, lonely Anna towards whom he has by no means ceased to feel nevertheless a tender loyalty. Against his will he has often found comfort in the companionship of Sasha, a young girl, the daughter of a rich, miserly mother. Her attraction for him is that of credulous, admiring, energetic youth for a tired, sceptical man who has lost faith in himself. To the neighbours it looks as though, disappointed in one rich marriage, he is preparing to make another; they know Anna is consumptive and cannot live long. She is on Ivanoff's nerves; and both the doctor, who attends Anna and is in love with her himself, and Ivanoff's neighbours think he is only too ready to hasten the poor woman's death by treating her badly. Ivanoff's self-accusations seem to bear them out.

Sasha is a character to be met in the pages of Turgenev, but here she is not idealized. She is in love with Ivanoff and it is she who does the wooing. Her passion is distinguishable from a longing to help him; she is the type of girl who loves a man because she believes she can 'save' him. But Ivanoff does not believe he can be saved; he feels on the contrary that he will drag Sasha down. The death of poor Anna is heavy on his conscience in the last act. On his wedding morning, though he refuses to go to church, Sasha will not release him. Is she in love with him or with her own goodness? Both. There is a comi-tragic competition in unselfishness between them, amazing to her plain-minded father, Lebedieff, and then – Ivanoff shoots himself.

Those who have not seen the play will wonder where in such a story comedy could come in. Well, the answer is, it is by Chekhov. It is in these humiliations and self-regarding scruples of the hero that the comedy lies; in the contrast between him and such simple, kindly souls as Lebedieff and such eupeptic, thick-skinned vulgarians as Borkin; in the fact, so true to life, that gossip makes the most private perplexities of the soul also, alas, the concern of people who conspicuously leave that element out in judging people. This vague hum of lively indifference and callous censoriousness of which gossip is composed was wonderfully rendered in the production. The party at the Lebedieffs' house was a masterpiece of stage craft. Indeed, the whole production was one which the playgoer can look back upon and say, 'I have seen Chekhov properly acted.'

MAJOR BARBARA

Major Barbara is the story of a woman who lives her religion and loses it; who, after enduring the desolation of seeing her own and all the world's hope hang torn before her eyes, finds at last a belief her passionate heart can live by. This account will seem ridiculous to those who heard only the crackle of wit, the rhetoric of theory, and brisk interchange of comment; yet it is the centre and significance of the play.

It is the first English play which has for its theme the struggle between two religions in one mind. And to have written upon that theme convincingly is a triumph which criticism cannot appreciably lessen. The second act is 'wonderful, most wonderful, and yet again wonderful, and after that past all whooping'.

Barbara is the daughter of the chief partner in the biggest cannon-manufactory in the world. Her mother is a lady of birth and position, 'well mannered yet appallingly outspoken and indifferent to the opinion of her interlocutors, arbitrary and high-tempered to the last bearable degree, full of class prejudices, conceiving the universe exactly as if it were a large house in Wilton Crescent, though handling her corner of it very effectively on that assumption'. Barbara's parents have been living apart for years.

When the play begins, the engagement of Lady Britomart's two daughters to young men without money has compelled her to ask her husband to call upon her in order that she may persuade him to make a fitting provision for them. The one daughter is a very ordinary society girl; the other, Barbara, has a genius for saving souls, and is already a prominent officer in the Salvation Army. She is engaged to Cusins, a professor of Greek, who fell in love with her and proposed under the impression that she was an ordinary Salvation Army lass.

The first act introduces these people, and its interest lies in the return of Undershaft to the bosom of his family. Lady Britomart was admirably played by Miss Filippi. On Under-shaft's being announced I had a vivid recollection of her adjusting her spectacles and settling herself in a chair facing the door with an admirable air of nervous decision. Mr Calvert's Undershaft was not nearly so good as his blusterous Broadbent or his balmy 'William'; for Undershaft is good-natured and easy-going on the surface but fuliginous and formidable under-neath, but Mr Calvert was complacent underneath and formid-able on the surface. Of all Undershaft's family Barbara alone interests him, and his heart goes out to her, though he would resent such a description of his feelings. They both have religious natures, but the beliefs of each are poles asunder. Each wishes to convert the other, and they strike a bargain; he will visit her Salvation Army shelter, if she will afterwards visit his gun-manufactory. The second act is laid at the shelter.

There is no space in which to dilate upon the pathos, passion, and significant realism of this scene, or upon the ironic ecstasy which Cusins contributes to it (imagine the difficulty of acting such a purely intellectual passion!); but one incident must be noted. Bill Walker, a bullying sort of ruffian, slouches in to recover 'his girl', who has been recently converted; and when one of the Salvation lasses tells him she has gone away, he hits her in the mouth. Now, this blow very nearly brings about his own conversion; for Jenny Hill does not resent it, and Major Barbara takes advantage of the shame which begins to stir in him to make him more and more uncomfortable. His impulse is to buy back his peace of mind and self-respect by getting thrashed by his girl's new Salvation Army 'bloke', and failing in this, he offers Jenny a sovereign. Barbara tells him he cannot buy his salvation; she wants to touch his heart, and if he were to think he had made amends, he would go away as stupid and brutal as he came. Her father all the while watches this soul-saving process with grim sympathy. His chance comes when the news arrives that Bodger, the whisky-distiller, has offered a £5,000 subscription if another £5,000 can be raised. The money is of vital importance to the Army; indeed this shelter will have to be closed if funds are not forthcoming. Barbara has already refused £100 from her father for the same reason that she refused Bill's twenty shillings – because she wants her father to give up manufacturing the means of death; and if he can ease his conscience by being charitable, he will go on making money out of the sufferings of men. But the Army does not attach so much importance to the saving of Undershaft's soul as to the power his money will give them to help many others; so when he offers to make up the other £5,000 they accept it with grateful thanksgivings and Hallelujahs. This is a terrible shock to Barbara, who realizes, for the first time, that the power of the Army rests ultimately on the support of its worst enemies, who make the money they give away out of the very misery and degradation which the Army fights. The other side to this view is put by Mrs Baines: 'Who would have thought that any good could have come out of war and drink? And yet their profits are brought today to the feet of salvation to do its blessed work.' Barbara sees that Bodger 'wants to send his cheque down to buy us and go on being as wicked as ever'; while Cusins exclaims with excited irony, 'The millennium will be inaugurated by the unselfishness of Undershaft and Bodger.

O be joyful!' The Army must accept the money, since they are powerless without it; but the fact that they are right to accept it shows that they are fighting a battle they can never win; since if once they begin to make real headway against Bodger, his subscriptions, which are their means of victory, will be cut off. Barbara realizes this on reflection; but at the moment it is the revelation of the spring whence the Army's power is drawn, coupled with the object lesson that the Army cannot afford to think of the individual soul while such supplies are in question, which tumbles her faith to the ground. She is quite certain that a crusade which draws its strength from the evils it wishes to destroy, cannot put the world straight. This is a criticism which hits all the churches and all charitable institutions in so far as they hope to do this. From a revolutionist's point of view, they are also objectionable, because they tend to keep the poor quiet, by making them less discontented with conditions which they ought to die rather than stand, and the rich from thinking they are just and honest, by offering them opportunities of being generous and kind; in short, because they keep those who should be indignant, servile, and those who ought to be uneasy, self-satisfied.

Undershaft's gospel, on its social side, is to preach socialism to the rich and rebellion to the poor, whereby he twists the same rope from both ends. The most important fact to insist upon is, therefore, the importance of money; tacitly, this is recognized by everyone; the possession of comfortable independence being everywhere the most universally powerful motive. But instead of blinking this fact and preaching 'Blessed are the poor', while taking care at the same time to have a reliable source of income ourselves, we must preach 'Cursed be the poor', so that every poverty-stricken man may either feel he has a grievance not to be borne, or be ashamed of the feebleness which keeps him so. The way in which Undershaft puts it is that poverty is literally *the worst of crimes*, and it follows from this assertion that a man is right to commit any other crime to avoid that one, should circumstances force him into such a dilemma. Now this is a doctrine that good sense refuses to swallow. How then did Undershaft or Mr Shaw come to believe it, and urge it with such vehemence?

The temperament and interests of a reformer drive him to look continually at results of actions and emotions in valuing them rather than at these things themselves; and since poverty and ill-health are probably the causes of more evil than is any single vice, the reformer slips more readily than other people into the mistake of thinking that these things are, in themselves, worse than any vice. But it is clear that what may be a cause of evil is often not even bad at all in itself, let alone not so bad as the evil; and equally, that the means to good are often valueless in themselves, compared to what they help to bring about. That poverty is not bad in itself – is no more a crime than is a broken leg – is so clear that if a man of Mr Shaw's talents had not said it was, no critic would bore his reader with a refutation of such a statement. Bunyan and Blake, whom Mr Shaw praises with such liberality of genuine admiration, were very poor; yet that they were among the most ignoble of criminals he himself would never admit.

It is clear that poverty, like ill-health, is only bad as a difficulty in the way of a fine life which a few surmount, and that therefore the pretext of escaping from it cannot justify the worst actions. Indeed, if Undershaft's doctrine were generally be-lieved, the only effect would be to make poverty the cause of much more evil, of many more acts of violence, oppression and meanness, than it is now. Dubedat took every means in his power – blackmailing, stealing, utilizing his wife's charms as bait – to escape poverty; yet I do not think Undershaft would have felt that he was doing much to bring about a better state of things.

And Undershaft himself? He talks very big about having been prepared to kill anybody as long as he was poor; but what did he *do*? Did he found his fortunes by knocking an old woman

on the head and stealing her watch, or by going into partnership with a Mrs Warren? No, of course not; he stuck to his
desk like a good young man, inched and pinched until he had
made himself useful to the firm, and then took good care not to
be put upon. Undershaft's weakness lay in talking big; that is
really what his sensible wife could not stand. In Act II he tells
his son that he and Lazarus are really the people who govern
England, and decide questions of war and peace; and in Act III
he explains to Cusins that he is a fool if he accepts the
partnership in the hope of power, since he and Lazarus are in
fact absolutely powerless. In both cases he is talking big.

In this third and last act Barbara and her family visit the
town of Perivale St Andrews. They find it is a clean, fine place,
where everybody is well-fed and well-clad. It is, in fact, a kind of
socialistic community with this great difference; instead of
being pervaded with a spirit of equality and independence, the
whole place is honey-combed with snobbishness and petty
oppression. This spirit is what Barbara will spend her life now
in fighting. Her work will be amongst uppish, vulgar, prosperous, self-satisfied people, and her last speech is a pæan of
rejoicing that she will in future never feel the humiliation of
knowing that the truths she has at heart are listened to because
she distributes alms at the same time.

The last act is weak on the stage; indeed the defect of the play
is that Barbara's conversion is much less impressive than the
loss of her old religion. Miss Annie Russell, who was so good in
the first two acts, could make little of the third.

The moral of the play filtered from Undershaft's plutocratic
gospel would run as follows: that the ideal state is one in which
no one is poor; that the ideal man is he who shifts vigorously for
himself; that the best cure for the present anarchic and miserable state of things, is that every individual should become
self-reliant and use the weapons which Undershaft manufac-
tures against those who oppress him; that those who have
already some wealth and independence are the people it is most

profitable to teach what is good; that to the rest it is more important to preach rebellion. If *Man and Superman* is in a sense the cry of reformer clinging to the idea of selective breeding of mankind in the wreck of his hopes, *Major Barbara* expresses the disappointed impatience of a pamphleteer who gives up his belief in persuasion and turns to the swifter agency of force. The fallacy which the play attacks with perfect justice, is that of preaching to or of helping the poor simply because they are *poor*.

The mistake into which Mr Shaw slips of saying that poverty is a crime far worse than murder or lust or avarice, since it is perhaps a more constant *cause* of crime and feebleness than any one of these, is a fallacy which in one form or other often occurs in his writings. His great defect as an artist-philosopher is that he does not distinguish between those things which are bad as means and those which are bad in themselves, or between what is good as an end and what is only good as a means to that end; that when he judges the actions and emotions or the lives and characters of men and women, his test is invariably – What use are they? If he feels them to be useful as a means to reforming society, then they are good; if they cannot be shown to be useful, or only to be less useful than something else, then they are judged to be comparatively valueless. But it is certain that qualities and things which are valuable as means are not necessarily worth having for their own sakes, and that things very good in themselves may not at the same time be important as means to something else worth having. And since this is indubitably true, it follows that any one who judges the values of things from the point of view of their results, and hardly ever asks himself whether they have any value in themselves, must often get his scale of values wrong. This is the most general criticism which can be brought against the morality of the Shavian drama. A great part of that originality of view which underlies the plays is due to the fact that he judges goodness and badness by their results alone. The transvaluation which follows is often startling; actions which nobody thought particularly bad are put in a class with the most heinous offences, and qualities not commonly allowed to be claims upon the respect of others are exalted above affection. In this he is often right, because the goodness of things as a means may be an important part of their total value; but he is, also, often wrong, because the importance of anything as a means to something else may be a very small part of its total value. For instance, what are the qualities most extolled in his plays? Vitality, pugnacity, political and intellectual honesty, fearlessness and universal benevolence: these are clearly useful. What are the qualities and emotions which on the whole are depreciated or pointedly ignored? Personal affections, admiration, and sensitiveness to beauty: these cannot be shown to be such powerful means towards bringing about a better state of society; but are they not essential elements in that better state itself? Mr Shaw ignores the question of ultimate ends so completely that when he defines Heaven, the ideal state, he describes it as a community of men working towards bringing it into existence. 'In Heaven you live and work, instead of playing and pretending, you face things as they are; you escape nothing but glamour, and your steadfastness and your peril are your glory. . . . But even as you [the devil] enjoy the contemplation of such romantic mirages as beauty and pleasure, so would I enjoy the contemplation of that which interests me above all things: namely, Life: the force that ever strives to attain greater power of contemplating itself.' Hell is a community in which personal relations and the contemplation of beauty are the supreme goods. Mr Shaw cheapens this ideal by assuming that the only kind of love which can compete with the fellow-service of heaven is a kind which might be worthily sung by Sedley, or set to music by Offenbach, or depicted by Fragonard. No one requires to be told that Mohammed's paradise, however intellectualized and refined, is not the highest good; but what is instructive in Mr Shaw's antithesis is that he sets so much store by the contemplation of what is both real and beautiful at the same time, raising this above the contemplation of beauty or goodness which is not accompanied by a true belief in the object. That this judgement is a true one nobody can doubt; what can be protested against with equal justice is the assumption that love between individuals always implies contemplation of goodness and beauty which cannot be believed to be real.

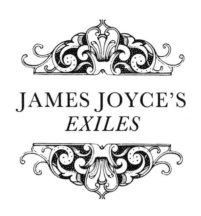

JAMES JOYCE'S
EXILES

Exiles is a remarkable play. I am more sure of this than of having understood it. I could never undertake to produce it unless the author were at my elbow; and when a critic feels like that about a play which has excited him it means he has not quite understood it. What I can do is to give an account of the play and show where I was puzzled. But first I must come to terms with a misgiving. It is a treat to be puzzled by a play, so perhaps I overrate this one because it has puzzled me? I do not think that is the case, but that possibility is the grain of salt with which what follows must be taken.

To be made to wonder and to think about characters in a play is a rare experience – outside the drama of Ibsen. It is a pleasure far excelling the simple pleasure of delighted recognition which is all that the character-drawing in the ordinary respect-worthy play provides. On the stage temptations to superficiality and exaggeration are so many, and the drama is a form which requires so much condensation of subject-matter and imposes so many limitations that, within those limits, all except duffers and men of genius are, alas, more or less on a level! Once a certain knack is learnt the happy proficient in play-writing finds he can produce a play with an expenditure of a fifth of the intellectual energy and emotion necessary to produce a novel of the same calibre. If he has more to give, it does not show; if not, it does not matter, for what he may still be able to produce may be on a par with the work of a better intellect. Hence there is so much truth in sayings like: 'In the art of play-writing construction is everything'; 'The idea of a good play should be capable of being written on half a sheet of note-paper', etc. They are certainly true of the common run of respect-worthy plays, but they are only true of them.

Exiles excited me for the same reason that the plays of Ibsen excite me – the people in it were so interesting. Ibsen's characters have roots which tempt one to pull at them again and again. And they are so deeply embedded in the stuff of experience that tugging at them brings up incidentally every sort of moral, social and psychological question, upon which those who would understand themselves and others can go on meditating, while feeling that they have still more to learn. The relations of Ibsen's characters to each other are presented with a sureness and brevity which gives the impression of masterly definition, and yet the complexity and obscurity of intimate relations between living people at intense moments are there too. If one lays a finger on a spinning rainbow top one discovers that the effect has been produced by a few discs of different coloured paper (red, green, yellow, and blue) superimposed upon each other; but while it was spinning that changing iridescence had too many hues to be identified. The rainbow top will pass as an emblem of the manner in which the plays of Ibsen satisfy at once the two prime contemplative pleasures – the exercise of the analytical faculty and delight in watching the movement of life.

I do not take Ibsen's name in vain in connection with the work of Mr Joyce. It is not (I beg you to believe) that habit so common in critics of chattering about anything but the subject in hand which persuades me to approach *Exiles* through the art of Ibsen. It is extraordinary, but the greatest of modern dramatists has as yet only had a destructive effect on the drama of this country. The plays of Ibsen have destroyed a certain amount of nonsense. Of late years his influence has been countered by the suggestion that he is a writer of problem plays, and 'problems', it is explained, have nothing to do with art. Ibsen is supposed to be out of date! Of all the verdicts which are now passed on the writers of the last century, this is the one which maddens me most. That great contemplative mind! . . . But the point I wish to make is that constructively Ibsen has had little influence. Few dramatists have learnt from his example. I hail Mr Joyce as one of the few who have grasped the value of two principles in dramatic art of which Ibsen is the master exponent.

The first is that on the stage, as in the novel, character (the individual) is the most interesting thing, the ultimate thing; for nothing *happens* at all unless it happens to a particular person, and action is dependent on character. The dramatist therefore must choose characters who illustrate his theme better and better the more he goes into them. Then, the deeper he digs the clearer will sound in our ears the running water of his theme. He cannot dig too deep, if he has chosen them well. But by what sign is he to recognize those characters? I do not know. His theme, intellectually stated, is certainly not the right clue. He usually finds them in himself – at least, a shaft which goes down any depth is nearly always, I think, opened from within, though afterwards sympathy and observation may continue the excavation and even control its direction; but that ground is not broken to any depth except by an author who has an inner life of his own to explore, is certain. Now what happens with most dramatists who are blessed with an idea is that they allow their theme to control their interest in character. In other words, either they have chosen characters which only illustrate superficially what they wish to show, or they only attempt to understand them in so far as they illustrate it. If they get really interested in human beings their theme becomes instead of clearer more obscure. I know no better test of a dramatist's imagination than observing if this happens.

One of the qualities which delighted me in *Exiles* was that evidently nothing would induce Mr Joyce to make his characters less complex and interesting than he saw them to be. He would rather obscure his theme than do that, and though a fault, it is a fault on the right side – on the interesting side. The second respect in which he has learnt from the master is his practice of intensifying our interest in the present by dialogue which implies a past. What a little scrap of people's lives a dramatist can show us – just an hour or two! In life it is usually what has gone before that makes talk between two people significant. If we did not add the days and months and years together our relations would be as empty as those of children, without being as delightful. The deduction is obvious: make people talk on the stage as though much had already passed between them. Dramatists are too afraid of mystifying their audience to use that obvious method of enriching their subject; for that there are not many people as quick and clever as themselves is a common delusion among them. Sometimes it may be no delusion; still, I am sure it is not necessary to temper their intelligence to the extent they commonly do. Besides, it is a writer's first point of honour not to write for people stupider than himself: let birds of a feather write for each other.

The merits of this play make it hard to tell its story. Summarized, that story would not distinguish it from many a play in which the love relations of two men and a woman wove the plot. Its distinction lies in the relations of the three points in that familiar triangle being complex and intense. Art is usually so superficial, life so profound. I admire Mr Joyce for having tried to deepen our conventional simplification of such relations and bring them nearer to nature. Now and then I lost my way in his characters as in a wood, but that did not make me think they were not true; rather the contrary. When I put my finger on his spinning rainbow top, I do not see the coloured rings which produced that iridescence so definitely as in the case of Ibsen. The theme of *Exiles* is not so clear to me. I conjecture that I get nearest to it in saying that the play is a study in the emotional life of an artist. (I am sure, at any rate, that I am giving the reader a useful tip in bidding him keep one eye *always* upon Richard Rowan, whatever else may be interesting him besides.) And when I say that the play is a study in an artist's life, I mean that its theme is the complication which that endowment adds to emotional crises which are common to all men. It makes sincerity more difficult and at the same time more vitally important. Imagination opens the door to a hundred new subtleties and possibilities of action; it brings a man so near the feelings of others that he has never the excuse of blindness, and keeps him at a distance, so that at moments he can hardly believe he cares for anything but his own mind.

When he acts spontaneously, he knows he is acting spontaneously – if not at the moment, the moment after – much as some people, thought modest, have hardly a right to be considered so, because they invariably know when they are. *Exiles* is a play in which two men are struggling to preserve each his own essential integrity in a confusing situation where rules of thumb seem clumsy guides; and between them is a bewildered, passionate woman – generous, angry, tender, and lonely. To understand Bertha one need only remember that she has lived nine years with Richard Rowan in that intimacy of mind and feeling which admits of no disguises, merciful or treacherous; that she has known all the satisfactions and disappointments of such an intimacy. Her nature cries out for things to be simple as they once were for her; but she, too, has eaten of the tree of knowledge and knows that they are not.

If you ask how Richard Rowan and Robert Hand stood towards each other, the answer is they were friends. There was a touch of the disciple in Robert. Richard was the intenser, more creative, and also the more difficult nature. He was an exile in this world; Robert was at home in it. But the essence of their relation was that they were friends, and friends who from youth had made life's voyage of discovery together. One was a journalist, the other an artist; but in experience they were equals. Both had lived intensely enough, and had been intimate enough to reach together that pitch of mutual understanding at which consciousness that each is still at bottom solitary is, in a strange way, the tenderest bond between them. Am I over-subtle? I think what I mean is recognizable. After all, it is in friendships of the second order (Heaven forfend that they should be held cheap!) that men are least troubled about the value of what they give. It is between these two friends that competition for the same woman rises, bringing with it jealousy, suspicion, and making candour – the air in which alone such a friendship as theirs can live – almost impossible. Well, very hard. Both make a mighty effort to preserve it; Richard succeeds best; how far Robert Hand failed is not quite clear to me. At first Richard thought his friend a common vulgar thief; against such a one he would protect Bertha tooth and nail. But he has misgivings which in different ways torture him more than natural jealousy. Perhaps Robert can give her something he cannot (O, he knows how unsatisfying and yet how much that has been!); something no human being has a right to prevent another having. This is the first thing he must find out.

The scene in Act II between the two men is wonderful in its gradually deepening sincerity. Hand is a coward at first, but he gets over that. Then Richard is tormented by misgivings about himself. Is not there something in him (for ties, however precious, are also chains) which is attracted by the idea that Bertha might now owe most to another – now, at any rate, that their own first love is over? How far is he sincere in leaving her her liberty? Is it his own that he is really thinking of? Bertha taunts him with that. And Bertha's relation to Robert – what is that? I think it is the attraction of peace. To be adored, to be loved in a simpler, more romantic, coarser way, what a rest! Besides, Robert is the sort of man a woman can easily make happy; Richard certainly is not. Yet, just as she decided between them years ago, in the end it is her strange, elusive lover who comes so close and is so far away whom she chooses. But was she Robert's mistress? The dramatist leaves that ambiguous. He does not mean us to bother much one way or another about that. Richard says at the end he will never know what they were to each other; but I do not think he is thinking of Divorce Court facts. He means how completely Bertha still belongs to him. Bertha tells Robert to tell Richard everything; but does he? She also tells him to think of what has passed between them as something like 'a dream'. That, I think, is the line on which one must fix one's attention to get the focus. Robert is happy; quite content with that. Perhaps because less hot for certainties in life than Richard, he thinks he has enjoyed a solid reality. I do not know.

I have left out much it would be a pleasure to mark. Richard's relation to Beatrice Justice (the other woman in the play) – I could write an article on that; but what I have written will be perhaps enough to persuade you that this is a remarkable play.

STRINDBERG

At eight o'clock on a May morning in 1912 a black procession of nearly 30,000 people moved down the streets of Stockholm towards the cemetery of the New Church where the poor are buried. The majority were students and workers, but among them walked also the Cabinet Ministers, artists, musicians, actors and authors of Sweden, foreign delegates, and a royal prince. They were following a hearse in which lay the body of a man who, at some period or other of his career had reviled, either personally or as a member of a class, every one of those who were now walking behind it.

With a description of this procession Mr McGill opens his life of Strindberg. He has done well to do so, for English readers need to be reminded that Strindberg in Scandinavia and mid-Europe was, and remains, a prodigious figure. During his lifetime no man of letters had roused more resentment by his writings or with more cause. He had attacked marriage, family life, education, revolution, tradition, science, religion, art, business, society, each in turn, with exasperated violence. He had repeatedly slandered in print not only his enemies but everyone who had befriended him. Gratitude indeed was an emotion he could not support. He had bitten the hand that helped him, and stopped with mud mouths that had praised him. As a thinker he had been the most shameless shifter of his point of view, and each of his pronouncements on social questions and morality, science and religion had been made with the intolerance of blazing conviction. Every time he had changed his mind he had declared he alone was right, he alone was honest.

Whenever he had annexed the allegiance and admiration of a new public he had proceeded to champion with ferocity what his latest admirers most detested. He had been a complete example of the literary Ishmael. He had been a weather-cock prophet, though it was the winds within him, not those without, that blew him round and round and round. He seems to have been possessed by an itch to destroy confidence and affection not only in his private but in his literary life, and to have resolved to live in enmity with everyone far and near, while cursing perpetually the hideous injustice of such a fate. Yet as soon as he was dead his dying words came true: 'Now everything personal has been cancelled.' Something for which men honour men, and honour them above their steady benefactors, remained. What was it that made the wild hate-directed career of this misery-scattering self-torturer worth while?

That is the question for his critic. The obvious answer, 'Strindberg was a genius,' though comprehensive, is too vague. Undoubtedly Strindberg was what we call a 'genius,' and a prodigiously prolific one. He wrote fifty-six plays, nine novels, numerous autobiographical works, lyrical poems, newspaper articles, historical and scientific treatises (the latter were apparently worthless); and although his work was often slap-dash and sometimes crazy, however poor he might have been at the time of writing, there had never been a 'pot-boiler' among them. He could only write out of himself. As a young man, though he had the intellectual energy of ten, he was repeatedly ploughed in examinations, for he could not master, even in an elementary fashion, a subject not vitally exciting to him at the moment. And he could not write at all unless his passions were engaged. Strindberg's intellect only functioned at the command of his emotions. This is a characteristic common in writers, in whom 'genius' predominates over all their other faculties. He possessed amazing insight without the power of weighing evidence; an astoundingly vivid imagination without being a great artist.

It is now commonly agreed that literary inspiration, at any rate of the first order, draws upon the subconscious; and the faculty of tapping this source, combined with power, is what we usually mean when we use the word 'genius'. But it is a writer's gift for selecting from the contents of that 'backward and abyss' of thought and passion in himself that makes him an 'artist'. The images, intuitions and ideas, which at the waving of his mysterious wand peer from those depths, are by no means necessarily of equal or indeed of any value. The spectacle of a poet emerging from a header into his subconsciousness, glistening and triumphant with an old boot or fruit-can in his hand is not infrequent today. Such objects come no doubt from the right place, but they are of small consequence. Strindberg's drama (his fiction is nearly all autobiography) is diver's spoil. But if we compare the attitude of his conscious judgement towards such strange treasure to Ibsen's attitude (he also was an explorer of the subconscious), we see the difference between a 'genius' who is an 'artist' and a 'genius' who is not.

The Norwegian and the Swede were antagonists. Ibsen had often given woman the *beau rôle* in his plays, divining in her more friendliness to 'the natural good'; women were not, he thought, quite so liable as men to be led from it by their idealistic noses. *The Doll's House* had moreover been hailed as a manifesto in favour of Woman's Emancipation, and given impetus to a movement which of all contemporary movements was to Strindberg the most permanently detestable, the most exasperating, the most riddled with lies. Incidentally, suspicion-mania drove him also to the absurd conclusion that *The Doll's House* was a satire upon his own marriage. But even apart from that insult Ibsen remained for him the arch-betrayer of his sex who had glorified those witless vampires – women. He flew at Ibsen's literary throat, and he was formidable enough to make the older dramatist feel some uneasiness, which is expressed in the Master Builder's dread of 'the younger generation knocking at the door'. But oddly enough Ibsen himself used to keep Strindberg's photograph together with a small viper on his writing-table. He explained that he did not keep it there because he knew Strindberg or sympathized with him, but because 'he found he worked better under that madman's eyes'. So Ibsen too felt that 'something' to which Strindberg's funeral was a vague testimony: an impetuous, selfless, never-flagging courage in the pursuit of the adventures of the brain and heart. Those mad eyes were a challenge to Ibsen's own exploring curiosity and resolve to face all things and speak out. Strindberg possessed in perfection that sincerity which lies in being loyal to every mood; but in the sincerity which allows for moods changing and seeks a stable point of view, and leads a literary craftsman to allow for changing moods and to temper them to artistic ends, he was abnormally deficient. His conceptions had the vigour of those of a man who flings himself whole into every emotion, every intuition, as though each was his first and each would be his last.

Imagine a man of profound excitability, violent passions, blazing temper, uncontrollable fastidiousness, seeing only one thing at a time as the emotional storm within him permitted, in whom a craving to enjoy a chivalrous worship of women, and an adoration of woman as a mother, struggled with an intense susceptibility to her as a mistress; imagine him planted in a society where many women were on strike against maternity, jealous of men, eager to emulate them, sick of being idealized yet perpetually on the defensive against criticism; remember, too, that this man is an imaginative creator and more than a little mad, perpetually overworked, frequently hallucinated by absinthe, and physically as nervous as a shying horse; and there you have the conditions out of which Strindberg's work springs. They are not those likely to produce perfect works of art, or even truthful pictures of life. Strindberg's works have not those virtues. But what he can give us are his torments, his madness, his struggles, shattered gleams of his ideals, guesses at the motives of others, half insane and half amazingly acute. It is not a *pleasant* experience thus to suffer with Strindberg, for he has the power to make his reader feel as though he himself were fighting for his own honour and his own sanity. But one can learn a good deal from him if one keeps judgement cool; and one has, at least, while thrusting at Hell's phantoms in the dark, the glow of identifying oneself for the time being with a man of undefeated courage.

The two most important psychological facts about him, apart from his genius, were his liability to violent attacks of suspicion-mania, and his inability to get on with or without women. He married wife after wife. He did not know how to live with women or how to quarrel with them, how to make it up or how to break with them. They threw him into a state of agonized bewilderment, shot with flashes of piercing hate-directed insight. Much of his work may be described as the torments of a henpecked Bluebeard. Possessing the lucidity of genius, he could also suddenly collect himself and see himself as mad or as impossibly exacting. He rightly named his longest account of such an intimacy *The Confessions of a Fool*, or to translate its title more accurately, *The Self-Justification of a Lunatic*. Being a poet, he could sometimes invest scenes with the tatters of a lurid beauty, making you feel, 'O what a noble mind is here o'erthrown'. But he could never keep the personal aspects of his subjects far enough off from his emotions; nor ever rid himself of resentment towards the creatures of his imagination on account of their resemblance to people who had made him suffer and served him as models. His intensely vivid recollection of all he had felt enabled him to fill his characters with vitality, but once on their feet, he could not allow them, as an artist should, liberty to live, however balefully, as independent beings.

This is discernible in even his best plays, and it degrades them from the category of the great to that of the remarkable. (I have not read or seen his historical dramas; perhaps they and his dream-dramas are different.) His art judged as a whole is of that kind which is euphemistically called 'cathartic', and which tends to be unduly exalted in periods of literary experiment, like our own, when the most blatant literary egotism is admired, and a sense of the importance in art of qualities of intellect and feeling which we call by ethical names, magnanimity, nobility, disinterestedness, has become dim or confused.

Mr McGill's biography, which is largely a paraphrase in American English of Strindberg's autobiographical novels, insufficiently supported by information from other sources, leaves nevertheless a real impression of the tempestuous career of a man of genius; of one who, if he was merciless to others, also never spared himself – except in one respect: Strindberg never could bear to see himself as absurd. Mr McGill disentangles his complexes ('mother-complex' and 'inferiority complex'), not a difficult task since Strindberg treated himself as a subject for psycho-analysis long before such processes were even dreamt of. Mr McGill shows how in childhood his passions were tied into knots which were wrenched tighter afterwards. He declares that his 'absolutism' is the key to his character and writings, that is to say, his furious refusal ever to compromise or excuse. 'To have sought God, and found the Devil,' thus Strindberg summed up the result for him of this absolutism. He was a never-resting struggler; but a man who is all struggle, though he may be gigantic, cannot be great.

THE ARTISTIC
TEMPERAMENT*

There is a saying that everybody has one book in him worth reading, which looks like an encouragement to memoirists and autobiographers. It is only an indirect way of saying that truth, however humble, is always interesting. It suppresses the fact that it is difficult to tell, cannot be told indeed, unless a writer has avoided telling lies to himself long before he ever thought of writing down his memories. With the best will in the world you can no more sit down and tell the truth than you can suddenly write a poem. Memoirists and autobiographers therefore are prudent to rely upon the general interest of their facts and avoid self-revelation. The candour which can make that worth attempting is either a gift of the gods or the reward of a lifetime. Some achieve candour; others have candour thrust upon them – with what worthless results! – by their publishers; a few are born candid.

To achieve self-portraiture a man must be both self-complacent and detached. Unmitigated self-complacency has produced some amusingly transparent autobiographies, but

* Review of *Memoirs of a Polyglot* by William Gerhardi.

those who have written best about themselves are, as a rule, men who have taken their work, or something in themselves, so seriously, and are so self-satisfied in consequence, that they have ceased to care a rap what impression they make in other respects.

In Mr Gerhardi self-complacency and detachment are fortunately balanced, and his *Memoirs of a Polyglot* is consequently a real piece of self-revelation. It is also an entertaining book, full of wit, malice, vivid impressions of people who are talked about, pathos, literary criticism, and acute spontaneous comment upon character and life. It is the book of a man who has found his way through the world by the light of his own lamp.

Like Mr George Moore he was born candid, and his subtlety springs from a kind of childishness. Like the author of *Ave atque Vale*, he values one thing in himself so highly that he can do without our respect on all other accounts. He makes an impression of social irresponsibility, and of loyalty to the artist in himself. No doubt you could bribe Mr Gerhardi into writing a rotten book (indeed, he has had a shot at it), but nothing could make him think that book worth writing, and he would despise you more for thinking so or bribing him, than himself for writing it for money. Valuing himself for having preserved – without the smallest effort, by the by – his integrity of vision through life, he naturally takes a detached view of his general behaviour, and can record his faults, follies and failures with amusement or unblushing curiosity.

The literary artistic temperament is apt to strike others as a queer mixture of conceit and humility, heartlessness and sympathy. His fellow human-beings meet with a deeper response in such a man than in others, yet he can do without them. He appropriates their joys and lets their sufferings prey on his mind and devour his nerves, and yet he may feel no obligation towards them. If he dissects them as though they were nothing to him, he is also prepared to destroy his joy in his own most precious emotions for the sake of a little clearer knowledge of life. If he cannot spare others, at any rate he cannot spare himself. This is perhaps why mankind tolerate in their midst this uncomfortable creature, who will not join one of the conspiracies or loyalties which tend to make things easier: though he may take bribes, he is unbribable. Even if you frighten him for a time, the truth may any day come snivelling out of him. This is not moral courage, in which he may be lamentably deficient, but he is so made that he cannot be interested in life, or do his work, on any other terms. He may be the most selfish of men, but willy-nilly he is compelled to be selfless in his work. In this book you will find the reflection of this temperament.

It is no surprise to learn that Mr Gerhardi, who was born of British parents in Russia, where he remained till the Revolution ruined his father, was considered the dunce of his family. Naturally, he would not take notice of the same things as other people; he could not help attending instead to what did not matter. And it was the same when he became a Derby recruit:

In the army, however, individuality is not encouraged. 'Jeerady,' the drill sergeant would shout, 'you innerve me.' Or, with reference to my equivocal movements, the hesitant figure I cut on the parade ground, he called me 'that Chinese puzzle'. My inefficiency was not cunningly planned, but was pure lack of interest in my surroundings. As in childhood I was unable to devote attention to that which others considered important, but unconsciously stored away trifles which illustrated particular aspects of the general, so here also I would note individual aspects which illustrated the tragic comedy of mankind at war. So interested was I in the expression of the drill sergeant's face that he said: 'I've got a picture of meself in me pocket. I'll show it to ye afterwards.' In a thundering voice: 'And *now* will you look to yer front!'

[235]

It is clear that he has been dodging 'the wrath of the collective spirit' all his life; in the family, in the Army, in official employment, at Oxford, in society. And, under cover of a mild propitiatory helplessness, he has escaped uncaught: no surrender, but no painful consequences. He has saved himself by appearing 'hopeless', thus preserving his faculties for their proper end. He has even escaped from the jaws of overwhelming patronage. A newspaper magnate took him up and carried him about in yachts and *trains de luxe*, told him he was a genius, attempted to make the fortune of 'Futility', dumped him down like a bag, took him up again, and left him, so to speak, in the cloak-room. Has all this made any difference to him? No: receptive but unalterable, he has been equally interested in the rise of his hopes and the flatness of his disappointment, while remaining as impartially observant of his patron as though he had never been either kind or indifferent.

When he flew to India with the Maharanee of Cooch Behar, and the flying-boat smashed on the rocks and the water gushed in, his feeling was: 'So this can happen to oneself also. Good God, how strange!' and he was inclined to remonstrate with Fate, 'This airplane trip was only a lark, you know; you really can't think of killing me for that.' And when someone shouted, 'Ladies first!' it became clear to him that it was most important *he* should not perish.

But sheer good manners kept me in check: I stood still and deferred to several passengers, through no love of my fellow-creatures, but dislike of panic and the fear of showing fear. . . . Nobody praised me; they were preoccupied with themselves. But I had merited my own approbation for behaving with composure. At the slightest encouragement I might have sacrificed my life, for of such emotion heroes are made. Or my nerves might have betrayed me. I don't know. Clearly, it would have been touch and go. It is fitting, therefore, that the deeds of heroes be immortalized in the memory of men, for their own exaltation lasts but a moment at the price of a lifetime.

The last comment is characteristic. Perhaps now, even without reading the book, you may begin to have an inkling of the author's detachment, which sometimes expresses itself as sharp irony, sometimes as delicate sympathy. It enables him also to sum up the situation in India better than most people who have studied it. What struck Mr Gerhardi was a feeling abroad in the country not unlike that which he had sensed in Russia on the eve of the revolution: 'Inarticulate, unfocused dissatisfaction with the present state of things, and no very workable alternative to take its place.' He noticed the morbid feeling of inferiority in the educated Indians towards the ruling English race; the divided feelings of the princes in attempting to reconcile their hurt pride with their interests which are protected by British rule; and he observed that 'the intellectual lucidity (though I should hesitate to call it vigour) of the Indians is insulted by the incurable hypocrisy of a certain English type (ridiculed by Bernard Shaw) who must needs identify his own interests with the supposed good of others.'

India's attitude towards England is like that of an adolescent daughter who can live neither with nor without her mother. And the position of the Viceroy is not unlike that of a mother of a young girl on board my homeward boat who complained to me that, whenever she corrected her daughter, the daughter did not answer back, but withdrew into herself or walked away – the attitude, I suppose, which old Tolstoy termed 'non-resistance to evil'. What, asked the conscientious mother, could she do with a daughter who met well-intentioned criticism with 'no cooperation' tactics? 'Give her a good hiding,' advised a passenger. 'What! For no apparent cause! The whole ship looking on! Never! Besides, don't forget, she is now seventeen. And if I hurt her she would dislike me more than ever.' . . . One thing emerges clearly: There is nothing to be done – and we are the very men to do it. That is, to 'hang on' to India, tentatively, complaisantly, almost absent-mindedly, while the Indians, a nation of barristers, exhaust themselves in garrulousness – hang on to India till the time comes when England will feel, without undue sentimental regret, that it is just as well, all things considered, to be rid of India. Since one day, 'in the fullness of time', there will be neither gratitude nor material advantage to be got from staying there any longer. . . . But we who believe in the recuperative, adaptive, improvising genius of the British race view the future with – yes, equanimity. To face realities, to deaden the shock, to bridge precipices is, after all, the essence of statecraft.

This is surely good sense, as good as any that has been written about the Indian situation. It shows, too, the value of detachment in practical affairs. But I am anxious about the future effects of such detachment upon Mr Gerhardi's creative power. A literary artist, besides being in a sense immune from experience, must also be at the mercy of it, so that he cannot tell afterwards whether he has owed more to the naïve impulses which drove him to meet life, or to the aloofness which softly and inevitably disentangled him again. In Mr Gerhardi artistic detachment has been reinforced by cultural rootlessness. There is therefore a danger that he may not care enough about anything except his work, to save that from becoming thin and fantastic. It seems to me rather ominous that he should already see in Proust's attitude towards experience a reflection of his own. Spontaneous response to life alone can nourish creation: he is too young to put up the Proustian shutters and regard the outside world as existing only for the sake of its reflection in his private *camera obscura*. The problem of every 'poet' (Mr Gerhardi prefers this word in the Greek sense to 'artist') is to strike a balance between devotion to his art and love for their own sakes of the things which feed it. Where that balance lies, depends upon the nature of his talents. If he loves life too much, he will never assimilate it properly; if he lives for his art alone, he will have next to nothing to write about.

LITERARY SNOBS

Dear Literary Snobs (how many of my readers will, I wonder, consider themselves as personally addressed? I think about fifteen hundred ought to do so – and among those will be many whose literary enthusiasms are most intense), if it were not for you, writers would receive less thrilling encouragement. You have introduced into the life of letters something of the excitement of politics or the Stock Exchange; those violent vicissitudes of fortune which, if they depress, also exhilarate and console, though they embitter. If after years of moderate renown an excellent author suddenly finds himself extremely famous, it is chiefly your doing. Your enthusiastic imaginations are the workshops where haloes, pedestals, animated busts, and ample, though not perhaps immensely lavish, royalties are manufactured. Only, the initiative is never yours. The diffidence of your separate judgements is as obvious as the genuine fervour of your collective admiration – fickle indeed but ardent, when once a suitable recipient has been recommended. Like Wordsworth's cloud, you 'move all together if you move at all'. But though it may safely be said that you never choose the recipient yourselves, the glow, the glory of the sunburst which sometimes surrounds the cloaked figure of the lone literary traveller (usually toward the end of his journey) is nearly always your work. Sometimes indeed those rays are positively scorching, so that the traveller's reputation begins to wither even while it ripens; and the very critics who most rejoiced to see fame thus following the pointing of their fingers, turn churlish and uneasy at the sight of such – of so much – docility. If they do not start blowing cold themselves, they will at any rate probably begin to remind you that your beneficent rays might be a little more evenly distributed. This is one of your great faults, that you ever exalt your chosen one to a pitch past bearing by those who compare and remember. A critical reaction inevitably results, and with it, round again you veer. How depressing it is, how disturbing to the judgement,

> When among the world's loud gods
> Our god is noised and sung!

I do not blame you; you can't help it. Still, it is hard on the traveller who has discarded his cloak to bask in adulation, that while he is perhaps actually mopping a grateful brow and murmuring, 'Too kind, too kind,' the sun should suddenly go in, and a chill from a quickly-blackening east should strike him. Small wonder if he then grows suspicious and mutters darkly of conspiracies against him; no one can stand his reputation being blown out and burst like a paper bag, unless he knows you for the flibbertigibbets that you are.

Your enthusiasms, your salaams, your acrobatic prostrations, your chops and changes have made me feel very old, older than my years. It is not natural that I should have seen quite so many literary reputations flourish and fade: I am not approaching my ninetieth year. And yet it is not a series of hasty blunders, which you have had, as hastily, to retrieve. No; your enthusiasms (thanks to a few good guides) have been, though sometimes excessive, nearly always admirably directed.

Tennyson, Browning, Carlyle, Swinburne, Meredith, Henry James, and now Thomas Hardy – these writers are worthy of admiration. You are not to be blamed for falling in love with them one after the other. It is the glory of the amateur to be susceptible. If there has been sin in you, it has been rather the sin of Amnon, who, after having eaten of the cakes that Tamar made, and having loved her, threw her away. You remember the passage? It is one of the most impressively moral passages in the Old Testament (II Samuel 13): 'Then Amnon hated her exceedingly; so that the hatred wherewith he hated her was greater than the love wherewith he had loved her. And Amnon said unto her, Arise, be gone.'

You know how those words are ever on your lips; how you cannot admire Dickens without abusing Thackeray, nor Dostoevsky, without directing destructive sniffs at Flaubert or Turgenev. To hear you talk about Tennyson at the present moment, one would think he never wrote a better line than,

The little town
Had seldom seen a costlier funeral.

Meredith, whose heightened reflection of the beauty and courage of life seemed to you, not so long since, to eclipse older novelists, you made, before he died, the Grand Old Man of English Letters. But now – 'Arise, be gone!' Ruskin and his magnificent prose? – 'Arise, be gone!' Carlyle (a writer born to the use of words if there ever was one)? Swinburne, who once made your judgement reel with his winding, surging melodies? 'Arise, be gone!' Those of you who are fascinated by recent attempts to compress poetry into hard, bleak conversational speech, invariably assert, I notice, that Milton was no poet – apparently without suspecting that this is a silly thing to say. Some of you have been arrested lately by the queer intensity of negroid art. Well, you have enlarged your aesthetic experience, and that is always worth doing. But you cannot express the satisfaction that a little dark pot-bellied squat-legged image gives you, without declaring that Phidias is a duffer. 'Arise, be gone!'

You have met in life emotionally poor natures who have only a sufficient stock of amity for one friend at a time; who, in order to make a new friend, must drop an old one. They are never sane judges of human nature. You resemble them aesthetically. Your minds are like little buckets which must be emptied of enthusiasm before they can be filled again, and you spend your lives running backwards and forwards from the well to the sink.

I should like, however, to end this letter on a more friendly note. It is true that your literary judgements are not interesting, but you get a great deal of fun out of your rapid revulsions and temporary admirations – and fun is human. Moreover, if you are always ludicrously unfair, you are at any rate unstinting in praise while giving it, which is, in a way, amiable. Well, now, I will give you a few tips after your hearts. You know how exhilarating it is to be among the first to scramble into the train of the latest literary fashion, and how depressing it is to find you have only got in at the last moment and will have to bundle out at the next stop. You know your fatal love of making G.O.M.'s. You were right to glorify the delicate art of Henry James; but you didn't sit long in the Jacobean train, did you? You are right to admire Hardy; but get out before the smash comes, before the aesthetic *sauve qui peut* begins. The smash will come, because no author can sustain the reputation of being 'the one and only'. Critics will point out that, though Hardy has a profound tragic sense, he often tries to express it through crudest melodrama; that though he writes with lovely originality, his books are full of inept sentences, such as, 'There was not a point in the milkmaid that was not deep rose-colour'; and that though he has written five or six perfect poems, most are only quaint lamenting tunes drawn from an old snoring 'cello. And then . . . well, you know how easily you are stampeded. Now, the

Tennyson train and the Walter Pater train are, on the other hand, practically empty; get your corner seats now, and you will have a nice long run.

LITERARY BOOMS

The other day I was walking down the Strand with a friend. He has written many books and some are very good indeed. Even those which died a natural death in infancy contained pages which showed what he could do, and an individuality of phrase which makes those who love his best books like even his worst. In short, he has a solid reputation.

We passed a poster; his name was on it in large black letters. He made a grimace. 'Angels and ministers of grace defend us!' he exclaimed, 'I hope I am not going to have a Boom.'

'What! don't you want to make money?' I said. 'Why, only half an hour ago, while we were sitting over lunch, didn't you say that you wished that a little man, bent double under a sack of gold would come in and dump it at your feet? And there is,' I said, pointing to the vendor of papers, who was holding the poster like an apron in front of him, 'there is the little old man, and you won't look at him!'

'A Boom,' he replied, 'is fatal to a man like me. Only the greatest can survive a Boom. When Goethe wrote *The Sorrows of Werther* all Europe wept and went into ecstasies, and Napoleon took it with him on campaigns. Goethe survived his Boom, I admit. *Pickwick* had a prodigious Boom, and Dickens towered till he died. But they were men of the first magnitude, and notice this, they were young, very young, when it happened. Goethe was twenty-one; Dickens twenty-three. Byron was a youth when *Childe Harold* made him a popular idol – "O the ivy and myrtle of sweet two and twenty!" The richest mines in them were unworked; they had immense surprises in them still, and how rich those treasure were!

'But a Boom for a middle-aged man like me, who has already expressed himself, is simply fatal. It may mean a year or so of big cheques and gratifying fuss, but afterwards heart-breaking, draggle-tailed disappointment. It means people will soon be sick of me; that they will take up my newest book with an unconscious prejudice against it. Everything that can be said in praise of my work having been said again and again, the intelligent will set to work to interest the public in their own cleverness by displaying my faults. I shall become a mark for detraction. If I repeat myself (and we are all musical boxes with a set of tunes), even with improvement, the public will still be told that my latest book is not a patch on my early ones. And the young (one minds this) will begin to hate the very sight of my name. They will chuck me with joy into the limbo of overrated reputations. No, thank you, no Boom, please, for me. It wouldn't, in the long run, even pay me in money. A hit to the boundary is all very well, but a Boom is "lost ball", six and out – I believe that's how the little boys score in Battersea Park cricket.'

I was impressed by the energy of his protest, and when we parted I reflected on literary Booms. How brief they were! That was the first thing that struck me; next, that they were getting briefer and briefer as the *machine à la gloire* became more resonant and effective. I had already seen the reputations of many novelists and poets, splendid spreading growths like Jonah's gourd, wither away. How unnecessarily cruel it was! I remembered how Stephen Phillips had once been hailed as the greatest of modern poets. The elderly pundits, whom the quality of his verse had reminded of the poetry which had thrilled them in their youth (it is horribly true, we only really understand the poetry we loved before we were twenty-five), had acclaimed him. I recalled, too, the silence which followed their fanfaronnades upon Fame's trumpet, and the contempt of the young generation for poor Phillips. I thought of X and Y and Z, of A and B. There was a whole alphabet of them! I remembered how hard it had been to get the generation which followed that which adulated Tennyson to recognize even his most indubitable beauties. I marked in myself a tendency to curl my mind into a prickly ball like a hedgehog when a work of some incessantly belauded contemporary came into my hands.

Then I thought of Martin Tupper. Byron said he awoke one morning to find himself famous; Martin Tupper awoke one morning to find himself a laughing-stock. And what a Boom he had had! He had sold many more thousands of the *Proverbial Philosophy* than ever Byron sold of *Childe Harold*. The *Spectator*, in reviewing it, said: 'Martin Tupper has won for himself the vacant throne waiting for him amidst the immortals, and, after a long and glorious term of popularity among those who know when their hearts are touched, has been adopted by the suffrage of mankind and the final decree of publishers into the same rank with Wordsworth, and Tennyson, and Browning.' The *Court Journal* declared it to be 'a book as full of sweetness as a honeycomb, of gentleness as a woman's heart; in its wisdom worthy of the disciple of Solomon, in its genius the child of Milton.'

'If men delight to read Tupper both in England and America, why', asked The *Saturday Review*, 'should they not study him both in the nineteenth and twentieth centuries?' The *Daily News* wrote: 'The imagination staggers in attempting to realize the number of copies of his works which have been published abroad . . . he may now disregard criticism.'

Alas, in his later years, this must have been hard to do. Lord

Melbourne had made him an FRS; the Court had patronized him; society had idolized him; the press had eulogized him; wherever he went he had received what he calls himself 'palatial welcomes'. 'I have experienced almost annually,' he writes in his autobiography, 'the splendid hospitalities of the Mansion House and most of the City Companies.' The Prince Consort invited him to Buckingham Palace. 'Ladies', he tells us, 'claimed him as an unseen friend.' He was so nearly being made a peer that with prudent foresight he had coronets painted on his dinner service.

Suddenly the bubble of reputation burst. Obscurity descended on him like an extinguisher. Years afterwards, writing in 1886 (he lived to be nearly as old as Queen Victoria), he mentions as a curious fact that 'it is taken for granted that the author of *Proverbial Philosophy* has been dead for generations.' He tells us how he and his daughter were at a party where someone, on hearing her name, had asked her if she were descended from the famous Martin Tupper, and how, on her pointing to her father, the inquirer had started as though he had seen a ghost. He had seen a ghost. For years Tupper had been leading a posthumous existence, and a posthumous existence of the most unpleasant kind. He had become an emblem of the fatuous-sublime, of early-Victorian absurdity; he was referred to as unconsciously, cruelly, and cursorily as if he had been a character in a book. Poor old man! Boom! There is something ominous in the very word. Boom! Boom! Boom! Listen, it is the sound of a cannon shattering reputations!

REVIEWERS
AND PROFESSORS

The English Muse is a commentary on English poetry from the earliest to modern times, excluding that of poets still alive. It is a book of 423 pages, and those not crowded ones. Considering the magnitude of the subject, it must therefore, be classified as a rapid review of it. Professor Elton would have exceeded the six volumes of his admirable *Survey of English Literature from 1730 to 1830*, had he attempted to discuss the origins of the poetry of each period; the social, moral, and intellectual influences which produced it. His latest book is a collection of comments on English poets arranged in chronological order. What he has aimed at is defining, and illustrating by brief quotation, the art of each poet in turn. It need not be read consecutively, yet it is not a book of reference. The purpose it serves is different and important. It is a book which it would be profitable to consult before reading, or, above all, before writing about, any of the poets mentioned in it. It contains concise statements of the qualities for which each poet was most remarkable. I can suggest its usefulness best by recording a reverie into which I fell after reading in it.

It seemed that I was again literary editor of the *New*

Statesman, and confronted with one of the many young men who were anxious in those days to obtain reviewing from me.

Editor (after examining applicant's credentials, all excellent): 'What sort of books do you think you could review best?'

Young Reviewer: 'Oh, well, history and biography, criticism – *belles lettres* of course, and fiction and poetry.'

Editor (mournfully, burying his face in his hands): 'You all say that. It tells me nothing, nothing – except that you are fond of reading. Many people are.' (Then, brightening a little) 'May I tell you how you ought to have approached me? If you want to get work on a paper, start by posing as a specialist. It may be bounce, but the standard of erudition is not high, and if you only *take trouble to read up your subject while reviewing a book upon it* – unless you have been foolish enough to pose as a specialist on a subject in which thorough grounding is essential – you can usually put up a fair show of knowing something about it. It is useless your coming up here and telling me that you can review five-sixths of the books that come out. When I asked you what you could do, you ought to have said: "Well, I've read a good deal in a general way, but I'm afraid I can only write about Jamaica – and, oddly enough, Sir Philip Sidney . . . Oh yes, *and* Disraeli."

'Do you see what might happen then? The editor, it might be myself or another, would be inclined to believe you capable of reviewing books on just a few subjects. He might try you at once with, say, a new edition of *Astrophel and Stella*, and if you got up the subject thoroughly and made a good job of it, when a Life of Drayton or a collection of Elizabethan sonnets came out, he would perhaps send you those books too. You would have begun to establish yourself as a reviewer of Elizabethan literature, outside drama – already a fairly wide field. Then, if you had also taken trouble, consulted the Encyclopaedia, visited public libraries, and had bounced him in the matter of the review of a History of Jamaica, then, since the editorial mind is streamily associative, you might have gradually established a lien on books upon Sugar, Negroes, British Colonies, Tropical Scenery, Governor Eyre and Carlyle, Giant Fish, and what not. Your claim to know something about Disraeli might, in the same way, have led to ramifications – to Gladstone, Corn Laws, Oratory, the Berlin Congress in one direction, and to political satire, Victorian fiction and Heaven knows what in the other. In short, starting from three subjects, you would have been on the way to obtaining that roving commission to comment on books at large to which your intelligence, no doubt, but not your knowledge, entitles you.'

At these words the dejected countenance of the applicant rose before me, and I added, 'Well, I'll give you a trial in spite of your not having bounced me. You are exactly in the position I was at your age. You are enthusiastically and ignorantly interested in literature. Your enthusiasm is to the good; your ignorance to the bad. But that can be overcome – if you condescend to crib from critics who know much more than you do. You say you can review criticism and poetry. Here is a monograph on Webster – try your hand at that. You have read *The Duchess of Malfi.*.? Good. His other plays?'

Young Reviewer: 'No; one need not drink a cask of wine to sample a vintage.'

Editor: 'Quite so. Yet one can't value a house by peeping into the dining-room window. You had better see what the house-surveyors have to say. An editor does not want merely *your* reaction to Webster. I can't fill these columns week after week with thoughtful idiosyncratic nonsense. You must find out, as well, what *others* have thought and felt about him. Your own sensibility is to the good – I don't want macadamized reviews. But you must also consult the Professors. And, if it came to a choice, I would rather that you took your review wholesale from them than *entirely* out of your own head; though the good review springs from both sources. Yes; if you are going to be a literary reviewer you must start by acquiring a Library of Criticism. You must lay down the Professors. Whom do you suppose

Professors Saintsbury, Grierson, Elton, Mackail, Raleigh, Ker, wrote their books for? If you imagine that they wrote for pupils, you are mistaken. They wrote in order to keep people like you and me *straight*. They believe in learning and culture. There-fore, when I send you a book on a literary subject, go first to the Professors. They are men with a passion for literature which (you may find this difficult to believe) probably once exceeded your own. But being, however, in positions of responsibility they could never allow themselves – simply because, say, they admired Dryden – to sniff at Milton. They had to cultivate a sense of proportion. And to be of any use to me, *you* must show it – even before you have earned the right to it. Meanwhile, be humble – crib.'

Then, in my reverie, I found myself antedating this book by Professor Elton. 'Here', I said, 'is a book which will help you. Suppose I were to send you a book on Drayton? I could hardly expect you to read Drayton's works through before reviewing it. (You would starve.) But I bet anything all you know of Drayton now is a sonnet or two, "Since there's no help, come let us kiss and part", etc. You would therefore do well to look at his *Nymphidia*, keeping what Elton says of it in mind; "everything is on the midget scale, has the precision and matter-of-factness that children ask for in such stories". You have probably come across Drayton's "Ballad of Agincourt" in Henley's *Lyra Heroica*. But you had better note that *The Virginian Voyage*, which you have never read, recalls Marvell's *Bermudas* and follow Professor Elton's summary:

Drayton's poetry is like a broad low plateau singular and pleasant to explore, though it sinks away into featureless plain; with a rich flora, often beautiful, and always strongly rooted; with many streams and meadows, and fairy rings where little beings can be watched at their tournaments; and with a high crest or two, jutting up abruptly. It is all good travelling, for the devout.

'That's central. Make for the centre – though, as an ignoramus,
I know you've no right to: I'd rather print the truth than what is
original any day. Suppose I send you a new edition of Suckling
to review – "natural easy Suckling"? *You* don't know that
Congreve's Millamant praised him admirably, but Elton does.
You don't know either that Lovelace in his *Lines to Lucasta* spoilt
one of them, by altering it in a later edition, from "the birds that
wanton in the air" to "the gods", significantly condescending to
fashion – but Elton *does*. Crib from him. That is what he is there
for; that's why he wrote – to make the culture of the average
critic a little more thorough.

'Do you want to write about Hudibras Butler? You will
probably wish to distinguish his merits, without ignoring them,
from those of greater satirists; well, Elton will help you. He will
draw your attention to the purely intellectual interest of Butler's verse, to his habit of mind at once "detached and destructive". And so on down the poets. Beddoes? Listen: "Often his
words are parted, by that thinnest film which makes all the
difference, from a pure series of beautiful sounds." There's a
theme for you! And it will be Elton who gave it you. Beddoes's
resemblance to Poe as well as to the Elizabethans? You'll find it
hinted at. Tennyson? You don't know that "Tears idle tears"
and "Now sleeps the crimson petal" were "a *new* species of
lyrics springing at once into perfection" – you haven't read
enough. And, again, note the importance of "the wonderful
surface in Tennyson's work, which, as in Pope's, covers a
varying depth of soil". You will react to Tennyson and dozens
of poets as a man from Mars, if you are not nudged. Buy this
book. I won't employ you unless you read the Professors. They
– we – are coral insects building the reef that protects the lagoon
of literature from the restless sea of nonsense and confusion.
Strong waves will burst against it, and part of them foam
over. That is well; but the reef must be built. If you are not
content to be an insect too, I won't employ you, and you
must try your luck as a genius. My dear, the sensibility of

your own generation is only the tick of a minute-hand. If you set up to read the clock, you must watch the hour-hand as well.'

ETON

Books that I have read are like old diaries to me. I find my old self in their pages. Do I want to be back in my School Library?* I have only to open some book I first read there and as I allow my mind to wander, I see again the long book-lined room; the busts, the model of the Acropolis, the large diamond-paned windows, the leather-topped tables, and the attitudes of the boys sitting at them. I hear the whispers and suppressed giggles. Again I see the look of well-simulated amazement on the face of the precise, tiny Librarian, when someone brings a Greek Lexicon down on the bowed head of a fellow-student. Do I wish to recall those twenty minutes of peaceful solitude (tea-time in my own room) between cooking for my fag-master and carrying up three flights of leaded stairs cans of hot water for his bath, and then running through dark streets to pupil-room? Well, I need only open some novel like *The Deemster* and dream upon its pages. Instantly I am in the past again. Back it comes to me: the look and smell of my indigestible new loaf,

* Before the South African War Memorial was built the School Library used to be on the upper storey of the New Schools.

whose doughy centre, well-squeezed, made such an excellent missile; its crust, which was a mere pretext for huge dollops of jam; my printed red-flannelette table-cloth, and even that after-football feeling in my legs – if I had played well, such a delicious tingle!

Eton is very great, very big, very old and very rich; certainly far more reminiscences of Eton are published than of any other school. This is not astonishing, for Eton stands near the main thoroughfare of the world, and often catches the eye; while her own public is the largest for which books of this special kind are written. Nevertheless I, who was at Eton, am sometimes made uneasy by the tone of these books. Many seem to take for granted that the greater public, if it does not share the Eton sense of proportion, will at any rate try hard to do so, and that they will all be glad to pretend for a while to be old Etonians. This does not appear to be unnatural, but experience has taught me that it is not always the case. I have been sometimes embarrassed by such books, as we are sometimes embarrassed abroad by the confident yet very proper sentiments of a fellow-countryman. Could I read a book describing the appearance and analysing the temperament of old 'Biped Brown' of Marlborough, or 'Pinker Dickson' of Winchester? Frankly, no. My inability is shown by the fact that I have actually had to invent these striking personalities; for, with the exception of 'Bowen of Harrow', I do not know even the name, let alone the nick-name, of one bygone master at any school but my own. I feel sure such ignorance is reciprocated by old boys of other schools.

I have just been reading Mr Percy Lubbock's *Shades of Eton*. Some of the figures, which do not require even a touch from his elegant pen to live for me, which need only be named to rise as vividly before my eyes as Nelson or Mr Micawber, must surely appear empty of significance to any but Etonians. How, then, are these unfortunates to know when Mr Lubbock has deftly hit off some characteristic? What interest would there be to the public were I to venture to correct his drawing, say, of a nose? These rhetorical questions answer themselves, or will be answered by my silence about those parts of the book which could not fail to be interesting to Etonians, but to them alone. *Shades of Eton* is, however, much more than a gallery of such portraits. It is, from one aspect, a self-effacing man's story of his own education, and raises questions of wider interest. It can be read as a book about Eton, or as a chapter of autobiography, or as a subtle discussion of public-school and classical education. Fortunate is the reader who can read it from these three points of view at once.

Mr Lubbock is one of the comparatively few contemporary prose-writers of whom it can be said that he has thoroughly mastered his craft. He writes with a beautiful precision. The suavity and the subtlety at which he aims he attains; though the kind of perceptions which he wishes to record are by no means always easy to convey. He can express his own sense of the beauty of outward things; and where character is concerned he has learnt the art of insinuating without being treacherous, of being even very kind without being very vague. His imagination in retrospect is deeply tinged with 'piety' in the Roman sense of the word. Close contact with Henry James may well have deepened in him this mode of feeling – Henry James who was so horrified at the offhand wasteful callousness of the world, and whose imagination often liked to rest beside considerate, scrupulous people in the quiet garden of tradition. I seldom notice in Mr Lubbock's use of words the imprint of that influence, but I detect it in his distrust of bare statements. In Henry James, revulsion from such statements, when they might hurt, led him into periphrastic and metaphorical hesitations which by delaying a perhaps fatal verdict often made it in the end more crushing. Thus in conversation when he had done speaking one was sometimes reminded of that comment upon Renan: '*le plus doux des hommes cruels*'. And yet Henry James was not cruel. He had a merciless eye and a tender heart, and in a style of delicate and prolonged ingenuity he strove to combine the reports of the one with the promptings of the other.

Mr Lubbock, also, is a writer of complex sensibility, but he attains unity by refraining rather than by combining. His charming book *Earlham* suffered in a measure from a too uniform diffusion of 'piety' and sweetness, and the *Shades of Eton* are bathed, to my understanding, in too still and golden an air. I suspect him of having explored his past only where he could bless and praise. A writer so sensitive, so responsive to whatever in our precarious muddled state of being is gracious, ordered, gentle and safe, must have been frequently excruciated at a public school; and a boy so precociously alert must have seen many shortcomings in those who educated him. But of such excruciations and such defects there are few traces in the story of Mr Lubbock's education, only a hint or two that he was often far from happy during it. It may seem odd, at first, that one who like myself enjoyed wildly every day of his school life – except, of course, those black intermittent days on which carelessly-provoked calamities trod him down – should complain of such omissions. Yet, after all, it is not strange. Whatever has given us massive satisfaction we can afford to criticize with ungracious freedom.

Mr Lubbock says that he who tells us he was happy at Eton tells us much about himself but nothing about the school. This is not so true as he thinks. If different kinds of boys are happy at a school, it tells us something most important about it. He and I were, I think, contemporaries, and yet in a sense we were not at the same school. His Eton is composed entirely of masters and traditions, mine of boys and places. He was educated by masters, I by boys.

This difference is a typical one, and one which confuses the whole discussion about public-school education. The boy-educated – and they are the majority – cannot understand these pedagogic heart-searchings. Mr Lubbock reports Arthur Benson as saying sadly, 'But we don't educate these boys.' 'I should think not,' the boy-educated is inclined to reply, rather impatiently. 'How can a handful of masters educate in any intense manner a thousand boys or more?' One young mind out of ten they can affect, certainly not more. Masters must, of course – and they can – prevent the community from degenerating into squalor, and drum some elementary information into those thousand heads; but what more can they do? And, after all, would more be generally desirable? There are grave deficiencies in the education of boys by boys, but the adultly-educated often suffer from a drawback: they cannot henceforth get on with, or get anything out of, anyone as young as themselves. There is something so restful and gratifying in the companionship and approval of a mature mind that they cannot afterwards stand the sharp illuminating crudity of their own generation. This, too, may be a disadvantage.

When I talk to a dog I am sometimes reminded of myself and my masters. Nothing could be seemingly more responsive than the dog; but at the sound of a distant bark its whole being is suddenly possessed by the quiver of a very different attention; I am forgotten. I, too, could once only attend to barks. I could be made for a few seconds to sit up with pendent paws for a biscuit, and if scratched behind the ears I capered and ran in circles with delight; when my masters talked to me I heard them, but I only listened to barks. Reviewing my contemporaries, this seems to have been the case with most of them. The yapping and baying and growling and belling, to me the most exquisite of concerts, is a pandemonium against even the memory of which Mr Lubbock stops his ears. Indeed, I can only recognize *his* Eton by recalling the impressions of my subsequent visits. Then I see that this master contributed this kind of culture, that one that; but I should never have known it had I not gone back. The doors which opened for him upon refuges, and revelations, and intervals of happiness, were doors I never even saw. Do I regret it? Hardly; there was so much outside – besides, I walked in later on. And yet we are both grateful to our school! That boys so different can both be grateful does tell others something important about it.

Some of the most enchanting and penetrating pages of this book are a discourse upon the value of that old-fashioned scholarship which transmutes the classics into something quite unlike themselves; presenting them not as expressions of human passions and adventures in thought, but as those queer static things, *books*. 'The Greeks and Romans, indeed, were remarkably trimmed and chastened', Mr Lubbock truly says, 'before they could settle down in the valley of the Thames.' 'To what purpose', he asks, 'have you loved those adventures of genius if you aren't a terror to all quiet minds? Others may dream and moon in repose upon a time-approved culture; but the learned Grecian is a man, he must be, of a restless and realistic temper, keen, mobile, immodest, grasping the good gift of life with avid hands. There is an image, indeed, of the scholar of Eton!' And yet Mr Lubbock has something to say, and to say exquisitely, in explanation of this process of domesticating the Classics, though he marvels at its queerness. But he does not marvel so much at the oddity of the actual process of imparting that culture to boys – and that is what I remember best.

I am again in a large, half-panelled room. At a raised desk sits a man in a university gown, and in front of him sprawl between thirty and forty little boys: the air hums with innumerable subdued noises. One of the boys is suddenly called upon to construe. After a hurried consultation with his neighbour he stands up with an air of apparent alacrity:

'*O Venus* – oh, Venus – *regina* – queen – *Cnidi Paphique* – of Cnidus and Paphus.'

'Os, os,' interrupts the master mildly.

'*Sperne* – spurn – *dilectam Cypron* – delectable Cyprus – *et* – and . . .'

'Well, go on, go on.'

'I can't find the verb,' says the small boy – then, suddenly, as though it had been dodging about, 'I've got it! *Transfer!* transfer

– *te* – thyself – *decoram in aedem* – to' (his voice quavers interrogatively) 'to the . . . decorated house?'

'Come, come. You know better than that. You know what *dulce et decorum est pro patria mori* means: It is sweet and fitting to die for one's country.'

'The well-fitted house?' the small boy suggests, smiling to make up for a possible blunder. The master smiles too: 'No, no. The word suggests reverence, something almost sacred. The adjective together with the noun, the phrase *decoram in aedem* really means a 'shrine', or, if you like, 'gracious house' would do here. Go on.' The small boy's eyes meanwhile have been fixed in absent-minded wonder of his face.

'*Vocantis Glycerae*' (should he risk it?) – 'of shouting Glycerine.' (General titters.)

'If you play the fool you'll sit down and write out the lesson. Sit down.'

'But, sir!'

'Sit down!'

'But, sir, *vocantis* does mean shouting or calling.'

'Sit down! I'll go on construing. Follow carefully and bring me a translation tomorrow. This is poetry "Of Glycera who invokes thee, *multo ture* – with much – or perhaps better – with a wealth of incense. *Fervidus tecum puer* – with thee may thy glowing boy." Who was her glowing boy?' (General mild astonishment.)

'Yes, who was the son of Venus?'

'Oh, Cupid,' another boy, lolling on hip and elbow, answers contemptuously.

'Cupid, of course. "With thee may thy glowing boy and the Graces and the Nymphs with unloosened zones" – are you following? – "hasten hither, and Youth, who lacking thee is not charming."' Here the master coughs, and ends rather lamely with 'And Mercury.'

'Quite a party,' says the small boy who has been made to sit down. (Laughter.)

'You will write out the lesson twice.'

'But, sir!'

'If you speak again you will write it out four times. Come up for a Yellow Ticket afterwards.'

Such were our frontal mass-attacks day after day, week after week, month after month, year after year, upon the barrier of that ancient language. How few of us won through to the scholar's ilex-grove and the placid fields of asphodel!

THE FIRST
WORLD WAR

I

August 4th 1914:
Nature, I believe, meant me to be a special reporter, but she forgot to endow me with the knack of being 'on the spot'. But sometimes so much worth noticing is going on everywhere that it matters little where you are. The night of August 4th was such an occasion. It does not disqualify me as a reporter that I was not in the pushing, yelling, chaffing crowds which thronged the Horse Guards or in the cheering ones outside the House of Commons.

I met at two in the morning, in the far and quiet West, and in a clean, lit, empty, residential street, an old, eager, one-eyed vendor of papers with a Union Jack in his billy-cock. A tattered bill fluttered before him as he shuffled wearily and hurriedly forward. 'Thrippence. Thrippence. Declaration of War.' He was trying to shout, but he only achieved a quinsied whisper. I stopped and bought. 'It's not in it,' he added, confidentially, pocketing my coppers, 'but it's true: God's truth it is – I couldn't get the latest. I was an hour and a quarter getting through the crowd.' I looked at him and felt as if I had been in that crowd myself, and could describe it, too. 'If Mr Disraeli was alive!' he croaked huskily. After this unexpected comment he lunged on again with bent knees, leaving me under the street lamp staring at the columns of the new, but already familiar, heavily-leaded type.

Though the region where I parted from my friends was fairly well known to me, I had lost my way, and after walking about half an hour I had come out somewhere below Holland Park. How late the buses were running! And the taxis were buzzing one after the other down the main thoroughfare, as if it had been ten o'clock and not two in the morning. This reminded me of public injunctions, already emphatic, concerning economy in petrol. But economy was impossible tonight; night of good-byes, of intimacies and friendships huddled into climaxes; night of sociable, equalizing forebodings; night ominous to the solitary, but gay, positively gay, to the gregarious.

I had noticed on my late ramblings and strayings that 'good-nights' from passing strangers had been frequent, and that they had had a different ring. People seemed to like being stopped and asked for a match or to point out the way; their eyes were more alive, less preoccupied, more conscious of one. When I joined a group round a coffee-stall to drink a cup of hot slop, I did not feel that customary embarrassment at not being suitably dressed. The silence round me was more friendly; some sort of barrier was down; no one asked me for money. Beside me as I drank stood one of those little, odd, undersized fly-by-nights, her grubby hands resting side by side on the oilcloth of the counter. She looked up under her feathers and smiled. It was not the usual smile.

As I crossed, striking southwards, some idea – what was it? – began to peep through these impressions.

A taxi packed with people waving flags whizzed by, down the now empty road. A girl in a pink jersey and a man, sitting on the half-open roof, set up a long hooting screech as they passed: I felt I had sampled the patriotic enthusiasms of Piccadilly Circus. What luck! How depressed I should have been in the midst of them! There is nothing so heart-damping as being out of sympathy with a crowd.

In a road of modest villas (it was quiet and dark) I passed first one and then another waiting taxi ... close on three o'clock, and in this region of prudent living! Suddenly behind some acacias shivering in the night air a door opened. A woman ran quickly down the steps, waving back at a man who was standing in the lighted oblong, signalling and nodding agitated encouragement. In she sprang, flinging herself back with that rapid preoccupied movement which is equivalent to exclaiming, 'This is life!' This hectic communal excitement, which overlay gloom and foreboding, which was expressing itself here in intimate ways and elsewhere in confused uproar – my peeping idea had something to do with that.

I had not come up against those blatant manifestations of it, that swaggering contempt for suffering which suggests such an ignominious combination of cowardice, stupidity, and cruelty. Clearly the great majority (unless they fear too much for themselves or those nearest them) loved war. There was exhilaration abroad tonight, but beneath lay forebodings of dreadful days, and deeper still a dumb resentment at the cold-blooded idiocy of diplomacy. Yet, there it was – and it was a kind of happiness. Why did a declaration of war make people unusually happy? Was it only love of excitement? Where exaltation roared and romped and streamed along the streets, it seemed it might be so; but where I had surprised it, in quieter eddies, there seemed to be another element involved. I caught the idea which had been peeping at me, and the irony of it was enough to make one cry: people seldom experience so genuinely that sense that life is worth living, which a feeling of brotherhood gives, as when they are banded together to kill their fellow-men; they are never so conscious of the humanity of others as when they are out, sharing risks, to smash the self-respect and mutilate the bodies of those who, but for a few politicians, might just as easily have been hoping with them, dying with them side by side.

Earlier in the night I had seen a party of French recruits doubling through the streets, singing. Everybody had hailed them as they went by. Coming towards me now under the lamps was a man in spectacles, with a small straw hat perched on his big square head. He looked Teutonic. '*Gute Nacht*,' I said, as we passed. He stopped for a second and wrung his hands: '*Ach Gott, Ach Gott! Mein lieber Freund!*'

II

November 11th 1918
The maroons went off as I was pulling on my boots. It was eleven o'clock, and the war was over. I went to the top of the kitchen-stairs and shouted, 'The war is over!' The washing-up clatter stopped for a moment; someone exclaimed, 'Thank goodness!' As I slammed the front door I said to myself, 'The war is over.' I repeated it again; but meeting with no response, I began to abuse myself. 'You clod, you dead-alive lump the war is over!' Still no response. 'Well,' I thought, 'at any rate I can go out and see how happy people are; that I shall enjoy.' In the street men and women were walking briskly with the same intent. Each looked to see how pleased the other might be, and each, having caught a reflected ray, beamed on the next passer-by. Apart from the few self-generators of high spirits, who were hooting and hailing others intermittently from bus-tops, most people, it struck me, were out to gather emotion. Here and there a few flags fluttered from the windows, and women came to doorways or up area steps to smile on every one that smile they usually reserve for their own children. A drum-and-fife band followed by some soldiers turned the corner; I felt inclined to cry. Should I follow, and in tears? 'No.

This time', I thought, 'I'll be on the hub of things; so on to Buckingham Palace.' Many were bound in that direction. The crowd, at first loosely flowing, began to congeal, then to solidify. Its current was strong enough, however, to sweep me some way up the Mall, in spite of the stream flowing down it. I caught at a cannon, crowded with people, and mounted. At last I could look round. The Mall was choked with vehicles invisible under their loads; on the pavements and between the traffic, heads were set as thick as cobblestones, and above them fluttered innumerable handkerchiefs and little flags. The statue of Queen Victoria caught my eye; up it black figures were swarming like ants over sugar. One youth, looking as small as a child's doll, already lay comfortably cuddled within her fat marble arm, another was pulling himself higher by the help of her nose and her veil. The chaotic din of yells, catcalls, tin-noises and squealers swelled now and then to a roar. Near me a block of Canadians kept chanting with rhythmic persistence, 'We-want-King George'. And there, sure enough, far away on the Palace balcony, appeared a little group of figures, male and female. One was doubtless the King; he was probably making a speech.

A crowd is usually the most incomprehensibly patient of beasts; but that day its particles were restless, and longing to disperse, move, recongregate, no matter where. It began to loosen and swirl, and I, too, was washed gently on under the Admiralty Arch into Trafalgar Square; caught now and then, like a straw on a rock in a stream, then pulled firmly away, on down Whitehall, where the housetops were trimmed with people, and the windows were blocked with faces. Sometimes a snowstorm of paper wavered down on our heads; it pleased me to fancy the scraps were once copies of DORA.

But it was time for me to exercise initiative; and like a swimmer who makes the bank but touches it lower downstream than he intends, I landed and reached my destination. There, in a high-perched room looking over the Thames, I was absorbed into private life. I became as a plant in a parlour-window whose leaves are still, though outside the wind is shaking bushes and trees to their roots. And looking out of the window I had to tell myself yet once again that the war was over at last. There was the river, there the black boats and the barges punching up or gliding down tide; there the familiar silhouette of warehouses, factories, chimneys, there the rayless London sun, 'shining like a new penny in a basin of soapy water'. Yet how often I had looked on that scene, feeling far happier than this! The distant howl, it is true, brought a faint glow of emotion. But it is lucky I haven't, say, a toothache, I thought; it would need but a little trouble to cover up all my joy. Then I thought of the recumbent figures in hospital-blue on Carlton House Terrace, pulling themselves by cords from their pillows to wave for a minute at the crowd in the Mall below; of the lorry-loads of nurses I had passed, jigging and cheering; of one anxious, impatient face – a woman's – in a taxi with luggage. Communal satisfactions are only a background to other feelings; that it should be well with the background is often vital to real happiness, but the sentiment of life within is so near and dear, that whatever impinges on this takes precedence, though not always in judgement, always in feeling.

When London went to lunch there must have been many luncheons close replicas of mine – luncheons with discussions about what this would mean to Germany or that to us; discussions more giddy than usual, stimulated by rather more wine, with the Kaiser and Hindy and Tirpy and Lucy bobbing up in them like apples in a warm, spicy posset; conversations almost entirely inane, childish, but pleasant. The company I was with being well-to-do, the word 'Bolshevism' also recurred, a name for a thing like the fog now at the window. For the room grew dingier and darker, the fire redder and redder, and the windows as brown as transparent brown paper, through which could be seen the black, dripping branches of trees. But the fire was ruddy and warm. It would not be bad after all to end nodding over a pailful of coke, guarding tools with a sack on one's shoulders; not so bad, at least so it seemed when in each of us was a glow that the infection of public rejoicing could turn to a blaze. We had all become shadows where we sat – just shadows, each with three points of light, two eyes, and one spark of a cigarette. Someone, with whimsical solemnity, thought fit to pour on my head a small libation of wine. I was thinking this was the last armchair I had sat in before going to France – what years, what ages ago! Time! Time? O yes, of course Time like an ever-rolling stream bears all its sons away – 'I must be off.'

The park was empty; the paths were shining wet; I walked in a bubble of mist. It was a no-man's-land of ghosts; not of the ghosts I would fain have talked to, who still looked wondrous like themselves, but of wispy, whimpering ghosts, anonymous ghosts – multitudes of them. And yet on the other side of no-man's-land I ran into a crowd, streaming home as from the Derby! Such a jolly crowd, every man and woman of which had apparently backed the winner! Then (for me), tea and exclamations: exclamations of whose banality it was impossible that day to tire: 'Isn't it marvellous? Isn't it *incredible*? Isn't it . . .' but words break down in gestures. It was pleasant to savour thus the inexhaustible obvious; but it was to the night I looked forward.

To set out with the expectations of a child at a pantomime, but never to be sure if the curtain had actually risen, whether or not what you saw might not prove to be only a drop scene; to push on and on, to wander hither and thither, in search of the spectacle, and then to discover that you, in virtue of being one of thousands and thousands, you just doing that, *were* the show – such in barest analysis was the night's experience. To become as a currant in a vast human plum-pudding, gaily bedecked, danced round by the flames of harmless good spirits and offered up at the table of the *Padre Eterno*, serves, as metaphors will, to bring back its sensations. A great gregarious good-humour was abroad, a solid fraternal satisfaction. It softened and made friendly-pathetic the squeakiest, thinnest, most self-assertive monotonous manifestations of joy. How inexpressive a creature is man! Left to himself, without the help of art, which he despises, he can only kick up behind and before, scream, 'Ow-yow, tiddle-diddle-ooo!' and change hats with his female.

On November 11th they said, 'We are so happy! We will show it and romp.' They did, and were happier still. On November 12th they said, 'We were so happy last night! We must romp again.' They made gestures more violent, lit fires, knocked hats off and charged each other in the streets. Were they happy? Perhaps. But I know I came between two men, facing each other, with the sulky semi-consciousness of bulls in their eyes, and with split lips and dripping noses. On November 13th they said, 'We must pump up jollity to the last dregs of all.' They rushed about dragging cannon to batter in doors of hotels, tore clothes off the backs of women, and tied one, it is said, to a lamp-post and danced round her. I deduce that they were not nearly so happy.

Unshaded street-lamps and lit windows, long unlighted, were enough that night in our eyes to make a glorious illumination. Piccadilly was a ballroom, where strangers ran at each other with a cry, hugged, took the floor, and twirled and jigged to no music, or only that kind which from earliest ages has been famed for keeping off devils.

We did miss a band. I met only one, it was a Belgian military band, travelling inside a bus. Behind the quivering windows they were blowing and banging it out, their energetic faces looking like dashing portraits by Franz Hals; while from the top of the bus men in steel hats and blue-grey coats leant, shouting, shaking hands with the air. Trafalgar Square was more sombre; processions of munition chits with flags trailed about, singing nasally, lazily, sometimes jeering and laughing at passers-by. A great revolving crowd of black loiterers sat about, ran about – did nothing, did anything – as happy and easily distracted as dogs. The door of St Martin's Church was open; there was a thanksgiving service going on. The quavering, throbbing and whining of the organ, and the people at the foot of the portico steps dancing 'Nuts and May', harmonized into a single appeal which made me feel I should like to go in, sit still and remember. Pews, a slightly foggy atmosphere, bright lights and soporific warmth – how familiar it all was! The service was composed of hymns and improvised prayers; the former were rather lugubriously triumphant, the latter moving because spoken naturally. We prayed for many kinds of people: the dead, the bereaved, the wounded, the saved, the relieved, for statesmen and Christians and reformers. I waited for the clergyman to tell us also to pray for our enemies; he was, I thought, the sort of man who might. But he did not. At the close we sang 'God save the King', and fixing my eyes upon the Lion and Unicorn above the altar, whereon stood a small brass cross, my thoughts turned to 'a highly respectable First Cause', whose views on Alsace and the Suez Canal were sensible and positive. Then I was once more absorbed into the paganism outside.

And so home, through the streets which were easy to traverse in the wake of charging wedges of humanity, among people who laughed when they were jostled, on into the quiet West, where the houses were dark, and dusky flags hung limply from the windows, as though in dumb show saying, 'It is finished.'

TWO TRIALS

'Max' once wrote a delightful essay called 'Dulcedo Judiciorum', in which he owned to finding the drama provided by the Law Courts superior to that provided by the theatres. At the same time, he said, he much preferred listening to civil cases:

> I cannot but follow in my heart the English law and assume (pending proof, which cannot be forthcoming) that the prisoner in the dock has a character, at any rate, as fine as my own. The war that this assumption wages in my breast against the fact that the man will, perhaps, be sentenced is too violent a war not to discommode me. Let justice be done. Or, rather, let our rough and ready, well-meant endeavours towards justice go on being made. But I won't be there to see, thank you very much.

I understand what he means, but I confess my curiosity is usually stronger than such qualms. I have only attended two sensational cases in my life, but if opportunity offered I should, no doubt, attend another.

The first was the trial of a woman for the murder of her child, a poor little creature about eight years old and subject to fits. The child was illegitimate, and a great burden on its mother. She was living with a man whom she hoped to marry, and he had consented to pay a few shillings a week to some home for such unwanted waifs, because no landlady would keep a child with fits. Perhaps the woman had discovered that more money was required for this than he would be likely to give; anyhow, she determined to spare his pocket by leaving the child with her parents, while telling him she was taking it to the home. With that end she went by train to Reading and set out to walk. It was a wet, windy day. She had twelve miles to go. Witnesses came forward who had passed her on the road, and according to them, she was sometimes carrying the child and sometimes pulling it along; one witness reported that the child was crying. They were all going in a direction contrary to hers – perhaps if she had been able to get a lift that crime would have never been committed. She became exasperated and tired; and when she approached her home it seems suddenly to have struck her that, after all, her plan could not work. She had already deposited another little mis-begot with her parents, and about that child she had not owned up to her man. If she left both children there, sooner or later, he would find out about the first, and then – would he marry her? So she turned back, lugging the crying child. What happened on the walk back we never learnt, but the child was afterwards found, strangled, in a wayside pool.

I did not pick out this painful case. I happened to be staying with the Sheriff, and so accompanied him to the Assizes. In Court that war of sympathies within the breast of which 'Max' speaks was considerably mitigated in mine by one little incident. The accused woman betrayed no emotion during the trial until the Judge asked the witness who had found the body to show the jury how the lace collar had been wound round the child's neck. The witness did so by putting the collar round his own. The prisoner then bent her head to hide a smile – the gentleman looked so funny! This seemed to betoken a degree of insensibility in the criminal type which relieves one from too acute a fellow-feeling.

The only historic trial I ever attended was that of Sir Roger Casement, and the impressions it left in me are as fresh as they were that day.

To me, when I attended the High Court on the last day of this trial, the prisoner was not a symbolic figure of Ireland's wrongs, nor was the court an embodiment of England's rights. He was a man, and I – one who looked on and listened. We all of us have a characterless percipient in us, though he is rarely active; indeed, it is only in the small sleepless hours of the morning that most of us are aware of him. Come with me, at any rate, in the spirit of those small hours. I cannot take you excitedly by the arm, as some reporters might do, and point to this or that; characterless percipients have no arms, and there can be no good-fellowship between us.

Imagine, however, that we have successfully 'seen', as the police call it, the policeman who keeps back the crowd, a crowd which lingers in the dark passage with the wistfulness of hungry urchins outside an eating-shop – resigned to not going in, but unable to tear themselves away – and that we have pushed together through these swing-doors.

So this is an historic trial! One day some future Carlyle or Macaulay may describe it in phrases which will make it vibrant with passion and life. How convincing his description will be, and yet how false! He will mention that the venerable ex-ambassador and historian, Lord Bryce, was there, looking down an interested spectator from the gallery; he will sketch the career of the young Lord Chief Justice, Lord Reading, destined to be an Indian Viceroy, and who was also once a ship's boy; and, perhaps, if he is a very learned historian, he will touch in lightly the careers of the two judges who sit on either side of the Lord Chief Justice. He will certainly paint the portrait of the

Attorney-General, whose political career had been deeply im-
plicated with Irish affairs, and who, as Lord Birkenhead, was
destined to take a most important part in the creation of the
Irish Free State. Yes, distinguished personages are there,
careers and all; but such accessories, out of which historians
create an atmosphere, seem at the moment of precious little
importance. The air of sleepy unreality which haunts the
Courts of Law broods over even this trial, too. Ramparted
behind desks, and raised above everybody, sit the judges in
scarlet; their dress denotes that it is impossible to speak to them
as a man to men. They have ceased, in a way, to be human.
They are embodiments of impersonal forces. When they speak
of each other they call each other 'brother', and the word
excludes the rest of mankind. Do they make a joke or pay a
compliment to counsel? The remark has a peculiar savour, as
though it were a kind of *lusus naturæ*. And there is the usual
contrast between the leisurely matter-of-factness of the proceedings and the excruciatingly vital issue at stake.

A long man in a black gown, with wig tilted off his forehead,
like a straw hat on a hot day, and an oddly undergraduate air, is
talking; talking as emphatically as his preoccupation with what
he is going to say next allows. It is the Attorney-General. He is
saying that it is not necessary to go into old, unpleasant
controversies, for an event has happened which has altered the
whole face of Irish politics: he means the war with Germany.
For a moment, my mood changes; I cease to be a detached
observer. I feel inclined to interject, 'But it didn't alter them –
that's the whole tragedy. And why "old", as though these
controversies were dead and buried long ago?' Then I slip back
into being a characterless percipient. The Attorney-General
goes on. His passion comes in irregular gusts, like the noise of
talking through a swing-door which is constantly opening and
shutting. There seems no particular reason why he should be so
moved one moment or so casual the next. His moral indignation appears something he can turn on and off with a tap.

These contemptuous gestures of abhorrence directed towards the prisoner – at whom he never looks – what kind of emotion do they represent? Is the speaker's heart really aflame? If so, how account for these sudden drops into the conciliatory casual tone of a sensible man addressing all sensible men?

The argument is sound enough and well arranged. It is clear as a pikestaff that Sir Roger Casement has committed treason; that he tried to land arms in Ireland, and to persuade Irish prisoners in Germany to fight against England. The verdict is a foregone conclusion. I keep wondering why the accused does not jump up and cry, 'Enough of this; I deny nothing; sentence me to be hanged and have done.' For the first time I look at him steadily and try to read him. He sits, fidgeting a little now and then, in a lassitude of composed impatience. I guess that he is suffering from an internal, churning sensation of anguish. He looks at his watch; occasionally he yawns a little. It is not a yawn of indifference – I saw that half-yawn on the faces of men in France, just before they were going into action, or when shells were beginning to arrive. But the prisoner does not jump up; he allows the Attorney-General to go on telling a perfectly clear story, which, nevertheless, as a human story, is quite incomprehensible. There are no motives in it! And he ends by telling the jury that they have a duty to perform as painful as that which is being performed by others, elsewhere, in these bloody and critical days, in the service of the Empire. Here, it strikes me that the Attorney-General is speaking as a civilian. I wonder if the Lord Chief Justice is really going to find charging the jury as painful as he would find charging the Germans at La Boisselle.

The Lord Chief Justice turns in his chair towards the jury with an almost confidential movement, which says as plainly as speech, 'Now I am going to make everything clear; you can't go wrong if you listen to my words, and they will be nearly all of one syllable.' He takes out his eyeglass and looks at them, while they crane forward as though fairly hypnotized. He begins by telling them that they must not think the counsel for the defence a wicked or disloyal man for having said what he did on behalf of the prisoner; that it is, on the contrary, the pride of the English Bar that the prisoner should be defended whatever the crime of which he may be accused; that it was a courageous, admirable speech. He then goes on to say that he has always felt anxiety in a Court of Justice when there was any possibility of political passions being introduced: 'Justice was ever in jeopardy when passion was aroused.' 'Yes, my lord,' a voice cried out within me (perhaps an Irish voice), 'that is true; but justice of the finer sort may be also in jeopardy when the existence of political passion is ignored.' He goes on explaining what is meant by 'aiding and comforting the King's enemies,' the clause under which the prisoner stands indicted. It covered (no one felt surprise) seducing the King's soldiers with a view to making them fight against England, also importing arms for the use of rebellious subjects from a country with which the King of England is at war.

'Put a coronet on a man's head, and the blood in his brain will start circulating in different fashion, flooding new channels, and changing in important respects his outward demeanour.' It is the same with a judge's wig. I hardly recognized in the Lord Chief Justice the advocate I remembered. His clear, ringing voice had become a minatory mumble; his delivery so weighty as to be almost indistinct. He seemed to have aged thirty years. The stand-firm, prompt-pouncing manner of the advocate had changed into the ominous formality of immemorial authority. I hastily remind myself that it is unfair to charge a man with insincerity for adopting a manner, not natural perhaps to him, but appropriate to his function. Yet sometimes circumstances arise which sharpen our contempt for acting of all kinds, and then. . . . Well, it was precisely this that was to happen after the luncheon interval.

Of course, during the morning I had looked from time to time at the accused. I noticed two things about him: First, he was obviously a foreigner. He might have been, for all one could tell, with his sallow face, black beard, and that peculiar lift – did it betoken vanity or pride? – of the eyebrow, a Spanish hidalgo. I decided he was very vain. Secondly, he was a type of man whose 'spiritual home', to use a phrase then famous, was certainly not a Court of Justice. Doubtless he would have been a better man, a more reliable one, had he had something of the final matter-of-fact sense of right and wrong which reigns there. He looked the sort of man who might put devotion to a purpose or an ideal so high that, when that emotion possessed him, nothing else, no virtues, consistencies, or loyalties, would seem to him of much consequence. There were, I knew then, grave inconsistencies in his career, and I learnt afterwards there was also a grotesquely morbid streak in his temperament. Somewhere, in some legal or political archives, his private diary is still kept, and the publication of extracts from it would effectively prevent the canonization of his memory. It would be itself a dirtier action than any private shame recorded in that diary, but it would be effective.

Looking at him, I realized how inevitable it was that, as he had accepted a knighthood from the King, he should have done so in a graceful letter. Such a man could no more be curmudgeonly than he could be raspingly rude. As for his living on a pension from a Government he was betraying, I said to myself he would regret he had done so, yet he would feel he had earned every penny of it in the past – and anyhow, loyalty to his cause came first. It was a miserable, irretrievable fact that 'his honour rooted in dishonour stood', but there was no helping it. Thus I explained him to myself. What those whom he had betrayed had a right to think of his conduct was another question. He himself would not expect mercy where he had betrayed confidence.

The jury were away about an hour. What they were hesitating about I could not conceive. When the hush of Court was disturbed by the jury's return and the curtain shook and the usher came in, we stirred uneasily. The prisoner smiled; he seemed happier now.

After the verdict the Lord Chief Justice asked him if he had anything to say. He was, of course, standing up between the warders at that moment, and he stepped to the rail with a manuscript in his hand: 'My Lords, as I wish my words to reach a much wider audience than this, I intend to read all I propose to say.' The new voice was very agreeable – a little uncertain and agitated; and the papers shook in his hand. It was the first perfectly natural voice we had heard in Court all day, and at the sound of it something very strange occurred: the dream-like formalism of the proceedings vanished; the tension relaxed; his judges turned to look at him for the first time, and with a kind of friendly curiosity, leaning on their elbows to listen.

What a different point of view, what a fantastically different point of view, was presented to us! 'If true religion rests on love, it is equally true that loyalty rests on love. . . . Loyalty is a sentiment, not a law. It rests on love, not restraint. The Government of Ireland by England rests on restraint and not on law; and since it demands no love it can evoke no loyalty.' Good heavens! either this was the most arrant rubbish, or Sir Frederick Smith and Lord Reading had left out a great deal. I felt that at bottom it was my view, too, but the difference between me and the rebel in the dock was that I loved England, and I could never have wished him success at the cost of England's downfall. Yet I could understand him. For, if instead of being a hyphenated Irishman, owing everything that makes life worth living to Englishmen and to living in England, I had been brought up in Ireland, could I have helped putting Ireland first? Would the legal aspect of my position as a subject of King George have seemed the absolutely final word on what my attitude ought to be during the War? I do not think so. But presently I was wondering far more at the strange world of romantic legality into which the condemned man seemed to be drifting. He was reading to us about Edward III, and the claim

of the English Crown upon French subjects! It seemed fantastic, till I grasped that, to him, it was an obvious fact that
England had no more claim over Ireland than she had over
modern France. The press afterwards commented on his im-
penitent and smiling departure from the Court. But, if this was
what he believed, what reason had he for repentance? To me
the relations of these two countries did not seem so simple that
they could be summed up by saying that they had nothing to do
with each other; but what I felt was that England had so ruled
Ireland that she had forfeited her right to expect loyalty as a
matter of course from all Irishmen.

He finished his speech; and as if by magic (one had not
noticed the attendants behind the chairs) three black squares of
cloth appeared on the wigs of the judges. The Lord Chief
Justice read out the death-sentence in low, even tones, while the
other two kept their eyes upon their papers.

The memory which will stay with one is that of a sincerity in
the prisoner at once more human and more idealistic than the
sincerity of the men who were sitting in judgement upon him,
and of its strange effect on the proceedings. At its touch, the
trial, even the solemnity of the death-sentence, seemed to lose
their significance – their power, at least, to brand as well as to
kill.

THE CROWDS AT
BURLINGTON
HOUSE

The tremendous crowd which gathers every day from all parts
of England to see the Exhibition at Burlington House is a most
curious phenomenon. It is a tribute to the prestige of art, not of
course a sign of love for it, or understanding of it. The National
Gallery remains empty. What then makes all these people rush
to get a peep between each other's shoulders at these pictures?
Curiosity – they like to glance at famous and very valuable
objects. Social obligation – owing to the dearth of conversational openings they find themselves incessantly asked, 'Have
you seen the Italian Exhibition?' or, 'Are you going to the Exhibition?' Vanity and uplift – a reluctance to admit indifference to
art, and a faint hope that it may be overcome. Lastly –
sheep-in-a-gap, follow-m'-leader instinct. The majority of
those streaming out (read their faces) have experienced a
'something-attempted, something-done' satisfaction; the
majority streaming in, feel 'I am doing what an educated
person ought to do.' Few of them, however, stop opposite any
picture for a quarter of the time they do in front of something for
sale at Selfridge's. They loiter round and round in a mazed
condition of vaguely elevated depression; and no mood can be

less propitious for art, since depression is a non-conductor, and
vague longing to be impressed destructive of discrimination. Of
pairs doing the Exhibition together, the one who reads in a low
halting gabble from the catalogue usually appears the happier;
but there comes a moment when he, or she, also, must gaze at
the picture described before passing on. Oh, that moment of
blank effort to respond; the muttered misery of his or her
ineptitudes! 'That's . . . don't you think? . . . I like. . . . Yes,
yes, a distinct look of Aunt Mary, and aren't the baby's legs
wonderful?'

The few but crowded benches display the unostentatious
stoicism of the railway waiting-room. There the old who have
won the game of musical chairs enjoy a mild sense of triumph,
but no view. They are to be commiserated least. The exhausted
sweetly-sour atmosphere has devitalized them, but they are
seated. Nor must we pity the children, who from a peep at the
pictures between thighs lift their faces to catch from their
parents appreciation of their artistic zest: they are buoyed up by
the pride of extreme youth in sharing what they suppose their
elders enjoy.

It was the great moving, muddled, middle-aged mass that
touched me. Why were they there? What had they come for?
In a fashion I have already answered those questions, and
in the study the answers satisfy. But in the presence of the
Phenomenon they seemed inadequate: there was no pushing
or thrusting; the public washed up gently against the walls
like driftwood sluggishly circulating in a current; their mutual consideration was perfect, and reminded me of journeys
in the Tube during the War when all were sobered down to
even kindliness by common calamity. Oh, Culture, what cruel-
ties are committed in thy name!

It is inevitable that the dogged pursuit of culture should
implant in the human heart a deep unconscious hostility to art;
and what is worse, arrogance. Art is a living force ever taking
new forms, and its transmigrations are least likely to be recog-

nized by those who have painfully approached it in the hope of self-improvement and not in pursuit of pleasure.

At this point I can imagine my reader interrupting me. 'Ah, I know you. You're one of those superior persons who, believing they understand art themselves, are anxious, with dog-in-the-manger vanity, to suggest that the perceptions they enjoy are beyond the reach of ordinary humanity.' Acute, but hypercritical reader, you are mistaken. Pictures have meant very little to me compared with the beauty which is transmitted through the written word. All I have obtained from them is a mild but constant pleasure. In the mildness of that response I resemble the crowd. For such as me, it is the constancy and reliability of the pleasures of the eye which constitute the chief part of its value. It is more detached from mood and circumstance than the satisfactions which literature can give, though it is far less strong. I have met in my life some half-a-dozen people of whom this was not true, who lived through the eye with an intensity which I can just imagine but can never experience. It is therefore as one of the crowd that I address those who resemble me.

Firstly, there is nothing disgraceful in being unable to appreciate painting; the disability is too common to be distressing. The important thing is to get rid of the idea that in such matters one's opinion and taste are of consequence. This at least will restrain one from tarring and feathering, either in conversation or in fact, anything new which has not yet prestige behind it. It has also a further advantage. Once rid of a sense of responsibility, one is free to enjoy what one can; and this freedom brings one nearer in spirit, though not necessarily in taste, to those to whom painting is really important. People seldom lie more flatly than when they utter with exasperating modesty the familiar formula, 'I know nothing about art, but I know what I like.' If they spoke the truth they would say, 'I have some idea what others think I *ought* to like, but I have not the smallest notion what I do.'

The safest approach to the art of painting is not through the gate of aspiration or self-improvement, but through the humble door of pleasure, and the first step to culture is to learn to *enjoy*, not to know what is best. It is not true that we needs must love the highest when we see it, only vanity ever convinced anyone that it was. Those who do not deceive themselves need no enlightenment on that point.

SHOOTING WITH
WILFRID BLUNT

Wilfrid Blunt was almost the last host who ever asked me down for a day's shooting. By the age of twenty-five I had become the sort of young man no one could possibly associate with sport; and I was not sorry. Why he continued to ask me to shoot at Newbuildings, since I was so poor a shot, I cannot guess – unless I was right when I sometimes suspected that was a qualification in his eyes. It was for the sake of his company and the sleeping beauty of his lovely small old house that I invariably accepted, not for his birds.

Although winter afternoons were short, luncheon was always leisurely and eaten in company with his Nurse. At table I would produce any scraps of political or social gossip I had brought down with me from London (he liked to be supplied with it, though I was a disappointing gossip), and when my little stock of news was out and he had made his comments, we usually fell silent. Then, a white Arab mare with a fountain tail would be brought to the steps from which the moss was never scraped, and he would slowly swing himself into the saddle, looking there I thought not unlike a photograph of the old Count Tolstoy I had at home – only more handsome and more worldly

– but the poet – yes, very much the poet – obviously enjoying the damp, still afternoon, the winter woods, and the elastic paces of his mount.

Thus we would set off, I walking at one stirrup with my gun, and a man-servant with a light bamboo chair over his arm at the other, and a keeper and a few beaters following behind. At the cover his chair would be placed at one spot while I was stationed at another, to await that distant tapping which heralds the rising of the birds. Then, my qualification, or disability, or whatever you like to call it, came into play. With a startled hiccup, a snapping of twigs, and whirring of wings a pheasant would presently fly out, followed by another and another. It was five to one (especially if they flew to the right of me) that I missed them. It was ten to one my host from his armchair brought them down: I think he enjoyed 'wiping my eye'. The bag was a matter of indifference. Once, at the close of such a day, he said: 'We may as well shoot two or three duck before we go in'; and off we went to a small pond on which a number of them were placidly swimming. It was not necessary to approach with caution, indeed they were hard to put up, being half tame. At last, after the manner of ducks, they began circling round and round their feeding-ground, ever higher and higher; and by a miracle my eye was in. Again and again as the flying wedge came over me, I pulled as by a string now a leader, now a straggler, out of the dusky sky. I was too excited and triumphant to notice that my host had stopped firing long ago. He was not pleased. He had meant the words 'two or three', and I had shot nearly a third of his carefully reared, hand-fed wild-duck! However, coals of fire were heaped on me next day in the shape of three brace in the railway-carriage rack above my head.

Wilfrid Blunt was suspicious of those in power (no one knew better how apt power is to make men stupid), and in his old age he was also jealous of the young. I am inclined to think that I owed his benevolence towards me partly to not being a shining specimen of youth. I was companionable without exciting envy. He used to say he detested young men; it would have been truer had he said they made him envious. He hated growing old. He never wrote more directly out of himself than in that fine sonnet which begins:

> I long have had a quarrel set with Time
> Because he robbed me. Every day of life
> Was wrested from me after bitter strife,
> I never yet could see the sun go down
> But I was angry in my heart.

Now, I was not the sort of young man who suggested successes in love, nor were my spirits of the towering sort. I could ride, play games, shoot after a fashion, but not with any skill that could remind him that his own heyday was over; and then, with reservations not hard to conceal, I admired him immensely. Admired? Well, it would perhaps be more accurate to say I relished him immensely: his personality, his bearded and bedouin handsomeness, his slightly daunting composure and good manners. No doubt he was vaguely aware that I did so, and more definitely that I appreciated enormously the beauty he had created round himself: Newbuildings Place was a house after my heart. Everything inside and out had been designed by one who knew that Time, the enemy, is also an artist. He understood the secret of creating habitable beauty: choose well, then let alone. I loved its dead-man's garden; and what would strike our plumber-pampered generation as its deplorable deficiencies were friendly features to me: in modern comforts I can find no dignity. I was attracted also by the freakish and fastidious collection of books the house contained, and by its pictures and the casual objects which lay about its tables. These, though often charming or curious in themselves, made you wonder first how they came there; they suggested stories.

Wilfrid Blunt was an aristocrat, and this, too, intrigued me.

Already, even in my youth, aristocrats were becoming scarce enough, and I had met but a few. There was much in an aristocratic temper of mind which attracted and interested me. Many of the effects on character of pride still please me aesthetically; I like the indifference to appearances it breeds, combined with perfectly frank ostentation if occasion demands; I like its traditional hospitality; I like the confidence of manner, whether gentle or peremptory, which is a product of ancient riches. Aristocratic pride seems to me the best social substitute for magnanimity; and to one incorrigibly preoccupied with human nature it is also amusing to observe where, when real magnanimity is absent (which may be found in any walk of life), the make-shift may break down. An aristocrat can prove on occasion a dirty fighter – we all know that. You cannot behave like a cad and claim to be a gentleman, but a good deal of caddishness and the aristocratic temper have sometimes been compatible: Byron is a good example. Shorn of his privileges, the aristocrat may easily go considerable lengths in that direction partly because he feels deep down he has a right to his own way, and partly because his self-respect has no connection with what others think of him. It is tucked away with pride of birth in an odd corner of his mind, which private conscience may or may not visit, but social timidity never invades. Perhaps he feels that, with the exception of the scrupulous among them, those whom he considers equals will be likely to forgive him lack of delicacy before they pardon want of spirit. Meredith made a flashing study of such a type of person in the Earl of Fleetwood in *The Amazing Marriage*. It is getting rarer and rarer. It needs, if it is to flower with fine carelessness, to be surrounded by a wondering romantic sympathy tinged with awe; vague democratic snobbishness is not sustaining enough. A man cannot go on believing confidently that there is a subtle all-important difference between himself and common humanity without corroboration, and the climate of the twentieth century is unfavourable to that.

But I am digressing. Wilfrid Blunt did not afford an opportunity for observing the aristocrat as a dirty fighter. In political activities he was invariably on the side of the weak against the strong, of primitive civilizations against the Empire and commercialism. Like Byron he was on the side of the rebels – without democratic sympathies. His championship of causes – they were usually lost – was chivalrous. He was imprisoned by Arthur Balfour in Ireland for addressing a prohibited meeting, and he suffered acutely from cold in his cell and not being allowed to wear his top-coat. Shortly after his release, however, he had the pleasure of helping into it, at a tennis-party, the Irish Secretary who was at the moment afraid of catching a chill. It was the sort of small incident that Wilfrid Blunt enjoyed, and no doubt he accompanied the gesture with a few appropriate words. Both as fastidious aristocrat and poet, he loathed mechanism, commercialism, luxury, and fiddle-faddle democratic regulations. On the way from Three Bridges station to his other home, Crabbet Park, which before he died he handed over to his only child, Lady Wentworth, you passed a well surmounted by two notice-boards. The one declared in the name of the Local Authorities that the water was unsafe; the other, a more lengthy statement, asserted that it had been analysed by Savory and Moore and found drinkable – that was signed 'The Lord of the Manor'. Why shouldn't cottagers get their water from a source which they had always used? The retort of the Local Authorities was to board up the well; and there the two notices remained for years, getting more and more mud-bespattered, typical of the conflict between fading feudal paternalism and the machinery of modern governing bodies, ostensibly democratic but often with their own little axes to grind.

On his own estate, however, he knew how to create the spirit he desired. That spirit was legible in his plump, rosy-gilled garrulous agent, with his 'Yes, Squire', 'No, Squire', 'Certainly, Squire, O certainly'; in his wizened coachman, with a round, alarmed, bird-like eye, who on the box of a shabby old barouche, behind a pair of light and lovely Arab horses, met you at Horsham station; in (one surmised) his labourers and old gaffers who, certainly at one time, went about their work in smocks. At any rate nothing was run on the estate with a view to squeezing money out of it – if that was compensation for the domination of the Squire, who also sympathized with and respected every sort of rural craft and skill. William Morris, who reinforced his love of traditional country life and craftsmanship; the Arab, whose independence and personal dignity made the average English 'swell' seem like a genial, shoddy oaf – probably with one eye askew upon the main chance; and recollections of days when the aristocracy was in a much more confident position, were the chief elements in the preferences controlling his behaviour.

In that delightful book *The Theatre of Life*, Lord Howard of Penrith recalls a Derby Day with him. There, every year, Blunt drove down a four-in-hand. This time he arrived too late to get to his place; whereupon he charged the police, galloped down the course, and swerved deftly into it. Towards the end of his life he was to drive a coach-and-four through conventions becoming to gentlemen; he published his Diaries in which he reported without scruple what friends had said of friends. There was an outcry; and one of them, looking back, has said with some truth, 'After all, it was Wilfrid Blunt who started the cad's chorus.'

Thus apart from their pleasantness, my visits gave me some insight into the effects of the aristocratic temper of mind on political opinions, country life, social life, and (but this requires separate treatment) on poetry. For Wilfrid Blunt, who remained an aristocrat when on the side of rebels, also remained one when writing poetry; he wore poetry like a ring on his finger. That is part of the charm of his verse.

UGLINESS

He was leaning with his elbow on the mantelpiece, gazing into the looking-glass, with his head cocked a little to one side. I heard him murmur: 'Ugly? Yes, but there's something attractive about the face!' The next moment he caught sight of my reflection behind his own, and spun round with an expression which any Macbeth confronted with the ghost of Banquo might have envied.

What, kind-hearted reader, would you have done in my place? Laughed? I hope not. I made a friend, or rather a devotee, for life. I went straight up to him and said: 'Perhaps you feel foolish, but what you said is *perfectly true*.' I have treated him, I fear, inconsiderately many times since then (he is an awful bore), but he is devoted to me still, and seldom meets me without delicately hinting that he will 'cut up' much better than people expect. The moral is . . . but it is not with worldly morals I am concerned; I want to talk about being ugly.

It is not the ugly we handsome fellows commiserate; it is the plain; the people who provoke in those they accost an impulse to say: 'I remember your name, but I cannot remember your face.' Most men are sensitive about their appearance, though few to the extent of the Roman Senator Fidus Cornelius, who, as every schoolboy knows, burst into tears (*circ.* AD 60) when Corbulo declared that he resembled a plucked ostrich. It is possible to be magnificently ugly, but you cannot be magnificently plain. And yet I can imagine circumstances in which it would be gratifying to overhear a comment upon the insignificance of your personal appearance.

Imagine a crowded railway station, and yourself an author whose fame is just beginning to sprout. The platform is lined three deep; there will evidently be a rush for seats, and all faces are turned towards the incoming train. Suddenly, at this absorbing moment, you hear someone behind you say:

'Look, look! Quick, there's X.'

'Who? Where?' replies another, unmistakably eager voice: 'Not the man who wrote . . .'

'Yes, there, on your left – behind you.'

And if the second voice were then to exclaim: 'What! *That* little man!' the very depth of disappointment expressed in its tone would be a proof of your literary talent. You would know you had written well.

Of course, if whiffs of fame kept coming your way in this form, it would, in the end, be depressing; but the first time I am sure you would tingle with pleasure.

But if the circumstances in which a plain appearance can be a source of gratification are rare, ugliness, on the other hand, real crushing ugliness, is a sort of distinction. You remember Lamb's discussion in his *Popular Fallacies* of the saying: 'that handsome is as handsome does'? Anyone who uses this proverb, he says, can never have seen Mrs Conrady without pronouncing her to be the ugliest woman that he ever met with in the course of his life. 'The first time that you are indulged with a sight of her face, is an era in your existence ever after. You are glad to have seen it – like Stonehenge. Lockets are for remembrance; and it would be clearly superfluous to hang an image at your heart, which, once seen, can never be out of it.'

The essay makes one envy the lady, and Lamb's conclusion, to which the reader inevitably assents, is that true ugliness, like true beauty, is the result of harmony. Lamb defies 'the minutest connoisseur to cavil at any part or parcel of the countenance' of the lady in question. Mrs Conrady convinced him that, if one must be ugly, it is better to be ugly all over, 'than, amidst a tolerable residue of features, to hang out one that shall be exceptionable'; in short, far better to be downright hideous. And I would add a gloss to this. Ugliness is not only a distinction; it may also serve as a palladium to its possessor, or as a weapon in the struggle of life.

In the terrible battle of Camlan, that fatal field where King Arthur fell with all his chivalry, only three Christian Knights survived: Sandde Bryd, who was so lovely to look upon that not one of the victorious heathen had the heart to strike him; Glewlwyd Gavaelvawr (or Great Grasp), the porter to King Arthur, whose prodigious thews made all unwilling to attack him; and Morvan ab Teged, who was so overwhelmingly hideous that the foe fled from him as from a demon out of hell. These three stalked through the battlefield, unscathed as gods.

The ugly should take this piece of history to heart. Let not, therefore, those dowered with an eye-searing ugliness reproach Nature, or throw away their singular endowment by attempting to mitigate their striking features. In dominating our fellows, the heavy lids and deliberate movements which suggest a saurian monster of the extinct world, the jaw which rivals the maxillary equipment of the larger apes, the complexion which in a savage tribe would render war-paint superfluous, these may prove important assets. To be as 'ugly as a mud fence', as they used to say 'Out West', is nothing; but to vie in appearance with the inauspicious monsters of the deep may be of incalculable advantage. Would Mirabeau, do you think, have dominated the beginning of the French Revolution if he had been a pleasant-featured man?

I am no nasologist, but who was not impressed by 'the

perpetual triumph, the everlasting bonfire-light' – to use Shakespeare's phrase – which accompanied the late Mr Pierpont Morgan's victorious career? And even those among the ugly whose longings are more amorous than ambitious, what need have they to be diffident? The obviously presentable among the male sex may shrug their shoulders at women's whimsies, but experience shows that the man 'with some architecture about him,' however Gothic, is in wooing more than the match of the comely suitor. Wilkes, who was considered easily the ugliest man of his day, and whose portraits bear this out, boasted that he could give the handsomest man in England half an hour's start in the race for favours, and beat him. 'Doesn't Mr Wilkes squint abominably?' someone asked a lady, who had met him. 'Yes, he does,' she replied thoughtfully, 'but not more than a gentleman ought to.' Review for a moment in your own mind the most successful 'ladies' men' you have known. What facial types predominate? The empty barber's block, the clean monkey, and the hairy gorilla. Fellows with pleasant, handsome human countenances stand no chance.

FROM A
CRITIC'S DAYBOOK

What is the critic? That he is only one kind of reader among thousands is obvious; and that he is the most useless of writers unless his faculty reaches a rather rare degree of excellence is obvious. A critic is one who has been given a pass-key into many rooms in the House of Art on condition that he does not dwell in any one of them. His part is to open a door, examine the furniture of the room, and compare the view from its window with those to be seen from others. He must stay long enough to see what the owner of the room saw – then he had better move on. He is a creature without a spiritual home, and it is his point of honour never to seek one. And his use? His use is that, thanks to an imagination above average strength, though of course weaker than the artist's, he is better able than the ordinary reader to interpret creative experiences; while his visits to other rooms enable him to know things about the work he is examining which the creator of it, who has never shifted from his own window, cannot know. The critic's first obligation is to permit himself to be absorbed in the vision of a writer, responding to it with all his emotions, and then to compare that vision with those of other writers. If asked what is the use of that, he can only reply that it is another way of doing what the artist does: his work, too, intensifies and multiplies experiences worth having.

I say he must respond with *all* his emotions, because I do not believe he should limit his response. It is true that some critics attempt to confine their comments to what they claim to be alone significant in a writer's work: its capacity for arousing 'aesthetic emotion' and its technical perfection. But one of the disconcerting discoveries connected with the study of literature is that beauty to which 'aesthetic emotion' is the response, resembles the shimmer upon a butterfly's wing; held to the light at a particular angle, it may dazzle and delight, but shift that angle and what before was a blaze of beauty turns dun and brown in our hands. Each generation holds the butterfly to the light at a slightly different angle. All changes in aesthetic response are caused by changes in beliefs and morals, and behind the new literature of the 1920s such changes lie. Even discoveries in technique are connected with them, for in art technique and substance can never be separated. It is because a writer wants to express something that has not been expressed before that he deviates from the methods of his predecessors; and it is because a painter wishes to draw attention to what has excited him in visible objects but has escaped the notice of his predecessors, that he alters his manner of painting. *Aesthetic taste is only further discrimination upon preferences determined by other causes.* Whatever the nature of the beautiful may be, and no man has succeeded in defining it, where and in what any particular generation will see beauty depends upon habits of mind and ways of feeling which, in their turn, are moulded by the condition of the world. The direction of our interests, whether intellectual or aesthetic, is decided by the times in which we live. And one of the main functions of the critic, when he is expounding the literature of the past, is to put the reader at the point of view from which its contemporaries saw that literature, at the same time, of course, judging it from his own; and, confronted by contemporary literature, to show its relations to the world today. He must therefore discourse upon current ideas and ideas once current; and the psychology of the reader of a book is almost as much a part of his subject as the book itself.

Woke early and to my dismal situation; I am sick of journalism. I must have a change. Resolved to write a discursive diary instead. Reminded myself that a diary must be very bright – and sighed. Tried to recall the flattest entry I had ever read in a printed diary: 'Oct. 23rd. Walked to Slapton with Brown' occurred to me. Couldn't well sink lower myself.

Robinson Crusoe has been my bedside book for some time. I am almost as fond of that book as the butler in *The Moonstone*, who used to refer to it whenever in doubt what to do, and wore out several copies. Robinson Crusoe's fervid thankfulness for small mercies is infectious; also his manful, forethoughtful simplicity of mind. Most complications (unhappily not all, but more than one might suppose) yield to Crusoe methods. Then, how delightful to contemplate the existence of anyone who has oceans of time! Crusoe is continually returning to this aspect of his predicament. Time is no object; indeed the longer everything takes him the better. How different the life of a journalist!

At the New Prince's Theatre I once heard M. Jacques Dalcroze lecture on 'Eurhythmics in Education'. His lecture was illustrated by some of his pupils. With the exception of some dances at the end – 'plastic realizations of music' is, I believe, the proper phrase to use – what we watched on the stage was M. Dalcroze taking a class of advanced pupils while he talked to us and explained his aims and methods. His audience was a large one, and very attentive. Most people who hear of new ideas at all have heard of M. Dalcroze and his college at Hellerau, near

Dresden; many of you must have seen photographs of its spacious, simple, almost forbiddingly hygienic architecture, and of the pupils dancing barefoot in the open air. Whether the pictures pleased you or not depended probably on whether or not you are the kind of person who readily believes that the secret of a happier, better life lies quite near to hand, and that the clue to its discovering it lies in the body. A great many people do nowadays believe this. Some of them think salvation is to be found in a particular diet, others in dancing –

He who is light of heart and heels
Can wander in the Milky Way –

others, again, in wearing fewer and looser clothes, or in seeing each other, if possible, naked (this last is now a favourite theme with novelists; conversion follows upon surprising someone bathing), or in repeating to themselves 'Life is perfect, I am perfect,' as they brush their hair every morning, drinking at the same time a glass of fair water. Personally, my first impulse (I prefer not to think the tendency congenital, but to attribute it to a public-school education) is to put down everyone who declares he has discovered a new contribution to the art of living as a cranky ass: occasionally it has been necessary to apologize afterwards.

That *Rasselas* and *Candide* should still be living classics seems to me significant. Both are monotonous, undramatic little stories in which each short chapter repeats the same lesson, that life is always empty and happiness is impossible. Now if the pessimistic view of life were a fantastic one and had no root in experience, neither of these certainly overcharged statements of its case would have continued to appeal to men. They continue to attract successive generations because they find much truth in them. Suppose, on the other hand, that the reiterated moral had been reversed, so that each short chapter was an episode of bliss and of hopes abundantly fulfilled, not even the austere eloquence of Johnson nor the quick precision of Voltaire could have kept those works alive. Such a surfeit of optimism would have been too repulsive to the average honest mind. Books of that kind no doubt get written, but they die like flies.

Touching pessimists in general, have you ever considered why they are not depressing – I mean the good ones? *Candide* and *Rasselas* certainly cannot be said to be cheerful pictures of humanity or hope-inspiring estimates of life; the gloom of *Rasselas* is even deeper than that of *Candide*. Schopenhauer, too, is far from a depressing author, indeed, quite the contrary. And why does not Ibsen, who is certainly not a bringer of good tidings, depress us, while we often go away in wretchedly low spirits from plays which are not nearly such formidable indictments of human nature or society? The explanation is that the pessimism of good writers is not the result of dejection, doldrums, discouragement, dumps, but of an unusual intellectual activity which becomes a temporary possession of our own while we are reading. One of my favourite critical principles is that a work of art must have somewhere in it a suggestion of desirable life. Yet it is often difficult to recognize this in stories which are nevertheless indisputable works of art, until one realizes that it *is* there, all the time – in the mind of the author, whose virtues of soul and intellect are infectious, and exhilarate more than the melancholy of his conclusions can depress. The contempt of the average hearty reader for 'face the facts' plays and novels is usually justified; they are seldom the fruit of intellectual power, but mildly pretentious projections of feeble, if sympathetic, moods of despondency. Away with them!

Looking into Professor Saintsbury's *Minor Poets of the Caroline Period* made me think what salutary reading it would be for modern poets, bringing home to them as it must the transience of fashion in thought and expression. It is clear that there was, for the contemporaries of these poets, a peculiar fascination in the quality of their diction; its intellectual quippiness and dry sparkle made them ask nothing more from poetry. Anyone who has read contemporary verse over some years will have noticed how quickly fashions in language follow and oust each other. Now it is for the rich, sensuous phrase, soon that is succeeded by 'a rage' (as sweeping as those which make every boy in a private school suddenly buy a pair of stilts or a squirt) for the brisk, crackling, conversational epithet, or for the emphatic yet non-committal generalized one; skies in turn are 'million-tinted', 'streaky' or simply 'amazing'. The pleasure which the mere flavour of a slightly new diction gives is brief; while it lasts, unfortunately, it is keen enough to conceal emptiness of inspiration both from writers and readers. It is, therefore, salutary to turn up from time to time the old forgotten poets, who draped themselves so skilfully in the idiom of the moment, and see what emptiness lay after all beneath. Seventeenth-century diction is up just now, the rich associative adjective having palled; but I am soon expecting the turn of the stately, smooth, limpid style, after we have masticated hair-brushes, Christmas-trees and hog's-bristles a little longer.

The language of art criticism is the queerest and most shifting of shorthand jargons. A word or phrase is taken up for a little time and then dropped, and the imprecision of these phrases is so great that it is often impossible to tell whether, or not, the slang symbols which replace them are synonymous. A few years ago the word 'amusing' was exceedingly common; it is used still but not so often. It was only in the context and in front of the picture to which it was applied that one could approach to understanding what was meant by it. It did not, of course, mean funny; a drawing of a crucifixion or of a solitary potato on a plate might be 'amusing'. It meant, or seemed to mean, that the critic was rather fascinated by the picture, but either did not really feel much when contemplating it or, for reasons unstated, regretted he was fascinated so much. It was the most subjective term imaginable. It is still possible, without laying yourself open to the charge of being as foolish as Ruskin, to speak of 'generosity' in the handling of a head, or shoulder, or what not. But what on earth does this mean if not that something in the painter's treatment of his subject gives one the same kind of satisfaction as generosity in the human being? A great deal of art criticism is still unconsciously Ruskinian.

When I travel I like to take a book of travel with me. It need not be about the places I am going to visit. I choose a book of travel because I like, at such times, the company of an observer; he teaches me how to make the most of my time. On my holiday I took with me Maupassant's *Sur l'Eau*. This is not one of his books which are oftenest read; yet, in a sense, it contains the whole of him.

Sur l'Eau is a reflective diary of one of Maupassant's cruises in his yacht, the *Bel Ami*. I chose it partly because I thought I should like on my own journeys the companionship of a strong, truthful man; partly because, being in a black mood, I thought I should prefer such a one to be also a pessimist. Thing in general would soon cheer me up quite irrationally, and meanwhile I should like to keep hold a little longer of a few grim truths (so they appeared to me) about life and the world, and a sincere pessimist (none of your lurid, bengal-light and gloom effects, thank you, with the philosopher raving and cursing magnificently above the wreck and roar) – a sincere pessimist, I say, would help me, in spite of the gentle allurements of change, to keep such facts before my eyes. There is the fact of death, for instance, which it is extraordinarily difficult to remember while bathing.

Clio is a Muse, and perhaps the most exacting of them; for she requires in her followers not only the gifts of an artist but fidelity to fact. If we cannot believe that the events which an historian describes happened, he is an impostor; if the importance he gives them is false, he is a deceiver; yet unless he interprets facts, his work, however conscientious, can only be a quarry from which some day an artist-historian may build real history.

Is Gibbon's account of that vast procession of events which he selected as his subject credible? The realist and the religious man say 'No'. Gibbon's method of interpretation is one which neither of them can accept. Its conventionality is obvious, but it works. Gibbon pulled together in his mind a mass of facts such as erudition never before, and seldom since, accumulated; and – here is the miracle – his attitude towards all those facts is consistent. If his account is remote from actuality, all its incidents are equidistant from the serene centre of this judgement.

By means of a balanced and ornate style, expressive of self-delighting detachment, he keeps events, and still more the passions behind them, far aloof. The cries of human agony and aspiration never reach to where, like an Epicurean god, he lies upon a cloud, watching the dumb show of a great and ancient civilization passing by. If he stoops to examine more closely one of the human atomies below, some emperor, prophet or general, with his thumb and finger he soon replaces him in that imposing march of circumstance, where he then resumes his proper ant-like stature.

Is this a truth-revealing attitude towards human-nature and history? Some critics have been at pains to prove it is not. Its value, its hold upon the imagination, lies in a congruity between such a method and the emotion which a long backward gaze across centuries naturally inspires, provided the mind makes no effort to recall the past as it was to the living, or to arrange events as a progress, whether under human or divine direction.

A new edition of that useful and entertaining work, *Burke's Peerage* has recently appeared. It is a book to be dipped into rather than read from cover to cover. When I turn these crowded pages I am reminded again, as I am whenever I try to get on a six o'clock bus in the Strand, that I am, at heart, a Malthusian. There are too many people in the streets, too many in the peerage. The population question is the one question on which I *cannot* see the other side. Every bachelor, every spinster, is in my eyes, *ipso facto*, a martyr in the cause of humanity, for to have children of one's own is a source of happiness. I would, if I were king, even at the risk of cheapening a little further that honour, give them each an OBE. We shall never be happy, kind and sensible, till we are less thick upon this planet. We shall never have a civilization of which we can be proud, never a State which we can each feel is a greater self, until the newspapers can report, with pardonable exaggeration as a most significant event, that 'a vast concourse of over five hundred people assembled to support the policy of the Government'.

There are even too many peers. The eighty-first edition of Burke has convinced me of this. It has 2,789 pages; the first edition published in 1826 had 400. To each name a number is attached, representing the precedence to which that person is entitled. However large your dinner party, the King, of course, goes in first; but I have failed to discover who, if you invited the whole peerage, would go in last. Mrs W. H. Williamson, I know, goes in 160,089th. I have not carried my researches further.

The interest of this great book, which satirists in their bitter way used to call the Englishman's Bible, is various. First and foremost it appeals to genealogists. Ancestor-worship is a passion of maturity. The young rarely have it, but it often breaks out in later life in people who were once extremely bored by discussions as to who was so-and-so's great-great-aunt. Another source of interest is looking up the real ages, when they are given, of ladies who give the impression of only having left the schoolroom a year or two ago. Then for those with literary sensibilities, there is pleasure derivable from the magnificent massing of high-sounding and glorious titles in the person of one man. This always gives me a thrill. The owners of multiple titles ought never to be announced by only one of them. I should like to hear, for instance, a butler roll out the words: 'The Duke of Hamilton, of Brandon, of Chatelherault; the Marquess of Douglas and of Clydesdale, the Earl of Angus, of Arran, of Lanark and of Selkirk; Lord Avon, Lord Polmont, Lord Machanshire, Lord Innerdale, Lord Abernethy, Lord Jedburgh, Lord Daer, Lord Shortcleuch and Lord Dutton'; and then – instead of a crowd of grandees, see a solitary unassuming gentleman, perhaps with a mother-of-pearl stud in his shirt-front, enter the room. It would appeal to my dramatic sense.

As the peerage and baronetage is so large now, I have decided to be unmoved by any title which is post-Waterloo. This increases my natural respect for the remnant.

When I come across some profound piece of criticism into which the critic has, I feel, been led by surrendering to his own temperament, I wonder if my own method of criticizing is not mistaken. One cannot get away from one's own temperament any more than one can jump away from one's own shadow, but one can discount the emphasis which it produces. I snub my own temperament when I think it is not leading me straight to the spot whence a general panorama of an author's work is visible. This point is often some obvious little knoll or terrace, which almost everyone would mount to get a view. Perhaps the other kind of criticism is more valuable, in which the critic wanders down a vista which he is impelled by personal impulse of curiosity to explore, ignoring what lies to the right or left of him, or what others see when they just look round them. But again how often the most alluring and mysterious little path in a garden leads only to the gardeners' privy!

I have always delighted in Montaigne and thought him a wise man; and in nothing wiser than in his attitude towards fear, a state of mind to be gently circumvented, if it cannot be outfaced.

The literature of fear has always been repellent to me, even when it is also the work of genius: for Dostoevsky admiration in me is mixed with dislike and contempt; he is too pathological, and terror too often inspires him. 'There is nothing more cheerful than wisdom; I had like to say more wanton. . . . In fine, we must live among the living and let the river flow under the bridge without our care, above all things avoiding fear, that great disturber of reason. The thing in the world I am most afraid of is fear.'

His early essays were commonplace books in which he copied out passages which struck him as he lazily read with his reflections upon them. But as time went on they began to achieve more and more completely an avowed intention – that of drawing a portrait of himself. In studying himself minutely he drew to our great gain a diagram of our species, while by dwelling curiously upon each experience as it passed he made his own life more rich. Thus we learn to know human nature better through knowing him so well, and if we can acquire his habit of self-observation we too can enrich our lives.

It is not in experience that our lives are poor, though sometimes it would seem so. If they appear to us limited and monotonous, it is because we do not watch what is happening to us or what we are feeling about it. Montaigne is a good master in the art of life because he teaches that detachment which enables us to be more conscious of life as it passes. Each day contains moments which could not be more pleasant or interesting even if our heart's desire had been fulfilled, or some longed-for piece of good fortune had befallen us. We do not wake up to this until our desires have been met or the luck is actually ours, when we are astonished to find after all how little difference that has made. The daily texture of our lives remains what it was, and in amazement we cry out that all is vanity! Since fortune is fickle and many things may come between a man and his desire, it is wise to make the most of those resources which good fortune cannot increase and only the worst calamities destroy. This is the lesson of Montaigne. Have not even the stricken sometimes marvelled to find themselves enjoying a fine day, a joke, a meal? There is comfort in this. Why dwell only on the humiliation in it? We may smile ironically with Montaigne at human nature, its 'flexibility' and 'diversity', but unless we learn from him to smile also gratefully, we have not caught his message.

INDEX